FROM SHADOW TO REALITY

*These are a shadow of the things
that were to come;
the reality,
however, is found in Christ.*

Colossians 2:17

Dr. John M. Oakes

FROM SHADOW TO REALITY

A Study of the Relationship
Between the
Old and the New Testament

www.ipibooks.com

ipi

From Shadow to Reality – A Study of the Relationship Between the Old and the New Testament

Copyright © 2005 by John M. Oakes

All rights reserved. No part of this book may be duplicated, copied, translated, reproduced or stored mechanically or electronically without specific, written permission of the author and Illumination Publishers International.

Printed in the United States of America
08 07 06   2 3 4 5

Reprint August 15, 2006

ISBN: 0-9745342-3-4

All scripture quotations unless otherwise indicated, are taken from the NEW INTERNATIONAL VERSION. Copyright ©1973, 1978, 1984 by the International Bible Society. Used by permission of Zondervan Publishing House. All rights reserved.

The "NIV" and "New International Version" trademarks are registered in the United States Patent Trademark Office by the International Bible Society. Use of either trademark requires the permission of the International Bible Society.

Published by
Illuminations Publishers International
www.ipibooks.com

ipi

Dedication

To:

My mother,

Ruth Oakes,

who taught me how to speak carefully,

and my father,

Harold Oakes,

who taught me how to work hard.

Acknowledgements

I would like to express my gratitude to a number of friends who have helped me with this project. First, thanks to Toney Mulhollan, my editor, for your hard work and encouragement. Also, thanks to Ruth Oakes and Tanya Okamura for providing editorial help. Phillip Lester provided inspiration and encouragement for this project. As a Christian who was raised in a Jewish home, he was able to provide invaluable insight into the Jewish perspective on the Hebrew Scripture and the Jewish concept of Messiah. I am also thankful to Phillip for much editorial help. Jeff Fisher did research on Jewish customs. Glen Giles gave helpful advice, as well as a great example as a teacher. Special thanks to Foster and Coco Stanback who have believed in this project and provided financial support. Greatest thanks of all go to my children Ben, Liz and Katie, and especially to my wife Jan for supporting me emotionally and putting up with my obsession with this project.

John M. Oakes, January, 2005

Contents

Foreword.	8
Introduction.	10
Chapter One.	19
Historical Prefigures	
Chapter Two.	56
Prefigures of the Messiah	
Chapter Three.	84
The Earthly Tabernacle and the Heavenly Tabernacle	
Chapter Four.	107
The Old Covenant Priesthood Foreshadows the Priesthood of the New Covenant	
Chapter Five.	121
The Mosaic Covenant Prefigures the New Covenant in Christ	
Chapter Six.	141
Old Testament Ritual Sacrifice Points to New Testament Sacrifice	
Chapter Seven.	166
The Old Covenant Feasts Prefigure Specific Aspects of the Christian Life	
Chapter Eight.	201
Prophecies in the Old Testament Predict Events in the life of Jesus Christ of Nazareth	
Chapter Nine.	240
Old Testament Prophecies Announce the Coming of the Kingdom of God	
Appendix One: The Limits of Biblical Interpretation.	263
Appendix Two: References.	271

Foreword

I began to read *From Shadow to Reality* and I could not put it down. It captured me with its clear presentation, showing the fulfillment of the Old Testament by the New Testament. It is more than a book about fulfilled prophecy. It is more than a chronicling of related passages between the two covenants. Dr. John Oakes has written a scholarly book which will be faith-building for Christians and non-Believers. *From Shadow to Reality* will build your faith in the Scriptures by showing the congruency and direct connections between Old Testament and New Testament. It will build your faith in God who does not change, in God who set in motion a plan for salvation since the fall of man to be fulfilled by Jesus Christ the Messiah. Your faith will multiply as you see the specific fulfillment of very detailed passages concerning Jesus in the first covenant brought to fruition in the second covenant. My faith grew as I read John's book and I realized in a deeper way how the Scriptures provide me with a description of the activity of God throughout the entire Bible that is consistent, planned and clear. I saw the loving character of our Father in heaven who has worked to have a relationship with us from the beginning of time.

This book is for Bible students of all levels of understanding and knowledge. The in-depth explanation of verses is a model of solid Biblical exegesis. I learned how to better explain many passages in the New Testament that require an understanding of the Old Testament counterpart. It is so beneficial to gain the "big picture" or outline of the entire Bible to supply the proper context for interpreting a particular passage. The book explains the overall structure of the Scriptures in a way that makes understanding the details in the Bible possible. *From Shadow to Reality* is a book for evangelism, discipleship and mature spiritual growth. It will help non-Believers gain faith in Scripture, God and Jesus Christ. The presentation of fulfillment regarding the Messiah, the tabernacle, the priesthood, the sacrificial system, Hebrew festivals, and the

Kingdom makes an undeniable case for faith in Christianity. No other conclusion except Jesus as Lord is reasonable after reading the extent and detail of fulfilled prophecies. No other explanation is plausible after seeing the scheme of redemption beginning with Adam and completed with Jesus. Difficult passages in both covenants are made plain through using the "lens" of understanding which Dr. Oakes provides in connecting the Old and New Testaments.

I have been privileged to witness the faith of John Oakes for over 25 years. We became brothers in Christ in the late seventies while he was working on his doctorate at the University of Colorado and I was an undergraduate. His faith was exemplified then as now through true discipleship to Jesus Christ. He has always been a scholar, servant and sincere Christian. I could not help but be inspired by the life behind the book. John captured a dream to change the world spiritually as a student. Praise God he is still doing the same as a professor. He has used his God-given talents as a scientist to explain and live the story of Christ. I know everyone who reads this book will gain faith and be blessed. May the reality of God and Jesus be present in your life as you read Dr. John Oakes' book, *From Shadow to Reality!* May any shadows of understanding be driven out by the light of this book as it reflects the truth of the Word of God!

Gregg Marutzky, Evangelist
Dallas, Texas

Introduction

The law is only a shadow of the good things that are coming—not the realities themselves.

Hebrews 10:1

Have you ever had someone tell you that it is difficult to come to a deep understanding of the New Testament teachings without a good understanding of the Old Testament? Perhaps you have discovered this yourself. The more one reads the Bible, the more this concept rings true. On the other hand, have you ever noticed that the overall message of the Old Testament only makes sense in the light of the New Testament? Sometimes, as a person quite familiar with the New Testament, I find myself wondering what the Jews thought about some of the passages they found written in the Old Testament. When David cried out *"They have pierced my hands and my feet,"* (Psalms 22:16) what must the reader of the Old Testament, or for that matter what must David himself have thought that the pierced hands and feet were about? The reader of the New Testament knows instantly that David is talking about—the specifics of the crucifixion of Jesus Christ.

So many of the teachings and even the events in the Old Testament only make sense when they find themselves fulfilled in the pages of the New Testament. It is almost as if the characters in the Old Testament are acting out a play, the meaning of which they are completely unaware. It is only the audience of the play, those who watch in light of solid knowledge of the New Testament, who understand the meaning of the words and events in this play.[1]

There is a paradox here. One can only fully understand the Old Testament in light of the New. At the same time, the events and teachings of the New Testament are only given full meaning to one well-versed in the Old Testament events, teachings and prophecies which foreshadow the New. If I need the Old Testament to understand the New and I need the New Testament to understand the Old, where am I to begin? Perhaps this book can help solve the dilemma.

If the Old Testament is a play, in which the actors do not fully realize the implications of their action and words, then what does that imply about the writer(s) of the play? Even the writers of the Old Testament were not fully aware of what the play was about. When Moses led Israel through the Red Sea, he had no idea that his actions in this drama would be a visible symbol of salvation from sin through water baptism. Those who splattered the blood of a lamb over their lintels on that fatal night in Egypt had no idea that they were performing a physical symbol of the redeeming sacrifice of Jesus, the lamb of God, on the cross. Only the ultimate author, God himself, was completely aware of the plot, from beginning to end. In this book you will be provided with hundreds of events, people, and prophecies from the Old Testament which clearly foreshadow New Testament events and teachings. An obvious question is how did the writers of the Old Testament know to put all these foreshadows of events into their writings when the events they anticipated would not occur for hundreds of years? That is an excellent question. Peter seems to have this question in mind in 2 Peter 1:19-21:

> *And we have the word of the prophets made more certain, and you will do well to pay attention to it, as to a light shining in a dark place, until the day dawns and the morning star rises in your hearts. Above all, you must understand that no prophecy of Scripture came about by the prophet's own interpretation. For prophecy never had its origin in the will of man, but men spoke from God as they were carried along by the Holy Spirit.*

Peter is telling his readers that we, i.e., those of us who live in the New Testament age, have the words of the Old Testament made even more sure by having seen their teachings and prophecies fulfilled through the events in the life of Jesus Christ and his kingdom. How else is one to explain the Old Testament without accepting that it was God who inspired the words to be written? According to Peter, having seen the prophecies and teachings of the Scripture worked out before the very eyes of the apostles and other eyewitnesses of the events, it has become obvious that the Old Testament Scriptures are from God, not men.

Another metaphor which can help one to understand the relationship between the Testaments is supplied by the apostle Paul.

> *Now to him who is able to establish you by my gospel and the proclamation of Jesus Christ, according to the revelation of the mystery hidden for long ages past, but now revealed and made known through the prophetic writings by the command of the eternal God, so that all nations might believe and obey him* (Romans 16:25,26).

In this passage, Paul describes the place of the gospel in the Old Testament as a mystery, revealed through the prophetic writings by God.

A parallel passage from Paul is found in Colossians in which Paul explains his commission to present:

> *The commission God gave me to present the word of God in its fullness—the mystery that has been kept hidden for ages and generations, but is now disclosed to the saints* (Colossians 1:25b,26).

According to Paul, the gospel remained a mystery for ages, but it is now fully revealed to the saints. In the New Testament, and in Jesus Christ, the Old Testament finds its full meaning.

Everyone likes a good mystery. In the best mystery stories, the reader is fully aware that there is a pattern behind the information being revealed to them, yet they are left guessing as to the connection between the clues. At the end of the story, that one last clue is revealed—the one which brings together all the others. The reader exclaims, "I should have known."

The Old Testament is like that. It is the greatest mystery book ever written, with a great variety of interconnected clues supplied by different authors, most of whom never talked to one another before adding their chapter to the book. It is packed full of clues about the gospel, yet it is hard for those who do not know of the life of Jesus to connect the clues—it certainly was for the Jews. Those of us to whom the mystery has been revealed through Jesus Christ can read the same Old Testament clues and understand what they point to. It is like reading a mystery book for the second time. Not only do the clues we saw before all make sense, we even find other clues hidden in the story which we did not pick up on before the mystery was revealed. A goal of this book is to help the reader discover those clues.

In looking at types and antitypes in the Old and New Testaments one important question is how one can know with confidence that the connections are legitimate. Could some of these connections be created in one's mind, rather than by God. Could we be looking at a spurious clue? The question of careful Bible interpretation as it relates to foreshadows and prophecies is dealt with in the appendix. Those for whom this is a major concern may want to read the appendix before preceeding to chapter one.

The purpose of this book is to show the historical, doctrinal and prophetic relationship between the Old and the New Testament. The conclusion is that in its essence, from Genesis to Malachi, the Old Testament is a foreshadowing of the New Testament. Let us reduce this to simple terms; the theme of the entire Bible is God's desire and plan for having a relationship with us. In the Old Testament God prepares a people through whom a Messiah will come. In the New Testament, that desire and plan are fulfilled in the birth, life, death and resurrection of Jesus Christ. To simplify it further, the theme of the Old Testament is THE MESSIAH IS COMING, BRINGING SALVATION. The theme of the New Testament is THE MESSIAH IS HERE, BRINGING SALVATION.

Isn't this what Jesus so boldly declared to the religious leaders and teachers of his day in John 5:39,46?

> "You diligently study the Scriptures because you think that by them you possess eternal life. These are the Scriptures that testify about me, yet you refuse to come to me to have life...If you believed Moses, you would believe me, for he wrote about me."

In this situation, "the Scriptures" Jesus' hearers have been studying diligently are, of course, the Old Testament. In this statement, Jesus was not just blowing off hot air. This is a bold statement of truth. The Hebrew Bible, from beginning to end, was written about Jesus. In the Old Testament, the Israelites had a priest, a prophet and a king. In Jesus we have all three. In the Old Testament there were sacrifices to express a commitment to the Lord and there were sacrifices to bring about fellowship with God. There were sacrifices to bring peace and sacrifices to bring about forgiveness of sin. We have all these things in Jesus Christ. How could Moses have known when he held up the bronze snake in the wilderness that he was holding up a physical prophecy of how Jesus Christ would also be raised up? Were David, Joseph and others aware that the very events of their lives were foreshadowing the life and the teaching of the Messiah? And speaking of acting out a play, what about the Levites and the priests as they served in the Tabernacle and later in the Temple? They had no idea that God had carefully set up every single detail of construction and ceremony so that they would be both symbols and foreshadows of the heavenly reality we have in Jesus Christ. Not only were the people in the Old Testament acting out a play: even the props were carefully chosen! Without revealing more clues, let it suffice to say that this is the outline of the book.

SOME DEFINITIONS

Before launching into descriptions of the myriad of ways that the Old Testament anticipates the New, it will be helpful to define a few technical terms which will be used throughout the book. One of the terms to describe how the Old Testament leads inexorably to the New is **foreshadow**. Foreshadow can be used as a noun or as a verb. Webster's dictionary defines the verb foreshadow as "to typify beforehand; foretell; prefigure." The noun, according to Webster (or at least according to his successors) is "an indication of what is to come." A foreshadow, then, is an object, an event, a person or a situation which stands for or represents something of greater significance which is to come in the future. We will see a great number of objects, events and people in the Old Testament which God used to foreshadow significant teachings and events in the New. Many times a physical object or situation is used by God to prefigure a spiritual truth. If one can demonstrate that these foreshadows in the Old Testament are legitimate examples, not just coincidence, and if one can assume that those who acted out or wrote down these events had no idea what they were foreshadowing, then one is left with a clear indication that the Old Testament Scriptures are inspired by God. This is exactly what Peter claimed.

As verbs, the words foreshadow and prefigure can be used almost interchangeably. To **prefigure** means to represent symbolically an object, concept or idea in the future. The distinction between a foreshadow and a prefigure is that, in general, in a prefigure, the thing anticipated by the prefigure has an almost exact correspondence, whereas a foreshadow represents a concept larger or broader than the original. For example, we will see that Moses is a prefigure of the life of Jesus Christ, while the manna in the wilderness is a foreshadow of Jesus' ministry.

Also similar to the concept of a foreshadow is the pair of terms **type** and **antitype.** A type, according to Webster, is "A person or thing regarded as the symbol of someone or something that is yet to appear." Webster defines antitype as "That which corresponds to or is foreshadowed in the type." Interestingly, the specific example Webster uses for a type and antitype is Jerusalem is the type of heaven. On an old-fashioned typewriter, the metal piece which strikes the page is the type, while the image which shows up on the page is the antitype. We will see many pairs of type and antitype in the Old and New Testaments.

Another term which is related to foreshadow is **symbol.** The word symbol has a broader meaning than foreshadow. One of Webster's definitions for the word symbol is "an emblem or sign representing something else." A symbol, then, like a type or foreshadow, stands for something else, usually larger than itself. The basic difference between a symbol and a foreshadow is that a symbol represents something which is presently real, while a foreshadow represents something which lies in the future. A symbol is a representation while a foreshadow is an anticipation. We will see many Old Testament persons and objects which God uses as symbols of things that were real at the time, but whose full meaning are made clear and more fully known in the New. As an example of this distinction, one could mention the story of Moses putting the bronze snake up on a pole (Numbers 21:4-9), allowing God's people to be saved from death even if bitten by poisonous snakes. In this case, Moses was holding up a foreshadow (anticipation) of the saving work of Jesus Christ (John 3:14). At the same time, one could call the snake on the pole a symbol, as it represented Jesus, who was in existence at the time Moses held up the snake.

Another term which is related to symbol and foreshadow is **prophecy.** We will look at a whole range of Old Testament prophecies which anticipated both general and very specific events recorded in the New Testament. It bears noting that the modern, Western usage of the word prophecy is very different from the normal sense it is given in the Bible. To the Jews, a prophet was not so much one who predicted the future (a fore-teller) as he or she was an instrument to reveal God's will for his people (a forth-teller). The prophets of Israel were the ones who spoke for God. They were God's messengers. In general their mission was two-fold: to give warnings of judgment on Israel and her enemies and to encourage God's people to repent of their hard-heartedness and sin. In the Old Testament, then, a prophecy in its most general sense was a statement of *"This is what the Lord says."* [NIV]

Having said this, however, it is clear that the prophets did make predictions of future events which would affect God's people. They predicted specific happenings both in what was for them the near future and in the distant future. Their predictions for the near future were provided by God as a test of the validity of their claim to the office of prophet, so the Jews could decide for themselves whether their message was from God.[2]

> *You may say to yourselves, "How can we know when a message has not been spoken by the LORD?" If what a prophet proclaims in the name of the LORD does not take place or come true, that is a message the LORD has not spoken. That prophet has spoken presumptuously. Do not be afraid of him* (Deuteronomy 18:21,22).

The message of the prophets to Israel was of great importance to the Jews. However, our focus will be on the Old Testament prophets' amazingly specific predictions of events which are played out in the New Testament. In the context of this book, then, the word prophecy will be used in its more narrow sense. A prophecy will be a specific written or spoken prediction of events which clearly lie in the future for the person making the prediction.

The theme of this book is that the Old Testament is a mystery. Its teachings, events, people, statements, ceremonies and celebrations, from the smallest detail to the broadest themes, are foreshadows, symbols, prophecies of the greater reality which is revealed in the New Testament and in its chief character, Jesus Christ. Is this all coincidence and luck? Or is it God's way of demonstrating that the entire Bible can be trusted and can lead us to a relationship with him? As one looks at the prophetic relationship between the Old and New Testaments, as it shows so dramatically that the the events of Jesus' life were a part of God's eternal plan, one can see that he truly is *"the Lamb that was slain from the creation of the world"* (Revelation 13:8).

Author's note: There will be a number of places in the text of this book where I will point out examples of the Jews' stubbornness or of their unwillingness to listen to those sent to them and so forth. The author would beg the reader to not read into such comments any sort of negative feeling toward the Jewish people in general. It is my belief that the Jews were no more stubborn or sinful than any other people would have been in the same circumstances then or now. The fact is that the Jews were God's chosen people. The Jews had a special place in God's heart. Paul may have spoken vehemently against the Judaizing Christians (for example in Galatians 5:1-12), but he expressed the most heartfelt love and compassion for his fellow Jews—even those who had not yet come to Christ. Paul's words in Romans 9:1-5 are some of the most poignant and emotional in the entire Bible.

> *I speak the truth in Christ — I am not lying...Theirs are the patriarchs, and from them is traced the human ancestry of Christ, who is God over all, forever praised! Amen.*

Jesus also had some strong words for the hypocritical Jewish teachers. For example in Matthew 23:1-36 one can find some of the most strongly critical words we have from Jesus. Yet, he followed up his condemning words against the Pharisee's hypocrisy with the beautifully compassionate statement about his beloved fellow Jews:

> "*O, Jerusalem, Jerusalem, you who kill the prophets and stone those...Blessed is he who comes in the name of the Lord*" (Matthew 23:37-39).

Jesus had a special place in his heart for God's chosen people, and we can assume he still does today. One should not interpret the fact that God offered a New Covenant as a rejection of the Jewish people in general, but as an offer of a better way to come to God. The entire tenor of the New Testament is one of hope, understanding and compassion for the Jews, especially for the common Jewish person who was not necessarily a teacher of the Law. It is a fact that many Jews did accept Jesus, and some do so today as well. Probably more Jews were won to Jesus on a percentage basis than any people in the first two centuries. While it is true that many Jews fell into idolatry, it is also true that the

Jews, as a people, were far less idolatrous than their neighbors. I have tried to keep from this book any statements or even a tone which comes across with any disrespect of the Jewish people. If I have failed in this intent, I apologize ahead of time for my error.

Endnotes

1 The movie, *The Truman Show*, starring Jim Carrey can serve as an example of this kind of play. In this movie, the Jim Carrey character is unwittingly living in a huge movie set, with all the events in his life set up by an unseen producer.

2 One can assume that many or most of the shorter-term predictions which the prophets made as proof of their office are not found in the Old Testament Scripture. A few examples of those which did find their way into the Old Testament are found in my book on apologetics: John Oakes, *Reasons for Belief—A Handbook of Christian Evidence* (Available at www.ipibooks.com), pp. 127-138.

Historical Prefigures

For everything which was written in the past was written to teach us, so that through endurance and the encouragement of the Scriptures we might have hope.

Romans 15:4

The Israelites had been grumbling again. *"They spoke against God and against Moses,"* and said *"Why have you brought us up out of Egypt to die here in the desert? There is no bread! There is no water! And we detest this miserable food!"* (Numbers 21:5). Suddenly, a great number of venomous snakes appeared among the people who were doing the complaining. Not surprisingly, the people now regretted their lack of faith and decided that repentance was the path to follow, but what was to be done about the snakes? Upon God's instruction, Moses made a bronze replica of a snake and held it up on a pole. Everyone who was bitten by a snake who then looked to the viper held up on the pole was miraculously healed.

This is a remarkable account with powerful lessons. There was much for the Jews to learn from the situation. Lessons can be gleaned from it about the human proclivity toward rebellion and our astounding tendency to forget the great gifts of God. One can also see a dramatic lesson about God's willingness to forgive those who turn to him for help.

That is well and good, but in the New Testament, what happened in the desert around 1430 B.C. becomes an historical prefigure of the saving power of Jesus Christ. As Jesus himself said, *"Just as Moses lifted up the snake in the desert, so the Son of Man must be lifted up, that everyone who believes in him may have eternal life"* (John 3:14). When God asked him to make a replica of a snake and hold it up before the people, Moses must have been tempted to question God. "You said idolatry is wrong. You told me to destroy the golden calf. How can you ask me to make an image of a snake for the people to look at it? Won't they be tempted to make this snake into an idol?"

When Moses held up the snake, he knew that he was obeying the command of God so that his people might be saved. What he did not know was that he was holding up a physical symbol of the *Messiah* himself. The snake in this story is clearly symbolic of sin. When people are bitten by the venomous snake known as sin, it is fatal. *"For the wages of sin is death, but the gift of God is eternal life in Christ Jesus our Lord"* (Romans 6:23). *"There is no difference, for all have sinned and fall short of the glory of God, and are justified freely by his grace through the redemption that came by Christ Jesus"* (Romans 3:22-24).

If one continues to read in Romans 3, one discovers that the only antidote for the venom of sin is to rely upon the *Messiah*, Jesus Christ. He is the one who was held up on that pole in the wilderness. In this one act of Moses in the wilderness we have both a symbol of Christ and a foreshadow of his saving grace.

But why was a snake held up? How can a snake, a symbol of sin, stand for Jesus Christ, the son of God? *"God made him who had no sin to be sin for us, so that in him we might become the righteousness of God"* (2 Corinthians 5:21). Jesus became sin for us. He took on all our sin, and in so doing, became our righteousness. He became the antivenin for the venom of sin. What a beautiful picture of the grace of God and of the saving power of Christ's blood!

Here is the central point. When Jesus pointed to what Moses had done in the desert over fourteen centuries before his ministry began, he was doing more than simply saying that the snake could serve as a symbol of what can happen when people look at him. What Jesus was telling us is that God told Moses to hold up the snake because he foreknew that many centuries later it would stand for the saving power of Jesus Christ. It is not that Jesus was scanning history to find interesting events which could serve as examples of his teachings. God caused Moses to hold up the snake, knowing that more than a millennium later, it would become a symbol of the saving power of Christ. The point is that God caused the event in the first place so that it could serve us who read the New Testament. It serves us as a prophetic picture of the Messiah. In his sovereign power, God entered human history to provide a symbol and message to us about his plan to send a Messiah to save us from sin.

Let me give an example to show how unique and amazing God's intervention is. It is a common human practice to use an historical event from the past as a symbol of a greater idea. For example, Americans use the heroic acts of the Minutemen at Lexington and Concord as a symbol of heroism and the American spirit of independence from tyrrany. The acts of these patriots serve as a great symbol of the American ideal. Let us change this scenario. Let us imagine someone wanting to have a really neat symbol of the American Spirit. Imagine this person saying to himself, "I know what I will do, I will get in my time machine, go back to the year 1774, talk to a group of those rebels and help them to form a plan so they can serve later generations of Americans as a symbol of the fight for liberty...." One can see right away that this scenario will not work. It is impossible to go back in history to create an ideal situation which one can later use as a symbol of a concept.

True, but in essence this is what God did, both in history and in his inspired word. God, knowing that the Son would come as a saving Messiah, had Moses hold up the snake and then miraculously healed the people from the effect of the snake venom. God knew that the event would be recorded. In fact, God caused it to be recorded in the Old Testament. Could there be any greater evidence that the Bible is the inspired word of God? Could there be any greater evidence that God had a plan all along to offer salvation to those who look to his Son Jesus?

If the story of Moses holding up the snake in the wilderness was the only example, one could argue that this is a fortuitous coincidence. In the previous paragraph, a rather large claim was made. In fact two claims were made, and these support the central theme of the book. First, in the snake in the wilderness, we see God's hand directing the events in the history of his people, Israel. We can see God causing his people to live through dramas which serve as a symbol to us of his saving grace in Jesus Christ. Second, it is claimed here that not only did God cause the events in question to happen, he also caused these events to be recorded in the Old Testament. In other words, the prefigures and foreshadows in Old Testament history provide proof positive that the Bible is the inspired word of God.

To the skeptic (and hopefully, we are all skeptics, at least to some extent) the one example quoted above would not serve as sufficient proof of this claim. It is the sum of the evidence which makes the case. In this chapter we will examine a great number of examples of God entering history to create a symbol, type or foreshadow which he would later cause to serve as a lesson to us, *"on whom the fulfillment of the ages has come"* (1 Corinthians 10:11). The Old Testament itself and the events recorded in it serve as a foreshadow of what we have in Christ.

Before turning to some of these examples, let us consider the Bible, and especially the Old Testament, as history. Among the world's religions, Judaism and Christianity are unique in that their teachings and theology are immersed in history. The Bible is a record of historical events—the story of God creating a people to whom and through whom to send the Messiah. The story takes place over thousands of years. Without the record of God working in history, the New Testament does not make sense. If the history recorded in the Old Testament is not true, then the hundreds of antitypes in the New Testament lose much or all of their power to teach.[1] None of the other world religions—not Hinduism, Buddhism, Islam, Confucianism, or B'hai—find their teachings worked out in history.

Historians scan human history to find examples of related events and themes which seem to tell a story about the human condition. In order to do so, the historian must inductively discover some sort of pattern of human behavior in the patchwork of recorded history. The student of the Bible has a much easier job. The Bible has a theme and a series of closely related events, not because the historian is searching for a pattern, but because God's all-powerful hand was reaching into history to create a story which can teach us about him. *"These things happened to them as examples and were written down as warnings for us, on whom the fulfillment of the ages has come"* (1 Corinthians 10:11). God caused these things to happen, made sure they were recorded in his word, and inspired the New Testament writers to use them as examples to teach us. Quite a bold plan!

GENESIS

I. ADAM AND EVE

Let us start at the beginning. Consider Adam and Eve. Admittedly, this is a somewhat risky place to begin. The Bible is the most accurate book of ancient history, without a rival.[2] Having said this, the first eleven chapters of Genesis cover events which occurred earlier than any existing written record (outside the Bible, that is). The historically/archaeologically confirmable material in the Old Testament begins with the life of Abraham in Genesis chapter twelve. One's faith in the reliability of the story of Adam and Eve is based on the very strong evidence for the reliability of the Old Testament in general, but not on historical confirmation.

The Old Testament begins with a great example of a type in Adam and Eve. It is assumed here that the reader is familiar with this story, but if not, please read Genesis chapter three. When Adam and Eve "fell" in Genesis three, in a very real sense they were representing all of us. Adam and Eve are the type. You and I are the antitype. The story of Adam and Eve is the story of every one of us. Adam and Eve were created to have an intimate relationship with God. God gave them freedom, but he also gave them choices which had consequences. Unfortunately, Eve and Adam abused that choice, as all of us do. The result of that choice was death—not immediate physical death as the first couple had perhaps been anticipating (the serpent created a lot of confusion here), but death and separation from God were the eventual result of their choice to trust their own wisdom over the loving admonishment of God. Can anyone relate to this scenario? Is this not, in a single, simple and beautiful story, the human condition? Many thousands of books, poems, songs, plays and the like have been produced by people to express the human condition, yet God outdid them all right in the beginning of the Bible using the simplest of stories.

The great thing about this story is that it actually happened, and yet it serves as an exact representation of every person's relationship with God. God is teaching us in this story and is laying the groundwork for the New Testament message of our need for Jesus Christ from the beginning. *"Therefore, just as sin entered* the world through one man, and death through sin, and in this way death came to all men, because all sinned" (Romans 5:12).

The type and antitype found in Eve and especially in Adam develop even further. When God creates a historical symbol/prefigure/type, he is able to do it in layers and on many levels.

> *Nevertheless, death reigned from the time of Adam to the time of Moses, even over those who did not sin by breaking a command, as did Adam, **who was a pattern of the one to come.***
>
> *But the gift is not like the trespass. For if the many died by the trespass of the one man, how much more did God's grace and the gift that came by the grace of the one man, Jesus Christ, overflow to the many! Again, the gift of God is not like the result of the one man's sin: The judgment followed one sin and brought condemnation, but the gift followed many trespasses, and brought justification. For if, by the trespass of the one man, death reigned through that one man, how much more will those who receive God's abundant provision of grace and of the gift of righteousness reign in life through the one man, Jesus Christ.*
>
> *Consequently, just as the result of one trespass was condemnation for all men, so also the result of one act of righteousness was justification that brings life to all men. For just as through the disobedience of the one man the many were made sinners, so also through the obedience of the one man the many will be made righteous* (Romans 5:12-19).

God uses Adam as a type of Jesus and in a very special way. They are the same and yet they are opposites. Notice the emphasized words, *"Adam, who was a pattern of the one to come."* The one to come, in this case, is Jesus Christ. This is one of the most profound passages of scripture. Entire books could be written on this passage and in fact they have been. Let us keep it simple. Just as the sin of Adam set a pattern and produced a terrible result for all who would follow him, so the perfect life and the sacrifice of Jesus set a pattern and produced a wonderful result for all those who would turn from the sin of Adam to the righteousness of Jesus Christ. There is profound truth here, but God caused an event to happen in the distant past which would later serve as a type of his saving grace in Jesus Christ. In a very real sense, the life of Adam serves as a living prophecy of the antitype; Jesus Christ.

There is still more prophecy in the story of Adam and Eve. The subject of messianic prophecy will be reserved for a later chapter, but it is hard not to mention what is certainly the first messianic prophecy in the Old Testament. This is found in Genesis 3:14,15. In this passage, God speaks to the serpent, or Satan, telling him that because he deceived Eve, *"I will put enmity between you and the woman, and between your offspring and hers; he will crush your head and you will strike his heel."* This is a prophecy concerning Jesus, the offspring of the woman, the "he" in this passage. Satan will do some damage to the work of God in Jesus Christ. He will strike the offspring's heel, but the Messiah will eventually crush the work of Satan through his willing sacrifice on the cross and through his resurrection from the dead. From the very beginning of mankind's fall, God had a plan to deal with the problem of sin. Yes, the consequences of Eve and Adam's sins were terrible, but God had a plan from the beginning to send a savior to crush the head of Satan who tempted Adam and Eve and who still tempts us today.

II. NOAH AND THE FLOOD

Noah's flood (which was really God's flood) is one of the most significant events recorded in the Old Testament. This story is deluged with types which find their fulfillment in the New Testament. In fact, that is Peter's point in 2 Peter 2:4-9:

> *For if God...did not spare the ancient world when he brought the flood on its ungodly people, but protected Noah, a preacher of righteousness, and seven others,...if that is so, then the Lord knows how to rescue godly men from trials and to hold the unrighteous for the day of judgment, while continuing their punishment.*

Of course, the story of Noah and his family stands on its own, providing great lessons to the Jews who read it. However, in addition, when God brought on the flood, he was creating a type whose antitype is Judgment Day. In fact, Peter uses the type (the flood) to explain what the antitype (Judgment Day) will be like in 2 Peter 3:3-7:

> *First of all, you must understand that in the last days scoffers will come, scoffing and following their own evil desires. They will say "Where is this 'coming' he promised? Ever since our fathers died, everything goes on as it has since the beginning of creation." But they deliberately forget that long ago by God's word the heavens existed and the earth was formed out of water and by water. By these waters also the world of that time was deluged and destroyed. By the same word the present heavens and earth are reserved for fire, being kept for the day of judgment and destruction of ungodly men.*

Every spiritual teaching in the New Testament has some sort of physical foreshadow in the Old. Judgment Day is no exception. Those who scoffed at Noah as he built the ark are a foreshadow of those who scoff at the idea of the second coming of Jesus today. When Jesus comes back, as when it started raining in the time of Noah, it will be too late to prepare for the impending judgment.

There is more detail to the foreshadow of Noah's flood. There is a silver lining in the cloud of the flood. The same silver lining is found in the New Testament teaching about Judgment Day. In this horrible flood which cleared the earth of sinful men, a few were saved through the water. As with the type, so with the antitype. Only a few, namely Noah and his immediate family, were saved from the flood through their faith and obedience to God's commands. Similarly, with the second judgment, only a few will be saved, this time through the water of baptism. The water of the flood is a symbol of the cleansing which God carries out for us in baptism.

> *God waited patiently in the days of Noah while the ark was being built. In it, only a few people, eight in all, were saved through water, and this water symbolizes baptism that now saves you also—not the removal of dirt from the body but the pledge of a good conscience toward God. It saves you by the resurrection of Jesus Christ, who has gone into heaven and is at God's right hand* (1 Peter 3:20-22).

As Jesus was raised from the dead, so Noah and his family were raised above the waters and saved through their faithful obedience to God. In the story of Noah we have the horrors of Judgment Day and the glory of salvation in the waters of baptism. This brings to mind the statement in Romans 15:4, *"For everything that was written in the past was written to teach us, so that through the endurance and encouragement of the Scriptures we might have hope."* There is warning and there is hope in the story of the flood.

III. ABRAHAM, ISHMAEL AND ISAAC

Volumes could be written just on the subject of the life of Abraham as a foreshadow and as a type of the fundamental teachings in the New Testament. Through his faith, Abraham became the father of many nations (Genesis 17:5). He also became the father of all those who through faith, receive the promise of eternal life in Jesus Christ. God used Abraham as perhaps the most important type in the Old Testament. Abraham is a type of all those who would be saved by faith under the New Covenant. Abraham's antitype is anyone who is saved, through faith, by the blood of Jesus.

> *We have been saying that Abraham's faith was credited to him as righteousness. Under what circumstances was it credited? Was it after he was circumcised or before? It was not after but before! And he received the sign of circumcision, a seal of the righteousness that he had by faith while he was still uncircumcised. So then, he is the father* (i.e., type) *of all who believe but have not been circumcised, in order that righteousness might be credited to them. And he is also the father* (type) *of all those who not only are circumcised but who also walk in the footsteps of the faith that our father Abraham had before he was circumcised* (Romans 4:9-12).

Abraham is the type of those who are saved, not by being born a Jew and not by being circumcised physically, but by faith and by being born again into Christ. Abraham was a living, walking, example and proof that we are justified by faith. In order to drive his point home, Paul reminds his readers that Abraham is the type, not only of the Gentiles, but also of the Jews who would accept Jesus Christ as savior: *"Those who not only are circumcised but who also walk in the footsteps of the faith that our father Abraham had."*

Paul makes his point very clear in Romans 4:16,17.

> *He is the father* (forerunner, but also type) *of us all. As it is written: "I have made you a father of many nations." He is our father in the sight of God, in whom he believed—the God who gives life to the dead and calls things that are not as though they were.*

When God saw the faith of Abraham, he also saw us. God saw Abraham, willing to leave his life of security to wander in the wilderness, believing the promise of a son, even though his body was as good as dead, and willing to give up his promised son. When he saw Abraham doing these things, in his heart God saw all of those who would in the future live out what Abraham foreshadowed: a life of faith in God. When God credited Abraham's faith as righteousness, he was, by a vicarious foreshadow, doing the same for us.

There is much more foreshadow to be found in the life of Abraham. Consider the birth of his children. Sarah had been promised a child despite her barrenness and advanced age. Unfortunately, she wavered in her faith and sent Hagar to lie with Abraham. *"Go sleep with my maidservant; perhaps I can build a family through her"* (Genesis 16:2). This unfaithful union led to the birth of Ishmael. Ishmael is a type of the nation of Israel and of the Old Covenant. The type is revealed in the fact that both Ishmael and Israel, the Jews, were the result of natural birth. Ishmael is a type of Israel, but Isaac serves as a type of the Church. Despite her unfaithfulness, God blessed Sarah with the promised child, Isaac. This scene is an amazing foreshadow of God's grace toward us. The promised son Isaac is a foreshadow of the promised adoption of the Church as God's spiritual family. As with Isaac, disciples of Jesus Christ become the people of God through miraculous birth— both the miraculous birth of Jesus and miraculous rebirth in baptism (more on that later).

It would be fair to say that the Jewish people would not easily be willing to see themselves as the antitype of Ishmael. This is especially true because the descendants of Ishmael became their traditional enemies: the Arab people. The Arabs have been the avowed enemies of Israel even to this day. Yet God, in his wisdom and foreknowledge made Ishmael, the child by natural descent, a type of Israel. Of course, the news for the Jews is not all bad because the promise of salvation—of spiritual circumcision and adoption into spiritual family line of Isaac—is available to the Jews as well if they will come to the Messiah, Jesus Christ.

Paul provides more details about the nature of the foreshadow God created in Ishmael and Isaac:

> *Tell me, you who want to be under the law, are you not aware of what the law says? For it is written that Abraham had two sons, one by the slave woman and the other by the free woman. His son by the slave woman was born in the ordinary way; but his son by the free woman was born as the result of a promise.*
>
> *These things may be taken figuratively* (as symbols or foreshadows), *for the women represent the two covenants. One covenant is from Mount Sinai in Arabia and corresponds to the present city of Jerusalem, because she is in slavery with her children. But the Jerusalem that is above is free, and she is our mother.... Now you, brothers, like Isaac are children* (antitypes) *of promise. At that time the son born in the ordinary way persecuted the son born by the power of the Spirit. It is the same now. But what does the Scripture say? "Get rid of the slave woman and her son, for the slave woman's son will never share in the inheritance with the free woman's son." Therefore, brothers, we are not children* (antitypes) *of the slave woman but of the free woman* (Galatians 4:21-31).

After Hagar became pregnant, Sarah was embittered and jealous. She drove Hagar off into the wilderness. An angel appeared to Hagar and told her to return to submit to Sarah, saying of Ishmael, *"He will be like a wild donkey of a man; his hand will be against everyone and everyone's hand against him, and he will live in hostility toward all his brothers"* (Genesis 16:12). Could any more accurate prophecy about the Arab nations have been spoken? It is deeply ironic that Ishmael became the physical father of the Arab peoples, yet God made him a biblical type of the nation of Israel.

Thirteen years later, the child of promise, Isaac, was born. Shortly after, in a fit of jealousy, Sarah said to Abraham, *"...get rid of that slave woman and her son, for that slave woman's son will never share in the inheritance with my son Isaac"* (Genesis 21:10). Little did Sarah know when she acted on her jealousy, that she would be acting out a foreshadow of what would occur over eighteen centuries later. Forty years after the birth of the church of Christ on the Day of Pentecost, Jerusalem was destroyed and the Old Covenant sacrificial system ended forever in A.D. 70. God judged his first child, physical Israel and instead blessed his younger, promised child, spiritual Israel—the New Testament Church.

Is there any possibility that this is all just a set of chance events? Could the writers of the New Testament have simply scanned the various stories in the Old Testament until they found ones appropriate to making their theological points? Again, if there were only one or two examples of this sort of thing, this might be a reasonable conclusion, but the weight of evidence is mounting, and we have a very long way to go!

In 1 Corinthians 10:11, Paul says that, *"These things happened to them as examples and were written down as warnings for us..."* Paul is claiming that God caused the events in the life of Abraham, Isaac, Moses and others to happen in a specific way in order to teach us how to live. We would do well to study the life of Abraham and imitate his faith so that we might become children of Abraham.

But there is still much more in the life of Abraham which serves as a foreshadow of things to come. Consider God's call to Abraham to sacrifice his son. What a wonderful picture of what God has done for us in being willing to sacrifice his own son! When God said "Abraham!", one surely would not have blamed him if he had replied "Go away and leave me alone!" God's call to Abraham often involved sacrifice. Instead, Abraham said *"Here I am."* Then God said, *"Take your son, you only son Isaac..."* (Genesis 22:24). Is this a foreshadow? How could anyone deny that it is? God sent his son and like Abraham, he was willing to sacrifice his only son for us. Did the Jews understand the true nature—the deep symbolism about our relationship with him—buried in this amazing story? Most probably did not.

We had a need. *"The wages of sin is death"* (Romans 6:23), *"...and without the shedding of blood there is no forgiveness"* (Hebrews 9:22). The need was sacrifice—blood sacrifice. In this heart-wrenching story, we can see Abraham's response to the call to sacrifice his son, his only son. *"Early the next morning Abraham got up and saddled his donkey."* In the face of this amazing foreshadow, can anyone reasonably claim that the life of Jesus was just an accident, or perhaps that God was making things up as he went along? God had a plan to send his only son to save mankind from the beginning and he inexorably carried it out.

Abraham was willing to give up his son, his only son. In this story we have a type and an antitype. Abraham the father of Isaac is the type. The antitype is God, the father of us all. When Abraham traveled those three arduous days to the Mount Moriah he was unwittingly demonstrating God's willingness to sacrifice that which is nearest and dearest to himself for our sake.

And it is not coincidence that the journey to Mount Moriah lasted for three days. This too tells us about God sacrificing his son for our sins. From the moment Abraham set out with his son to make the sacrifice, Isaac was as good as dead. Three days later, Abraham received his sacrificed son back from the dead. This prefigures the three days between the crucifixion of Jesus and his resurrection, when God received his son back from the dead. For many years, I puzzled over the phrase in 1 Corinthians 15:4, *"that he was raised on the third day according to the Scriptures."* I always asked myself what prophecy in the Old Testament predicted that the Messiah would be raised from death on the third day. Genesis 22:1-14 is one such prophecy. Another is the three days that Jonah was in the belly of the big fish.

In this dramatic scene, Isaac serves as a type as well. God allowed the son of Abraham to stand as a foreshadow of the Son of God. One aspect of this amazing story which is often missed is seen in Isaac's behavior. How did Isaac feel about all this? We do not know when he caught on to what was happening, but at some point, he said, *"Father?"..."The fire and wood are here, but where is the lamb for the burnt offering?"* (Genesis 22:7). Jesus was led like a lamb to the slaughter, as was Isaac. Abraham did not have to knock Isaac out or drag him on top of the pile of wood. Both sons willingly offered themselves as a sacrifice.

It is not just an accident that God called Abraham to travel all the way to Mount Moriah. Why Mount Moriah? Moriah happens to be the same hill on which the Temple was later built (2 Chronicles 3:1). The place where Abraham offered up his son is now part of the city of Jerusalem, where Jesus was condemned. It is only a short distance from the place where Jesus was sacrificed for our sin. God asked Abraham to live out a play on the same stage which he planned to use eighteen hundred years later to reenact what Abraham did in offering up his son. Abraham was unaware of the impact of his example. He simply obeyed God. The writer of Genesis was also unaware of the amazing future symbolism he was recording when these words were recorded. Did Abraham want to sacrifice his son? Did God want to sacrifice his Son? Did Isaac want to be sacrificed? *"Not as I will, but as you will"* (Matthew 26:39). Jesus was a reluctant but willing sacrifice, as was Isaac.

We have seen that from God's view, sin requires sacrifice. When Abraham raised the knife, Isaac's life was forfeit. At the last moment, God supplied a lamb so that Isaac need not be killed. Without Jesus, we are destined for death. Fortunately for us, *"at just the right time, when we were still powerless, Christ died for the ungodly"* (Romans 5:6). God used these events to illustrate his relationship with us.

IV. SODOM AND GOMORRAH

When God judged the cities of Sodom and Gomorrah, the symbolism was not subtle. Even for those with virtually no exposure to the Bible the names Sodom and Gomorrah have strong implications. The word sodomy derives from this story. God is serious about sin! We should remember that what God did to these cities, he did *"as examples, to keep us from setting our hearts on evil things as they did"* (1 Corinthians 10:6).

The cities of Soddom and Gomorrah stand as types of the horror of sin. The situation in these cities was so bad that it was virtually impossible, even for a person with a good heart, to remain uncorrupted.

> *Before they had gone to bed, all the men from every part of the city of Sodom—both young and old—surrounded the house. They called out to Lot, "Where are the men who came to you tonight? Bring them out to us so that we can have sex with them"* (Genesis 19:4,5).

Is the point of this story the horror of the specific sin they wanted to engage in? That may be one point of the story, but the main point is the pervasiveness of sin and how we can be corrupted if we allow ourselves to become immersed in a culture where people have given themselves up to sin.

If the city of Sodom is symbolic of sin, then what happened to the city is a foreshadow as well. *"He condemned the cities of Sodom and Gomorrah by burning them to ashes, and made them an example of what is going to happen to the ungodly"* (2 Peter 2:6). The message of Sodom and Gomorrah is that unrepented sin will not go unpunished. No less a teacher than Jesus Christ himself preached this message. *"It was the same in the days of Lot. People were eating and drinking, buying and selling, planting and building. But the day Lot left Sodom, fire and sulfur rained down from heaven and destroyed them all"* (Luke 17:28,29). Normally, God will allow the sin of individuals to go unpunished, at least for a time. He does this in order to give them an opportunity to come to their senses. In the case of Sodom and Gomorrah, God decided to set for us a graphic example of what is in store for the wicked who abuse the patience of God.

The story of Sodom and Gomorrah is not all doom and gloom. Even in the very darkest hour, when sin appears to be in total control, the love and the grace of God is working. Among the horror that was Sodom, there was one righteous man. Never mind the fact that Lot had no business being there. He should have moved out of there a long time before. In this story, Lot is a type. Lot stands for those who would remain righteous in a wicked and depraved world which takes every opportunity to drag us down. Lot was not perfect, but Lot still clung to his relationship with God. As with Lot, so with those of us who are willing to remain unstained by the world. Lot is the tattered but surviving remnant. Lot is the one who makes it to heaven, but in the words of Paul, *"...only as one escaping from flames"* (1 Corinthians 3:15). Lot is the disciple of Jesus who just barely hangs in there. Just barely hanging in there is not great, but it beats giving up by a mile! Abraham is greater than Lot, but Lot makes it to heaven! That counts for something. It is telling that God called Lot, a person who just barely made it, a righteous man (2 Peter 2:7).

Lot's wife is a type as well. As is typical, God can make even the smallest detail of history stand for a great truth and teach us about a relationship with him. *"But Lot's wife looked back and she became a pillar of salt"* (Genesis 19:26).

Lot's wife is a foreshadow of someone who would leave their

life of sin, become a disciple of Jesus, but later turn back. What is God trying to teach us about turning back to our old life of sin after deciding to follow him? Jesus put it simply, *"Remember Lot's wife!"* (Luke 17:32).

This story actually happened.[3] In fact, I hesitate to use the word story because in common English usage the word story often implies something made up. This story is not a fable. In the story of Sodom and Gomorrah we have sin and God's judgment on sin. We also have the grace of God. The same flames which destroy many can purify the one who barely escapes them. We see the opportunity to flee from a life of sin. However, contained in that opportunity is also a warning. Leaving your life of sin is not enough. *"No one who puts his hands to the plow and looks back is not fit for service in kingdom of God"* (Luke 9:62). Again, an event in the Old Testament foreshadows a teaching in the New.

V. JACOB AND ESAU

God gave another object lesson about his relationship with us in the lives of the twins Jacob and Esau. In fact, even before they were born, these two were teaching us about the sovereignty of God. In Israelite custom, the first born son received a double portion of the inheritance from his father. In this case, the father was Isaac, who stood in the direct lineage of Jesus Christ. The birth of Esau and Jacob represents a major fork in the road for God's plan to bless humanity through the seed of Abraham. In a foreshadow of things to come, as Esau came forth from his mother Rebekah first, Jacob grabbed his heel. Jacob was not about to concede anything to his older brother! From that moment forward, Jacob spent his life trying to grab from Essau what rightly belonged to the first born.

God used Esau as a type of Israel and the Old Covenant, while Jacob is a type whose antitype is the New Covenant church. Israel came first, and was, by rights, the first-born child of God. Yet God, in his sovereign will, chose to take the right of the first born son and give it to the Gentiles—to those who become sons of God through the blood of Christ. Hundreds of years before God established the first Covenant at Mount Sinai, he foreshadowed that a later covenant would supersede it.

God demonstrated and prophesied this fact in the lives of

Jacob and Esau. The story of Esau selling his birthright for a bowl of lentil stew is proverbial. When Esau came home famished from a hunting trip, Jacob tricked him into trading his right as first born son. In a statement which would echo through human history, Esau said:

> *"What good is the birthright to me?"*
> *But Jacob said, "Swear to me first." So he swore an oath to him, selling his birthright to Jacob.*
> *Then Jacob gave Esau some bread and some lentil stew. He ate and he drank, and then got up and left.*
> *So Esau despised his birthright* (Genesis 25:32-34).

The Jews under the Old Covenant who read this story identified themselves with Jacob. All along, God had a different intention. Paul explains what God had in mind in Romans 9:10-13:

> *Not only that, but Rebecca's children had one and the same father, our father Isaac. Yet, before the twins were born or had done anything good or bad—in order that God's purpose in election might stand: not by works but by him who calls—she was told, "The older will serve the younger." Just as it is written: "Jacob have I loved, but Esau have I hated."*

Paul is quoting Genesis 18:10,14 and Genesis 25:23, and applying the story to Gentile Christians and Jews who do not accept faith in Jesus Christ. The application of the story of Jacob and Esau to New Testament theology is worked out in detail in Romans. God chose Israel first, but he replaced the Old Covenant (Esau, the law of Moses) with the New Covenant (Jacob, the law of Christ). It was God's intention all along to make the former the servant of the latter.

This is exactly what happened with Jacob and Esau. In fact, we say Jacob and Esau, not Esau and Jacob, even though Esau was born first. Esau lost more than the right of the first-born to Jacob's machinations. Genesis twenty-seven records the deceitful means by which Jacob, at the encouragement of his mother, pretended to be his hairy older twin, bringing in his father's favorite dish as he lay near death. Jacob took advantage of Isaac's blindness, fooling him into giving him his final blessing. As Isaac said:

> *"I blessed him—and indeed he will be blessed!"*

> When Esau heard his father's words, he burst out with a loud and bitter cry and said to his father, "Bless me—me too, my father!" (Genesis 27:33,34).

Esau begged for at least some sort of blessing, but:

> Isaac answered Esau, "I have made him lord over you and have made all his relatives his servants, and I have sustained him with grain and new wine. So what can I possibly do for you, my son?" (Genesis 27:37).

Even today, God's blessing is found under the children of Jacob—those adopted into the family of God through the blood of Christ.

It is not surprising that Esau was jealous of his brother. In a scene which is a foreshadow of how the early church was treated by the Jewish community, Rebekah told her favorite son, Jacob, *"Your brother Esau is consoling himself with the thought of killing you. Now then, my son, do what I say: Flee at once to my brother Laban in Haran"* (Genesis 27:42,43).

It is not just coincidence that the second son received the blessing. God intervenes in history and God intervenes in families in order to bring about his master plan to bless all people through Abraham and his descendant, Jesus Christ. Again we can see Old Testament events foreshadowing a fundamental truth found in the New Testament. There are a number of lessons to be learned from the story of Jacob and Esau (remember, Paul said these things occurred as examples to us). It is instructive to notice that Jacob was far from perfect. God did not choose Jacob because he was so much more righteous than Esau. It is the same with anyone who is saved under the New Covenant. It is not that any of us are better than those who are lost. It is only the grace of God which gives us access into the blessing of Jacob—abundant life in Christ. There is no cause for boasting here.

Remember as well that Esau had the blessing of God at one time. In Hebrews 12:16, God warns us not to become *"like Esau, who for a single meal sold his inheritance rights as the oldest son. Afterward, as you know, when he wanted to inherit this blessing, he was rejected. He could bring about no change of mind, though he sought the blessing with tears."* Many have lost sight of the blessings they have in God's family and have sold their salvation for things as insignificant as a single meal; a better job, a one night stand, a better reputation and the like. It is possible to lose one's salvation. Let us take warning from Esau.

There is a great deal of symbolism contained in the remainder of the Genesis account. One could mention the symbolism contained in the incident of Jacob wrestling with the angel (Genesis 32:22-32). God had a New Testament teaching in mind when he renamed Jacob as Israel. The life of Joseph, the favorite son of Jacob stands as an amazing prefigure of Christ, but we will leave that for a later chapter. It is time to consider the exodus of God's people from Egypt.

THE EXODUS

I. SLAVERY IN EGYPT.

When Jacob's family fled to Egypt to escape the famine in Canaan, little did they know they were beginning a saga which would create an amazingly vivid image of all the stages by which God pursues a relationship with each of us. Remember that the theme of the entire Bible is God's desire and plan to have a relationship with each of the people he has created. The entire history of Israel is the acting out of an intricate play showing God's plan to have us in a relationship with him for eternity.

When Jacob, his eleven sons, their wives, children and servants fled to Egypt, initially it seemed to be a wise decision. In fact, if the sons of Jacob had not gone down to Egypt, God's plan to bring the Messiah through Abraham's descendants would not have come to fruition. At first, the Israelites flourished in Egypt. They became perhaps the single largest non-Egyptian segment of the population in Egypt. Ultimately, out of greed and out of fear that the Israelites might rebel and set up their own independent power in the Nile delta, the Pharaohs began a policy of subjecting Israel to slavery. Israel ended up in brutal bondage.

God uses the bondage of Israel in Egypt as a type. Throughout the New Testament, bondage in Egypt is used as a symbol of an individual's bondage to sin. Israel in Egypt is symbolic of any individual in bondage to sin before they are freed from sin through the blood of Christ. As Jesus said, *"I tell you the truth, everyone who sins is a slave to sin"* (John 8:34).

> *So they put slave masters over them to oppress them with forced labor, and they built Pithom and Rameses as store cities for Pharaoh. But the more they were oppressed, the more they multiplied and spread; so the Egyptians came to dread the Israelites and worked them ruthlessly. They made their lives bitter with hard labor in brick and mortar and with all kinds of work in the fields; in all their hard labor the Egyptians used them ruthlessly* (Exodus 1:11-13).

Truly, sin is a hard task master. It enslaves us and makes us participate in thoughts, attitudes, and acts we never thought we would do.

If there is one thing God hates, it is when the people he created are in bondage to sin. When we are in sin, we are not in fellowship with God. When God saw his people crying out under the misery of slavery in Egypt, he sent them a savior. We were enslaved to sin. In response, God sent a savior, Jesus Christ. Israel was enslaved in Egypt. In response, God sent Moses to free them from captivity. There is a clear type/antitype relationship here. God decided to do something about the slavery (sin) problem and he chose Moses as "savior" of Israel.

God set apart Moses from birth. Because Moses is a prefigure of the Messiah, we will discuss this aspect later in detail. Look, however, at what God said to Moses:

> *The Lord said, "I have indeed seen the misery of my people in Egypt. I have heard them crying out because of their slave drivers, and I am concerned about their suffering. So I have come down to rescue them from the hand of the Egyptians and to bring them up out of that land into a good and spacious land, a land flowing with milk and honey—the home of the Canaanites, Hittites, Amorites, Perizzites, Hivites and Jebusites. And now the cry of the Israelites has reached me, and I have seen the way the Egyptians are oppressing them. So now, go. I am sending you to Pharaoh to bring my people the Israelites out of Egypt"* (Exodus 3:7-10).

God refuses to let his people continue to suffer in bondage, just as he cannot accept us being enslaved to sin. When God heard them crying out, he had to do something, so he sent a savior.

Through the ministry of Moses and through the mighty power of God, Israel escaped slavery. (The Passover events are a significant part of the means of by which God freed Israel. The Passover as a foreshadow will be covered in chapter seven.) But how did they escape Egypt and the clutches of Pharaoh? How will we escape the life of sin? Thanks to ten plagues, Pharaoh's heart was softened sufficiently for him to let God's people go. But Satan does not give up easily, and neither did Pharaoh. When Pharaoh realized that he was losing his vast pool of free slave labor, he decided to call out his army and pursue Israel into the desert to bring them back. Sin is not only irrational, but it is often stubborn as well. Following God's direction, Moses led the people right up against the waters of the Red Sea.[4] He must have wondered why God led him into a death trap. "God, where has putting my trust in you led me?" Actually, what God led him into was a wonderful foreshadow of how we escape from a life of sin.

In one of the most memorable miracles in the Bible, when Moses raised his hands over the water, the Red Sea parted. Israel was able to escape slavery in Egypt by passing right through the midst of this great body of water. The waters of the Red Sea are the type, and the waters of baptism are the antitype. Is it any coincidence that God had his people escape slavery in Egypt through water? When it appeared that Moses and the people were lost in the desert, God was leading them right where he wanted. When the people escaped through the sea, the Egyptian army, the enslavers of Israel were quite literally washed away, as are our sins when we are "washed" in baptism. This is no accident!

> *For I do not want you to be ignorant of the fact, brothers, that our forefathers were all under the cloud and that they all passed through the sea. They were all baptized into Moses in the cloud and in the sea. They all ate the same spiritual food and drank the same spiritual drink; for they drank from the spiritual rock that accompanied them, and that rock was Christ* (1 Corinthians 10:1-4).

Being baptized into Moses by miraculously passing through the Red Sea must have made a lasting impression on the Jews. Being baptized into Christ (Galatians 3:27) is a life-changing experience as well.[5] There is a pattern here. When God's people are saved, there is a recurring tendency for it to involve water. We see this in

Noah's flood and in Israel's escape from Egypt, and this will not be the last time. Another recurring theme in the salvation events for Israel is that it required faith on the part of Israel to be "saved."

After escaping through the Red Sea, the nation of Israel, under the leadership of their "savior" Moses traveled to Mount Sinai where they received the Law. This is when the Old Covenant was given. Israel had escaped from slavery. Now they would be established in a relationship with their God. This is a foreshadow of a New Testament happening as well. When one is baptized into Christ, that person enters a new relationship with God through Christ. Much will be said in chapter five about the Law of Moses and the ways in which it provides a foreshadow of what we have in Christ.

II. Wandering in the Wilderness.

After Sinai, Israel wandered in the desert for forty years. What were they doing all this time? There are a number of possible answers to this question, but one thing we can be sure of: when Israel wandered in the desert, they were acting out a foreshadow for us. The wandering in the wilderness is a foreshadow of the life of a Christian. It tells us about being a follower (disciple) of Jesus. When one is baptized into Christ, one does not immediately leave the earth and go to heaven. When Israel left Egypt, they were still not prepared to enter the Promised Land. In fact, slavery in Egypt, wandering in the wilderness and entering the Promised Land are all types of aspects of the relationship with God one has under the

Old Testament Type	New Testament Antitype
Slavery In Egypt	Lost, Slave To Sin
Wandering In The Wilderness	Saved, But Living Life Of A Disciple
Entering The Promised Land	Entering Heaven

New Covenant, as illustrated on the chart on the previous page.

What was the purpose of wandering in the wilderness? At the end of the forty years, right before entering the Promised Land, God provided an answer to this very good question!

> *"Be careful to follow every command I am giving you today, so that you may live and increase and may enter and possess the land that the LORD promised on oath to your forefathers. Remember how the LORD your God led you all the way in the desert these forty years, to humble you and to test you in order to know what was in your heart, whether or not you would keep his commands. He humbled you, causing you to hunger and then feeding you with manna, which neither you nor your fathers had known, to teach you that man does not live on bread alone but on every word that comes from the mouth of the LORD. Your clothes did not wear out and your feet did not swell during these forty years. Know then in your heart that as a man disciplines his son, so the LORD your God disciplines you"* (Deuteronomy 8:1-5).

What a great description of the life of a follower of Jesus! The life of a Christian is made up of a series of opportunities to learn to rely on God. The Israelites were not ready to enter the Promised Land because they had not yet learned to trust God. Had the people of God marched from Egypt straight into Canaan, they would have been tempted *"...beyond what they could bear"* (1 Corinthians 10:13), to trust in their own power to save themselves. Instead, God sent them out into the desert for forty years. The desert wilderness south of Palestine could never support the physical needs of two million people. Israel was forced to rely on God for both food and water.

The message to those under the New Covenant is clear. If we feel we have "arrived" after being saved by the blood of Jesus, we are fooling ourselves. We must constantly be trained to rely on God for our spiritual food and water or we will never enter our spiritual Promised Land: heaven.

One can imagine how at first, the people of Israel were excited to be led by the pillar of fire in the desert. They were astonished and encouraged to receive their food out of the sky in the form of manna and to get their water out of a rock. Later on however, the amazement dulled and these blessings seemed like normal everyday things and the people longed to return to Egypt. *"If only we* had meat to eat! We remember the fish we ate in Egypt at no cost—also the cucumbers, melons, leeks, onions and garlic. But now we have lost our appetite; we never see anything but this manna!"* (Exodus 11:4-6). Did they forget that they had been slaves in Egypt? They told themselves that the food in Egypt was free. True, but it was free only because they were slaves and had no money! Did they forget that they worked fourteen hour days, seven days a week? Did they forget that Pharaoh had decreed that all the male Israelite children would be slaughtered? Yes they did. Followers of Jesus should remember that Israel in the desert is the type, but Christians are the antitype. It is really inspiring to see some of the types and antitypes in the Old and New Testaments, but when the antitype is yourself, that is a good reason to pay attention. We must be very careful to not become like these ungrateful people. We will respond just like them if we do not take the warning offered by this challenging episode. We must rely on God, not self, to make it to heaven, and we must continue to appreciate the daily blessings we have from being in a relationship with God.

This is the message of Hebrews 3:14-4:2 (indeed, it is the message of the entire book of Hebrews [see also Hebrews 2:1-4, 6:4-12 and 10:35-39]):

> *We have come to share in Christ if we hold firmly till the end the confidence we had at first. As has just been said:*
>   *"Today, if you hear his voice,*
>   *do not harden your hearts*
>   *as you did in the rebellion."*
> *Who were they who heard and rebelled? Were they not all those Moses led out of Egypt? And with whom was he angry for forty years? Was it not with those who sinned, whose bodies fell in the desert? And to whom did God swear that they would never enter his rest if not to those who disobeyed? So we see that they were not able to enter, because of their unbelief. Therefore, since the promise of entering his rest still stands, let us be careful that none of you be found to have fallen short of it. For we also have had the gospel preached to us, just as they did; but the message they heared was of no value to them, because those who heard did not combine it with faith.*

"The promise still stands" because of the type/antitype

Historical Prefigures

relationship between the Old and the New Testament. Remember, those *"whose bodies fell in the desert"* are those who become disciples, receive the Holy Spirit, but later turn back. They never enter the Promised Land. They never enter heaven. It could happen to anyone who does not pay attention to the message!

A common teaching in the Christian world is that once a person is saved by the blood of Jesus, it is impossible for that person to lose salvation. However, the type set up by God makes it crystal clear that once someone enters the freedom implied in a relationship with God through leaving slavery to sin (Egypt), it is entirely possible to lose that salvation—to figuratively return to Egypt. Leaving Egypt does not necessarily imply entering the Promised Land. Similarly, leaving the life of sin does not mean that a person cannot return to it, thereby losing an opportunity to enter the Promised Land: heaven.[6]

What do followers of Jesus need to do to sustain their walk with God? Let us look at the type—wandering in the wilderness—to find the answer. Israel needed food and water. God provided food in the form of manna. By now, the reader will not be surprised that the manna was a foreshadow as well. After performing the miracle of multiplying bread for a crowd in the wilderness, Jesus was asked to perform another miracle. Instead, Jesus took the opportunity to teach them about himself:

> *"What miraculous sign then will you give that we may see it and believe you? What will you do? Our forefathers ate the manna in the desert; as it is written: "He gave them bread from heaven to eat."'*
>
> *Jesus said to them, "I tell you the truth, it is not Moses who has given you the bread from heaven, but it is my Father who gives you the true bread from heaven. For the bread of God is he who comes down from heaven and gives life to the world."*
>
> *"Sir," they said, "from now on give us this bread."*
>
> *Then Jesus declared, "I am the bread of life. He who comes to me will never go hungry, and he who believes in me will never be thirsty"* (John 6:30-35).

Manna is the type, and Jesus is the antitype. For the Christian, Jesus is spiritual food. In fact, as with Israel in the wilderness for whom manna was all they had to eat, Jesus is our only spiritual food. This concept is easy to understand, but hard to put into practice. Christians, like the Israelites, are sorely tempted every day to forget where their spiritual food comes from.

Jesus was absolutely right in reminding the Jews that Moses did not give them bread. It fell out of the sky while Moses was asleep! However, God did use Moses as his agent to call forth water for the people out of a rock.

> *But there was no water to drink. So they quarreled with Moses and said, "Give us water to drink."*
>
> *Then Moses cried out to the Lord, "What am I to do with these people? They are almost ready to stone me."*
>
> *The Lord answered Moses, "Walk on ahead of the people. Take with you some of the elders of Israel and take in your hand the staff with which you struck the Nile, and go. I will stand there before you by the rock at Horeb. Strike the rock, and water will come out of it for the people to drink"* (Exodus 17:1,2,4,5,6).

The waters at Meribah are the type, but what is the antitype in this case? It is the Holy Spirit which God pours out on all those who believe. As Jesus said:

> *"If a man is thirsty, let him come to me and drink. Whoever believes in me, as the Scripture has said, streams of living water will flow from within him." By this he meant the Spirit, whom those who believed in him were later to receive. Up to that time the Spirit had not been given, since Jesus had not yet been glorified* (John 7:37-39)

While wandering in the wilderness, the Hebrew people had all their physical needs provided directly by God. For those who have been called out of their old life by Jesus to walk in the "wilderness" with him, all their spiritual needs—their spiritual food and drink—are met in Jesus Christ and in the Holy Spirit. The challenge, of course, is to not lose sight of this fact and to act on it on a daily basis. Unfortunately, the Israelites did not do this and many of them fell in the wilderness. Let's not follow their example!

III. Entering the Promised Land.

After they had wandered in the desert for forty years, God had refined a people who were more or less faithful and trusting in him. At last, they were ready to enter the Promised Land! This fulfilled the promise given to Abraham, centuries before.

> *The Lord said to Abram after Lot had parted from him, "Lift up your eyes from where you are and look north and south, east and west. All the land that you see I will give to you and your offspring forever"* (Genesis 13:14,15).

Entering the Promised Land represented victory to God's chosen people. This was the ultimate. The Promised Land—Canaan—was pretty good. In fact it was more than good—it was awesome.

> *"For the Lord your God is bringing you into a good land—a land with streams and pools of water, with springs flowing in the valleys and hills; a land with wheat and barley, vines and fig trees, pomegranates, olive oil and honey; a land where bread will not be scarce and you will lack nothing; a land where the rocks are iron and you can dig copper out of the hills"* (Deuteronomy 8:7-9).

The type was pretty good, but the antitype is far better. God promised Israel that he would provide all they needed in the Promised Land. However, Canaan was only a foreshadow of something far greater. The physical Promised Land of Israel is a foreshadow of the spiritual promised land: heaven. God's goal for Israel was for them to dwell in the land—to experience a blessed and fulfilled life in fellowship with him. That is what the Promised Land was all about. And that is what heaven is all about. As Jesus said:

> *"Do not let your hearts be troubled. Trust in God; trust also in me. In my father's house are many rooms; if it were not so, I would have told you. I am going there to prepare a place for you. And if I go and prepare a place for you, I will come back and take you to be with me that you also may be where I am"* (John 14:1-3).

The Promised Land was a place to experience the blessings of God. It was a place to rest, secure in God's arms. That is what heaven will be for those who enter the heavenly Promised Land. However, God wants to remind us one more time, that we must make every effort to enter that rest.

> *It still remains that some will enter that rest, and those who formerly had the gospel preached to them did not go in, because*

> *of their disobedience. Therefore God again set a certain day, calling it Today, when a long time later he spoke through David, as was said before:*
>
> > *"Today if you hear his voice,*
> > *do not harden you hearts."*
>
> *For if Joshua had given them rest, God would not have spoken later about another day. There remains, then, a Sabbath-rest for the people of God; for anyone who enters God's rest also rests from his own work, just as God did from his. Let us, therefore, make every effort to enter that rest, so that no one will fall by following their example of disobedience* (Hebrews 4:6-11).

The people of God clearly could not enter Canaan on their own power, as we cannot get to heaven by our own strength. Nevertheless, God wants us to make every effort to hold fast to him so that we will not fall in the desert. Our effort is never enough to enter heaven, but without effort, we will not reach the Promised Land.

God used Moses to lead the people right up to the verge of Canaan. However, God was not done teaching his people about relying on him. The people of God were right on the border of the Promised Land, but there was the matter of a little river.... The Jordan was at flood stage. God wanted to provide one more reminder that they could only enter Canaan by his miraculous power. Naturally the same applies to the antitype. None of us will enter heaven on our own power. A response is required, but human effort is not sufficient to be saved. It is not as though the Jews could have taken a running start and cleared the Jordan at flood stage. The stage was set for another miracle (and another foreshadow).

> *So when the people broke camp to cross the Jordan, the priests carrying the ark of the covenant went ahead of them. Now the Jordan is at flood stage all during harvest. Yet as soon as the priests who carried the ark reached the Jordan and their feet touched the water's edge, the water from upstream stopped flowing. It piled up in a heap a great distance away, at a town called Adam in the vicinity of Zarethan, while the water flowing down to the Sea of Arabah was completely cut off. So the people crossed over opposite Jericho* (Joshua 3:14-16).

Just as God's people had required a "savior," Moses, to leave slavery in Egypt, they required a savior to enter the Promised Land.

This new prefigure of the Messiah was Joshua. We see a recurring theme here as God's people enter a covenant relationship with God in the Promised Land by passing through water.

The type is the Promised Land. The antitype is heaven. We can learn from the type that heaven is a place where we can live in fellowship with God. It is God's goal to make us into his people so that we can dwell with him. From the foreshadow we see that heaven is a place where we will be blessed beyond our wildest dreams. Canaan represents heaven; a place where we will be able to rest with God from our labors.

IV. IN CANAAN: A MIXED SYMBOL

Once God's people entered the Promised Land, the type changed. Therefore the antitype changed as well. Up to the time God's people entered Canaan, God was using it as a symbol of our Sabbath-rest with him in heaven. Once the people actually entered the land under Joshua, the type (being in Palestine) no longer fit the antitype (being in heaven). Although Canaan was truly a place flowing with milk and honey, it was no cake walk for Israel to conquer and occupy the land. From the beginning of the book of Joshua on—throughout the rest of the historical books of the Bible—living in the Promised Land becomes a type, not of heaven, but of the church: the Kingdom of God.[7] We will see much more on this in chapter nine. Israel's corporate battles with its neighbors will become a symbol of our individual battle with sin. Israel's kings, especially David, will become a symbol of the king in heaven: Jesus Christ.[8]

Because the symbolism attached to Canaan changes, depending on where it falls historically in the Bible, it is easy to become confused. In order to help keep things straight it is helpful to think of the Promised Land as a symbol of heaven in the Pentateuch (the first five books of the Old Testament), but to think of Israel in Canaan as a symbol of the kingdom of God and our personal relationship with God from the book of Joshua through the rest of the Bible.

With this in mind, it becomes easier to make sense of the symbolism of the crossing of the Jordan River. As Israel was baptized into Moses when they passed through the waters of the Red Sea, so they were baptized into Joshua when they passed through the waters of the Jordan. It is true that this is never actually stated in the New Testament, but the symbolism is fairly obvious.

If one is not completely convinced of this claim, what God commanded Israel to do immediately upon passing through the Jordan will make it much clearer.

> *At that time the Lord said to Joshua, "Make flint knives and circumcise the Israelites again." So Joshua made flint knives and circumcised the Israelites at Gibeath Haaraloth* (Joshua 5:2,3).

Although God had commanded every Israelite male to be circumcised on the eighth day, for the forty years of wandering in the wilderness, the Jews had not circumcised their male children. Why is that? God may have had a number of reasons, but it just so happens that in doing so, God made the events at Giveath Haaraloth to be a type of one of the important concepts in the New Testament.

Circumcision is a type whose antitype is baptism. For the male Hebrew child, circumcision is what made them part of Israel. Under the Old Covenant, the Jews were born into a relationship with God. For the male Israelite, this relationship was consummated on the eighth day when the child was circumcised. Under the New Covenant, one is born again into the kingdom of God in baptism.

> *In him you were also circumcised, in the putting off of the sinful nature, not with a circumcision done by the hands of men but with the circumcision done by Christ, having been buried with him in baptism and raised with him through your faith in the power of God, who raised him from the dead* (Colossians 2:11,12).

Paul makes it very clear that circumcision is the type, while baptism is the antitype. Baptism is spiritual circumcision. For the Jews, circumcision occurs soon after birth, while baptism is a rebirth. As Jesus said, *"I tell you the truth, unless a man is born of water and the Spirit, he cannot enter the kingdom of God"* (John 3:5). Israel had to be circumcised in order to enter the type, which is Canaan, a type of the kingdom of God. Circumsion was a physical sign of being part of physical Israel. It did not require faith on the part of the one receiving it. Those who come to God through faith in Christ must enter the spiritual kingdom of God through the spiritual circumcision, which is baptism.

In order to enter Canaan, God's people had to pass through water and they had to be circumcised. Could God have created a more clear symbolism than he did? What makes the event and its symbolism most amazing is that when Israel acted out this play for us, they had no idea of the significance of their acts. It was a mystery to them, but the mystery is revealed to us in the New Testament. When the writers of the Old Testament recorded this history, they too had no idea how God would turn all this into a dramatic representation of how we enter a relationship with him under the New Covenant.

There is more prefigure to be found in the entrance of the twelve tribes into the Promised Land. We have already seen that *"...as soon as the priests who carried the ark reached the Jordan and their feet touched the water's edge, the water from upstream stopped flowing"* (Joshua 3:15,16). It took great faith for the Levites carrying the ark to march right into the river at flood stage. The moment the ark reached the river the water stopped. This was not some sort of natural phenomenon which God somehow used to stop the flow of the river. This was a supernatural event. We will see in the chapter on the Tabernacle that the ark is a type of the presence of God. God was showing Israel and us that it is only his power which can part the waters, allowing us freedom to enter his presence. It is the same with the antitype to the waters of the Jordan. *"Having been buried with him in baptism and raised with him through your faith in the power of God."* In both the type and in the antitype, God is telling us that only through a combination of his power and our faith can we pass through the waters into a relationship with him.[9]

Consider one more prefigure in the entry of God's chosen people into the Land. Who was it that led them into physical Israel—into the presence of God? It was Joshua. As we will see in chapter two, Joshua is a type of Christ. The Hebrew name Joshua is the Aramaic name Jeshua, transliterated into Greek as Jesus. I suppose one could argue it's coincidence, but given all the other parallels between the Old Testament and the New, one can detect God's work, even down to the names involved. The name of he who led God's people into a covenant relationship with God in the Promised Land in the Old Testament is the same as he who leads God's people into the New Covenant relationship with God.

In the story of the entry of Israel under Joshua into the

Promised Land the Bible has given foreshadows of the place of baptism, of faith, of the power of God and of the work of Jesus in bringing people into a relationship with him.

CAPTIVITY AND SALVATION OF GOD'S PEOPLE

There is a great deal of type and antitype found throughout the periods of the Judges and of the Two Kingdoms. These will be covered in other chapters. The Jews should not have been surprised that if they turned their backs on God, it would result again in captivity and slavery similar to what they had experienced in Egypt. God prophesied this to them in very clear and graphic terms. In his parting words to the people, Moses said to Israel that if they were unfaithful to their God and did not obey all his commands and decrees:

> "The Lord will drive you and the king you set over you to a nation unknown to you or your fathers. There you will worship other gods, gods of wood and stone. You will become a thing of horror and an object of scorn and ridicule to all nations where the Lord will drive you....
> Because of the suffering that your enemy will inflict on you during the siege, you will eat the fruit of the womb, the flesh of the sons and daughters the LORD your God has given you.
> The LORD will scatter you among the nations, from one end of the earth to the other....Among those nations you will find no repose, no resting place for the sole of your foot. There the LORD will give you an anxious mind, eyes weary with longing, and a despairing heart" (Deuteronomy 28:36,37,53,64,65).

Tragically, this prophecy was fulfilled in all its detail. Despite Moses' warning in Deuteronomy and despite God's repeated efforts to warn his people, they continued to rebel against him. They turned aside from the commands in the Law of Moses, turning to the idols of their pagan neighbors. Repeatedly, God tried to save them from being "lost" by sending kings and judges to "save" them. Besides this, he sent preachers of righteousness: prophets such as Elijah, Isaiah, Jeremiah and many others. Unfortunately, despite God's repeated loving call for his people to return to him, the great majority of Israel became hardened to their sin.

Soon after the death of Solomon, King David's son, the

kingdom was divided by the rebellion of Jereboam. The Northern Kingdom, or Samaria, was extremely idolatrous from the beginning. They worshipped at the Asherah poles. They set up shrines to Baal. They ignored the pleadings of Elijah and Elisha, so God fulfilled his words to them. Samaria, the capital of the Northern Kingdom, was destroyed by the Assyrian armies under Sennacherib in 722 B.C. Of those not killed in the conflict, the majority were deported as slaves and scattered throughout the Assyrian Empire. Israel was back in slavery.

The Southern Kingdom, Judah, was more faithful, at least outwardly. The temple was in Jerusalem, the capital of Judah. Many of the most faithful Jews migrated south. With time, however, even Judah became corrupt, turning to idolatry and every form of prideful rebellion against God. True to his word in Deuteronomy and to many other warnings, God sent Nebuchadnezzar, king of Babylon, to devour and conquer Judah. After repeated attacks and deportations, Jerusalem was finally captured, burned and its wall destroyed in 586 B.C. Again, thousands were deported into slavery in Babylon and other cities of the empire. At the same time, most significantly, the temple was destroyed and sacrifice for sin in Jerusalem at the temple came to an end. God was no longer dwelling with his people.

What a horrific foreshadow to contemplate! What is God's message in this turn of events? To the Jews, of course, the message is that God hates sin and rebellion. In this case, the type is the return of Israel to slavery. The antitype is anyone who takes on Jesus Christ as Lord, thus entering a relationship with God. The message is that once we come into a relationship with God through Jesus Christ, if we turn back to our old ways, God will return us to the same slavery we came from. In fact, if the type is accurate, the second slavery is worse than the first. God used the lives of tens of thousands of Jews at the time of Sennacherib and Nebuchadnezzar to teach us a lesson. May that lesson not go unlearned! The words of Peter describe the antitype:

> If they have escaped the corruption of the world by knowing our Lord and Savior Jesus Christ and are again entangled in it and overcome, they are worse off at the end than they were at the beginning. It would have been better for them not to have known the way of righteousness, than to have known it and then to turn their backs on the sacred commandment that was passed on to

them. Of them the proverbs are true: "A dog returns to its vomit," and, "A sow that is washed goes back to her wallowing in the mud" (2 Peter 2:20-22).

Remember the words of Paul, *"Now these things occurred as examples, to keep us from setting our hearts on evil things as they did"* (1 Corinthians 10:6). Amidst the very sobering message, let us be sure to get the lesson of the type and the antitype clearly understood. It is not as if Israel sinned once and boom—off to captivity. It is not as if we need to live in daily mortal fear of losing our salvation. The New Testament assures us, and the foreshadowing in the Old Testament demonstrates to us, that as long as we remain faithful, God will not put us away from his presence for sinful setbacks. In fact even a major offense will not send us back onto slavery to sin. God appealed to Israel time and time again. He sent messengers into their lives, he gave them second chances, he listened to their death-bed repentances, and still he withheld his judgment. He will do the same with those under the New Covenant. However, God's grace is not without limit when we turn our backs on him. The destruction of Samaria and Jerusalem are stark reminders of this fact.

The destruction and deportation of Israel and Judah are not unique examples in history. Many ancient peoples experienced such a thing. However, the restoration of Israel to the Promised Land is another thing entirely. Again, God had prophesied to his people almost a thousand years before these events:

> *"When all these blessings and curses I have set before you come upon you and you take them to heart wherever the LORD you God disperses you among the nations, and when you and your children return to the LORD your God and obey him with all your heart and with all you soul according to everything I command you today, then the LORD your God will restore your fortunes and have compassion on you and gather you again from all the nations where he scattered you. Even if you have been banished to the most distant land under the heavens, from there the LORD your God will gather you and bring you back. He will bring you to the land that belonged to your fathers, and you will take possession of it"* (Deuteronomy 30:1-5).

When God proposes, he also disposes. After seventy years of

captivity, as prophesied by Jeremiah (Jeremiah 25:8-12), God used Cyrus the Persian to conquer the Babylonian Empire. When Cyrus had finished off Babylon, he gave permission for the captives of Israel to return to Jerusalem to rebuild the temple and to reestablish worship there. Ezra chapters one and two record the decree of Cyrus and the list of exiles who returned to repopulate Jerusalem and reestablish the priestly sacrifice. There is virtually no parallel in history of a conquering power allowing formerly dispossessed people to travel great distances to return to their homeland in order to restore their national identity and religion.

What does the historical restoration of Israel to the Promised Land tell us? Given the fulfillment of prophecy, we can learn from this that the Old Testament is inspired by God and that God rules the nations. God caused Moses to prophecy the restoration of Israel when they repented almost one thousand years before it happened. He also raised up Cyrus and put it on his heart to send the Israelites back to their homeland.

There is another lesson here as well. In this case, Israel and its relationship with God is the type, while individual Christians in their relationship with God are the antitype. The captivity of Israel under Assyria and Babylon tells us that it is possible to have God withdraw his blessing, but the miraculous return of the Jews scattered across the Babylonian Empire shows that God will go to great length to make an opportunity for us to return. If we leave God, he will let us go. We can lose our close fellowship with God. However, we can come back. This is reminiscent of the parable of the lost sheep.

> *"What do you think? If a man owns a hundred sheep, and one of them wanders away, will he not leave the ninety-nine on the hills and go to look for the one that wandered off? And if he finds it, I tell you the truth, he is happier about that one sheep than about the ninety-nine that did not wander off. In the same way your Father in heaven is not willing that any of these little ones should be lost"* (Matthew 18:12-14).

If God would go through all the trouble to set up a prophetic symbol of his willingness to take us back—if God would take a repentant Israel back after they had turned from him to gross idolatry and every other kind of sin, then surely we should not give up on anyone who has left God.

CONCLUSION

Many theologians and critics of the Bible over the years have claimed that the essential message and theology of the Old and the New Testament are radically different from one another. For example, some have charged that the Old Testament describes God as angry and judgmental, whereas the New Testament envisions a God who is loving and full of grace. Some would go so far as to claim that these two views of God are so opposed that the two Testaments cannot be theologically harmonized with one another. Does this claim hold up to careful scrutiny?

It is obviously true that one finds a progressive revelation of God to his people in the Bible. In the earlier books of the Old Testament, the nature of salvation by grace and the concepts of heaven and hell are taught principally by foreshadow rather than by direct statement. Gradually, as one moves through the Old Testament, the teaching about the resurrection and Judgment Day become more clearly stated, especially in the book of Daniel. Finally, God completes his revelation to mankind about his nature, about the final resurrection, heaven and hell in the New Testament.

It may be true that God's revelation is progressive, but the claim that the picture of God and his relationship with man is different in the Old and New Testament simply does not agree with the facts. When one looks at the symbolism of the events which happened to Adam and Eve, to Noah, Abraham, Isaac, Jacob, Joseph, Moses, Joshua and to the people of Israel, a clear picture emerges. From the very beginning, God had a plan. From looking at the types and foreshadows in the Old Testament, one finds a crystal clear message. God has always wanted an intimate relationship with us. He always had a plan to deal with the problem of the sin which destroys this relationship. The human cost of having a relationship between God and man has always been a decision to leave a life of slavery to sin and to cling to God in faith, trusting in him to bless our lives. The cost has always included sacrifice on the part of God. In the next chapter, we will see this plan unfold in the form of a Messiah, sent by God to his people Israel.

Endnotes

1 The evidence for the historical reliability of the Bible is, in general, outside the range of this book. For material which deals with this question, see John Oakes, *Reasons For Belief: A Handbook of Christian Evidences* (available at www.ipibooks.com.) pp. 189-232 and Randall Price, *The Stones Cry Out* (Harvest House Publishers, Eugene, Oregon, 1997)

2 Again, see many examples supporting this claim in my book: *Reasons for Belief—A Handbook of Christian Evidences.*

3 For archaeological evidence which supports the historical accuracy of the biblical story of Sodom and Gomorrah, see John M. Oakes, *Reasons for Belief—A Handbook of Christian Evidences*, pp. 203-205, (available at www.ipibooks.com).

4 Literally the Sea of Reeds. There is some controversy over whether this was the Red Sea, the Bitter Lakes north of the Red Sea, or even the Gulf of Aqaba. The symbolism behind this crossing is not affected in any case.

5 There is a common belief in some Christian denominations that baptism in water is only a symbol of the forgiveness that has already occurred when one "accepts" Christ. This doctrine violates a number of clear teachings in the Bible, but it also violates the type/antitype as God set it up. In this case, the symbol/foreshadow is the baptism of Israel into Moses in the Red Sea. The New Testament fulfillment of that symbol is the real cleansing which occurs in the waters of baptism for those who have decided to turn to Christ. When Israel passed through the waters, they escaped Egypt at that point. It was not some sort of symbol of what had already happened! Baptism is not a symbol. It is a cleansing.

6 For example, Hebrews 6:4-12, Hebrews 10:26-31, 35-39.

7 It is common to assume that the Church of Christ on the earth is the Kingdom of God. In fact the Kingdom of God is a far greater concept, which takes in much more than the church. The kingdom is God reigning in an individual's heart. The Kingdom of God is heaven. The Kingdom of God is the church. To put it in a form which is perhaps a bit too simple: the church is part of the Kingdom of God, but the Kingdom is something far greater. This will be discussed in more detail in chapter nine.

8 A good discussion of Israel in Canaan as a foreshadow of a relationship with God in Jesus Christ is found in, Satterthwaite, Hess and Wenham, *The Lord's Anointed* (Baker Books, Grand Rapids, Michigan, 1995) Chapters 3,4.

9 Those who teach that New Testament baptism is just a symbol of something which has already happened should take note. God is consistent in teaching through foreshadows that it is his power at work in the water. Being baptized is not a "work" of man, as some would say, but an act of submission and an expression of faith. As with the waters of the Jordan, the work is done by God.

Prefigures of the Messiah

"For as Jonah was three days and three nights in the belly of a huge fish, so the Son of Man will be three days and three nights in the heart of the earth."

Matthew 12:40

One of the most incredible miracles recorded in the Old Testament was when Jonah spent three days and nights miraculously preserved within a huge fish. Jonah was a prophet whose life taught Israel many lessons about the nature of God. From Jonah the Jews learned that when God commands one of his prophets to speak he is very serious and will not take no for an answer. They also learned that God will go to great lengths to see that his message is preached. God provided a massive storm and an unusual fish to give Jonah a strong message and to preserve his life. One of the great lessons of the book of Jonah is that God loves the Gentiles as well as the Jews. Surely this was a hard lesson to swallow, not just for Jonah, but also for the Jewish people.

The book of Jonah had much to teach its primary audience; the nation of Israel. In fact, during the *Yom Kippur* holiday, Jews read the entire book of Jonah during the afternoon service as a reminder of God's judgment and their need of repentance. However, with the entrance of Jesus Christ onto the world stage, much of the hidden message—the mystery—in Jonah came into the light. Jonah was a living prefigure of the Messiah—Jesus Christ.

Jesus made it clear that he saw Jonah as a prefigure of his own life and ministry. When Jesus was pressured by the Pharisees into performing a public miracle he answered:

> "A wicked and adulterous generation asks for a miraculous sign! But none will be given it except the sign of the prophet Jonah. For as Jonah was three days and three nights in the belly of a huge fish, so the Son of Man will be three days and three nights in the heart of the earth" (Matthew 12:39,40).

Jonah spent three days and nights interred in a huge fish. At the end of that time he was spit out onto dry ground. In an unmistakable parallel, Jesus spent three days and nights in the heart of the earth. Jonah was preserved for three days and was miraculously delivered from his presumed grave. Jesus was also delivered from death on the third day and miraculously freed from his grave when the angel moved the stone. Coincidence? No! Jonah was a prophet—a spokesman for God. Besides that, his life was a living prophecy. He was living out a prefigure of the life and, in this case, the death of the Messiah.

The three days and nights in the belly of the huge fish is not the only aspect of Jonah's life and ministry which foreshadowed that of Jesus Christ. Consider his birth. Jonah was born in Galilee; in Gath-Hepher in the tribal territory of Zebulun. This town is very close to Nazareth, where Jesus was raised. One of the criticisms of Jesus during his ministry was that the Messiah could not possibly come from Galilee. The Jews of Judea were very prejudiced against their hillbilly brothers up there in Galilee. *"How can the Christ come from Galilee? Does not the Scripture say that the Christ will come from David's family and from Bethlehem, the town where David lived?"* (John 7:41,42). In criticizing Nicodemus, they taunted him; *"Are you from Galilee, too? Look into it and you will find that a prophet does not come out of Galilee"* (John 7:52). Not only were they prejudiced, they were wrong. They forgot about Jonah. In fact, God had prophesied through Isaiah over seven centuries before:

> "In the past he humbled the land of Zebulun and the land of Naphtali, but in the future he will honor Galilee of the Gentiles, by the way of the sea, along the Jordan....He will reign on David's throne and over his kingdom, establishing and upholding it with justice and righteousness from that time and on forever" (Isaiah 9:1,7).

Both Jesus and Jonah are reminders to the Jews that God will be moving his focus away from Jerusalem.

Another detail in the life of Jonah which stands as a prefigure of the life of Christ is how he ended up in the belly of that huge fish in the first place. While on the ship fleeing to Tarshish, a great storm blew up which threatened to destroy the transport ship on which Jonah had hitched a ride, with all its occupants. In a scene which is reminiscent of the guards casting lots over Jesus' clothing, the sailors on the ship cast lots to see which of their number was responsible for their danger. The lot fell to Jonah. In both cases, a three-day interrment was preceeded by the casting of lots. Because of this discovery, and at Jonah's suggestion, they threw him overboard. Jonah was killed by his enemies (at least they thought so) so that they could be saved from death. In fact, Jonah willingly offered his life to save them. As the story develops the parallel to the saving death of Jesus becomes clear. *"Then they took Jonah and threw him overboard, and the raging sea grew calm."* Jonah, like Jesus, calmed God's anger when he was sacrificed in order to save the Gentiles who had been in the boat with him. Again, is this coincidence, or is God creating a miraculous prefigure of the work of the Messiah, Jesus Christ? Let the reader decide.

Still another foreshadow of Jesus found in Jonah is that, unlike the other prophets of Israel, Jonah offered repentance and a relationship with God to the Gentiles. Is it a coincidence that the prophet who was a prefigure of the Christ is also the one who broke the ingrained taboos of Judaism to bring repentance to Nineveh? Was it Jonah's idea? Definitely not! When God asked Jonah to go east to Nineveh to preach repentance (and presumably salvation) Jonah fled to Tarshish; the westernmost city in the known world! Jonah was a reluctant prophet. Jesus was not so reluctant.

> *"For as Jonah was a sign to the Ninevites, so also will the Son of Man be to this generation...The men of Nineveh will stand up at the judgment with this generation and condemn it, for they repented at the preaching of Jonah, and now one greater than Jonah is here"* (Luke 11:30,32).

Again, in this statement, Jesus acknowledges that he is the fulfillment of the prefigure established in Jonah. Through Jonah, God was telling the Jews that his Messiah would offer repentance and forgiveness to the Gentiles. God had to prepare the hearts and minds of the Jews for this revolutionary teaching. In case anyone is still holding out for coincidence here, he or she should bear in mind that the people who recorded this story of God reaching out to the Gentiles were at their core extremely prejudiced against the Gentiles. The Jews were very resistant to outreach to the Gentiles, right up through the first generation of the New Testament church. In order to get the apostle Peter to offer salvation to the Gentiles, God had to theologically hit him on the side of the head (see Acts 10). Despite this ingrained prejudice, God caused this account of the messianic prefigure Jonah preaching repentance to the Ninevites to be included in the Old Testament.

Jonah is the first of several examples of messianic prefigures we will examine. Two striking claims about the Old Testament have already been made. First is that the theme of the Old Testament is "The Messiah is coming." The second is that the Old Testament is filled with foreshadowings and prefigures of New Testament teachings. If both of these are true, then it stands to reason that the Old Testament should be riddled with prefigures of the coming Messiah. If one scans the Old Testament looking for characters whose lives God shaped into symbolic prefigures of the life and work of Jesus Christ, one will certainly not be disappointed.

In preparing prefigures of the life and ministry of Jesus Christ, God left out very few details. As we will discover, God has given us symbolic foreshadows in Old Testament figures of some of the smallest details of the life of the Messiah who, in God's eyes, was *"slain from the creation of the world"* (Revelation 13:8).

In creating a theocracy (religious government) for his people, God gave them three offices to provide spiritual and political leadership. Israel had prophets, priests and kings. The prophets were spokesmen for God, providing warnings and encouragements to keep Israel on the right path. The priests provided some spiritual teaching, but their primary role was to make intercession for the sins of the people of God. They were to perform the ritual sacrifices which kept the nation of Israel in communion with their God. The kings of Israel were to set a spiritual example to the people. However, their primary role was to lead the government and to protect the people of God from their enemies.

All three roles foreshadow what we have in the Messiah. God combined the three roles: prophet, priest and king, in the one man; Jesus Christ. Some of those in the Old Testament who are foreshadows of the Messiah were prophets, like Jonah. Others, as we will see, were priests. Still others were kings (or judges or governors, depending on the political setting). The amazing thing is that God was able to combine all three prophetic aspects of ministry to his people in one amazing individual: Jesus of Nazareth.

I. ADAM

Adam is unique as a prefigure of the Messiah. Rather than being a copy of Christ, he is, in a sense, the mirror image of the Messiah. As German theologian Leonard Goppelt put it,[1] "Adam and Christ are related to one another as a photographic negative to its positive print or as a mold to the plastic shaped by it." What Adam did, Jesus undid. Yet, even in that, the two are parallel.

Adam was the first born of physical humanity, whereas Jesus is the firstborn from the dead (Colossians 1:18). In other words, Jesus is the first to be raised from the dead for eternal life. Both were the product of a miraculous creation. Where Adam was the first human to sin (well, technically he was the second), and therefore brought death to all men, Jesus was the first human to not sin, and therefore brought release from death. In both cases, the act of a single person had an effect on all humanity. As Paul put it:

> *Consequently, just as the result of one trespass was condemnation for all men, so also the result of one act of righteousness was justification that brings life for all men. For just as through the disobedience of the one man* (Adam) *the many were made sinners, so also through the obedience of the one man* (Jesus Christ) *the many will be made righteous* (Romans 5:18,19).

In fact, Paul states the matter with Adam quite simply. He calls Adam *"the pattern* (prefigure) *of the one to come"* (Romans 5:14).

Romans chapters five through seven are meaty reading, but the essence of the message is that what was caused by the sin of Adam could not be undone by the Law of Moses, so a second Adam—Jesus Christ—had to come to undo the destructive effect of Adam's sin.

The typological relationship between Adam and Jesus is also discussed by Paul in 1 Corinthians 15:20-23:

> But Christ has indeed been raised from the dead, the firstfruits of those who have fallen asleep. For since death came through a man, the resurrection of the dead comes also through a man. For as in Adam all die, so in Christ all will be made alive. But each in his own turn: Christ, the firstfruits; then, when he comes, those who belong to him.

It would appear that for Paul, looking for types in the Old Testament to explain New Testament teachings is a common mode of biblical exegesis. In other words, Paul is saying that, given that death came to humanity through one man in the Old Testament, one should not be surprised that the cure for the problem would have come through the life of one man under the New Covenant.

II. MELCHIZEDEK

Melchizedek is one of the most intriguing and mysterious figures in the entire Bible. He is also a prefigure of the Messiah. We are introduced to Melchizedek in Genesis fourteen when he meets up with Abraham:

> *Then Melchizedek king of Salem* (Jerusalem) *brought out bread and wine. He was priest of God Most High, and he blessed Abraham, saying,*
> *"Blessed be Abram by God Most High,*
>   *Creator of heaven and earth.*
> *And blessed be God Most High,*
>   *who delivered your enemies into your hand."*
> *Then Abraham gave him a tenth of everything*
> (Genesis 14:18-20).

As already mentioned, Jesus combines in one person: a prophet, priest and king. Melchizedek was both priest and king. Melchizedek was the temporal king of physical Jerusalem, while Jesus is the spiritual king of the spiritual Jerusalem. When queried on the subject, Jesus said to Pontius Pilate, *"My kingdom is not of this world"* and *"You are right in saying I am a king"* (John 18:36,37).

As great as Abraham was, we have in this mysterious character Melchizedek one greater than Abraham. To quote the relevant passages in Hebrews:

> *This Melchizedek was king of Salem and priest of God Most High. He met Abraham returning from the defeat of the kings and blessed him...First, his name means "king of righteousness;" then also "king of Salem" means "king of peace." Without father or mother, without genealogy, without beginning of days or end of life, like the Son of God, he remains priest forever.*
>
> *Just think how great he was; even the patriarch Abraham gave him a tenth of the plunder! Now the law requires the descendants of Levi who become priests to collect a tenth from the people—that is their brothers—even though their brothers are descended from Abraham. This man, however, did not trace his descent from Levi, yet he collected a tenth from Abraham and blessed him who had the promises. And without a doubt the lesser person is blessed by the greater. In the one case, the tenth is collected by men who die; but in the other case, by him who is declared to be living. One might even say that Levi, who collects the tenth, paid the tenth through Abraham, because when Melchizedek met Abraham, Levi was still in the body of his ancestor* (**Hebrews 7:1-10**).

Melchizedek, figuratively, was like Jesus. Jesus is the prince of peace (Isaiah 9:6). Melchizedek was the king of Salem. Salem is the Hebrew *shalom,* which means peace. Melchizedek was literally the prince of peace. Melchizedek, like Jesus (and unlike the priests descended from Levi), is a priest forever. Apparently, like Enoch (Genesis 5:24), Melchizedek did not die. According to the Hebrew writer, when Abraham bowed to Melchizedek and paid him a tribute from the war booty he had gained, he was figuratively paying tribute to the spiritual Melchizedek, Jesus Christ.

There are many more parallels between Jesus and Melchizedek. The Levites were priests by birth. By contrast, Jesus, like Melchizedek, was a priest by direct appointment of God. The Hebrew writer continues:

> *If perfection could have been gained through the Levitical priesthood...why was there still need for another priest to come— one in the order of* (prefigured by) *Melchizedek, not in the order of Aaron? For when there is a change of priesthood, there must also be a change of law...And what we have said is even more clear if another priest like Melchizedek appears, one who has become a priest not on the basis of a regulation as to his ancestry but on the basis of the power of an indestructible life. For it is declared:*

> "You are a priest forever in the order of Melchizedek."
> And...
> "The Lord has sworn and will not change his mind:
> You are a priest forever."
> Because of this oath, Jesus has become the guarantee of a better covenant (Hebrews 7:11-22).

The writer of Hebrews quotes Psalms 110:4, proving that he is not just conveniently making up the connection between Melchizedek and the Messiah. David had prophetically mentioned the same connection over one thousand years before.

God was prophesying to us through Melchizedek that the Messiah, the ultimate priest of God, would not be a priest by natural descent—that he would not be a Levite. As usual, the foreshadow in the Old Testament is very precise in its representation of the New Testament reality it prefigures. In Melchizedek, God was telling us before the Aaronic priesthood was even established, that a greater priesthood would later replace it, in the order of Melchizedek. God knew and revealed to us before the first covenant was even established that he would have to offer a second covenant. This is pretty deep stuff, but that is what God did through Melchizedek.

It is interesting to note that in Genesis 14:18, quoted above, what Melchizedek brought as an offering to bless Abraham. He brought bread and wine. This, too, is a prefigure of the sacrificial offering of Jesus' body and blood. The writer of Genesis had no idea how accurate a picture of the Messiah he was portraying. The mystery is revealed in Jesus Christ.

From Melchizedek we learn that the Messiah would be priest and king, that he would be king of Jerusalem, that he would bring in a priesthood, not by natural descent, but by divine choice, that the Messiah would offer body and blood, that he would bring in a New Covenant. What a great picture of Jesus we have in Melchizedek.

III. JOSEPH

As already pointed out in chapter one, we could mention both Abraham and his son Isaac as types of the Messiah. Instead we will skip to Joseph. Joseph is one of the clearest of messianic prefigures. The parallels between the events in the lives of Joseph and Jesus will leave no doubt that God had a plan to teach us about Jesus through his ancestor Joseph.

Joseph was the eleventh child of Jacob, the son of Isaac. God had changed Jacob's name to Israel. The Jewish nation eventually was named Israel after their "father" Israel. Joseph was Jacob's favorite son (Genesis 37:3). So Jacob was the physical father of physical Israel, and Joseph was his favorite son. Similarly, God is the spiritual Father of spiritual Israel, and Jesus is his favorite and only son. Joseph tended sheep (Genesis 37:2), while Jesus is the good shepherd (John 10:14). Joseph was betrayed and sold into slavery in Egypt by his brothers for twenty pieces of silver. Jesus was betrayed and sold by one of his apostles for thirty pieces of silver.

Joseph was brought to Egypt by God to protect him from the jealousy of his brothers. *"I am your brother Joseph, the one you sold into Egypt! And now, do not be distressed and do not be angry with yourselves for selling me here, because it was to save lives that God sent me ahead of you"* (Genesis 45:4,5). Similarly, Jesus was taken into Egypt to protect him from the jealousy of Herod, who tried to kill him (Matthew 2:14,15).

Many other details in the life of Jesus are foreshadowed in the life of Joseph. God prophesied through his dreams that Joseph would rule as king over his brothers. *"Do you intend to rule over us? Will you actually rule us?"* (Genesis 37:8). In fact, that is exactly what happened. When God raised up Joseph, his brothers did indeed bow before him, calling him lord (Genesis 44:16). Similarly, Jesus, though born into a humble family, was raised up by God to become Messiah and king of the true sons of Abraham.

> *And being found in appearance as a man, he humbled himself, and became obedient to death—even death on a cross! Therefore God exalted him to the highest place and gave him the name that is above every name, that at the name of Jesus every knee should bow, in heaven and on earth, and every tongue confess that Jesus Christ is Lord, to the glory of God the Father* (Philippians 2:8-11).

Joseph's brothers conceived a plan to kill him out of jealousy (Genesis 37:17-19). Similarly, Jesus' brother Israelites conceived a plan to kill him, and jealousy was clearly one of the motives. God turned Joseph's brother's plot to kill him into an opportunity to save Israel and his family, and therefore to save the entire nation Israel. Despite having been sold into slavery for no fault of his own, God miraculously raised Joseph up from prison to become the second in command of all Egypt. From this exalted position, Joseph was able to save his family from a terrible famine which struck the land. *"For two years now there has been famine in the land, and for the next five years there will not be plowing and reaping. But God sent me ahead of you to preserve for you a remnant on earth and to save your lives by a great deliverance"* (Genesis 45:6,7). These prophetic words certainly do ring down through the ages. The parallels between Jesus and Joseph are striking. He, too, was taken from a position of honor to live in a very humble situation, which God used to save spiritual Israel. God used the successful attempt by the Jewish leaders to have Jesus executed *"to preserve for you a remnant on earth and to save your lives by a great deliverance."*

Notice even more detail here. Joseph was sent into slavery in Egypt, a prefigure of being "in sin" in the New Testament, for no fault of his own so that he could save Israel. Similarly, Paul said of Jesus, *"God made him who had no sin to be sin for us so that in him we might become the righteousness of God"* (2 Corinthians 5:21).

When Joseph revealed himself to his brothers, from their perspective they were receiving him back from the dead. In fact, Israel had already mourned his dead son (Genesis 37:34). This is a prefigure of the resurrection of Jesus Christ. Even though his brothers had conceived a plot to kill him and had sold him into slavery, Joseph recognized that God had used their jealousy to save Israel and forgave his brothers. *"Then he threw his arms around his brother Benjamin and wept and Benjamin embraced him, weeping. And he kissed all his brothers and wept over them"* (Genesis 45:14,15). As with Joseph, so with Jesus. *"Father, forgive them for they do not know what they are doing"* (Luke 23:34).

To summarize, Joseph, like Jesus, left his position at the right hand of his father to take on the lowest position as a slave, but was raised by God to the right hand of the king. Joseph was savior of physical Israel, while Jesus was savior of spiritual Israel. The writer(s) of Genesis had no idea they were recording an amazing prefigure of the life of Jesus in the story of Joseph.

IV. MOSES

Another amazing parallel between a figure in the Old Testament and the life of Jesus Christ is found in Moses. Of all the patriarchs, Moses is held in highest regard by the Jews. It is hard for this author to imagine how modern Jews who read the story of Moses' ministry to Israel can fail to grasp that his entire life was a foreshadow of Jesus Christ. In fact, God told Moses that *"I will raise up for them* (Israel) *a prophet like you* (an antitype of you) *from among their brothers; I will put my words in his mouth, and he will tell them everything I command him. If anyone does not listen to my words that the prophet speaks in my name, I myself will call him to account"* (Deuteronomy 18:17-19). God was telling the prophet Moses that his life was a foreshadow of the great Prophet he would send to Israel.

To demonstrate that Moses is a prefigure of Jesus Christ, let us go back to the beginning of his life. *"Then Pharoah gave this order to all his people: 'Every boy that is born you must throw into the river, but let every girl live'"* (Exodus 1:22). It is hard to miss the parallel here to the birth of Jesus. When Herod learned from the Magi that a king was born in Bethlehem, *"he gave orders to kill all the boys in Bethlehem and its vicinity who were two years old and under, in accordance with the time he had learned from the Magi"* (Matthew 2:16). It is striking to note that in the case of both Herod and Pharoah, God even used those who were hard-hearted enemies of his to fulfill his plan to bless the world. In both cases, a king's jealousy for his own power nearly caused the savior of Israel to be killed as an infant.

Perhaps one could argue the parallel between the births of the savior of physical Israel (Moses) and the savior of spiritual Israel (Jesus) is just a coincidence, but this would be an incredible coincidence! By the time we examine the other parallels between these two men, coincidence will no longer be a reasonable explanation. In the case of both baby Moses and of baby Jesus, God protected them from those who sought their life.

It is very interesting how God saved Jesus from his persecutors:

> When they (the Magi) had gone, an angel of the Lord appeared to Joseph in a dream. "Get up," he said, "take the child and his mother and escape to Egypt. Stay there until I tell you, for Herod is going to search for the child to kill him."
> So he got up, took the child and his mother during the night and left for Egypt, where he stayed until the death of Herod. And so was fulfilled what the Lord had said through the prophet: "Out of Egypt I called my son" (Matthew 2:13-15).

In this case, Matthew is quoting the prophet Hosea (Hosea 11:1). This very interesting prophecy of Hosea is both looking back to what God had done to save Israel from slavery, and looking forward to what God would do to save spiritual Israel from slavery to sin. God called his son out of Egypt, both when Moses led Israel[2] through the Red Sea and when Jesus came out of Egypt after the death of Herod. Again we see that God made Moses a prefigure of the Messiah.

The writer of Hebrews certainly saw a parallel between Jesus and Moses. Just as Moses was the most faithful in all of God's house on earth (Israel), Jesus was faithful to the one who appointed him over God's spiritual house (Hebrews 3:2). As with other type/antitype relationships, the antitype is greater than the type: *"Jesus has been found worthy of greater honor than Moses, just as the builder of a house has greater honor than the house itself"* (Hebrews 3:3). The writer of Hebrews specifically says that Moses' faith as a servant of God was a prophecy of the future ministry of Jesus: *"testifying to what would be said in the future"* (Hebrews 3:5).

The parallels between Moses and Jesus are many. As we have already seen, both were prophets. Both were raised by God from poverty to lead a nation: one a physical nation and the other a spiritual kingdom. By the miraculous design of God, when Moses' mother hid him in the reeds by the Nile to save him from death by Pharaoh's agents, Moses was found by the daughter of the Pharaoh and raised by her family. Moses was raised as the adopted son of the most powerful ruler in the world at that time. What did Moses do with his exalted position? He gave it up in order to identify himself with his lowly, enslaved people.

As with the type, so with the antitype.

> *Your attitude should be the same as that of Christ Jesus: Who, being in very nature God, did not consider equality with*

God something to be grasped (i.e. clung on to), *but made himself nothing, taking the very nature of a servant, being made in human likeness. And being found in appearance as a man, he humbled himself and became obedient to death—even death on a cross!"* (Philippians 2:5-8).

Both Moses and Jesus willingly stepped down from an exalted position—one as son of the king of Heaven, the other as son of the most powerful king on earth—to serve among an enslaved people in order to save them from their slavery. Moses came to save from physical slavery, Jesus came to save from spiritual slavery. We continue to see this pattern repeated in the Old Testament. God uses a physical example in the Old Testament to prefigure a spiritual reality in the New Testament.

God the Father prepared Jesus for his ministry to Israel by sending him for forty days into the wilderness. During this time he was tested both physically and spiritually (Luke 4:1-12). As God prepared Moses for his ministry to Israel, he was sent into the desert for forty years of testing (Acts 7:30). Moses needed much more time in the desert to be refined for his ministry, but notice the number forty in both cases!

Because Moses was insecure and slow of speech, God appointed Aaron to prepare the way. *"What about your brother Aaron, the Levite?...You shall speak to him and put words in his mouth"* (Exodus 4:14,15). God made Aaron to be Moses' prophet (spokesperson): *"your brother Aaron will be your prophet"* (Exodus 7:1). Jesus had his cousin John the Baptist as a prophet to prepare the way. *"There came a man who was sent from God; his name was John. He came as a witness to testify concerning that light"* (John 1:6,7). Or as Isaiah prophesied concerning John the Baptist:

> *A voice of one calling:*
> *"In the desert prepare*
>   *the way for the* LORD*;*
> *make straight in the wilderness*
>   *a highway for our God"* (Isaiah 40:3).

Moses had his Aaron and Jesus had his John the Baptist.

Moses proved his commission from God by performing miracles (Exodus 4:29-31). Jesus proved his right to speak for God by performing miracles (John 10:37,38, Acts 2:22).

Israel was baptized into Moses when they passed through the Red Sea, leaving slavery in Egypt (1 Corinthians 10:2). Followers of Jesus are baptized into Christ in order to be freed from their slavery to sin (Acts 2:38, Romans 6:3-7). Moses gave them bread (manna) in the wilderness as physical food (although as Jesus pointed out in John 6:32 that it really was the Father, not Moses who gave the manna). Jesus fulfilled the prophecy contained in this foreshadow, by producing both physical and spiritual bread. Jesus miraculously produced sufficient bread to feed five thousand men plus those who were with them (John 6:1-13). Having produced physical bread, Jesus showed his authority to make the claim to be the bread of life; spiritual food for God's people: *"I am the bread of life. He who comes to me will never go hungry"* (John 6:35).

The nation of Israel which Moses led through the desert numbered about two million souls. God's people needed both bread and water in the wilderness.

> *So they quarreled with Moses and said, "Give us water to drink..." The Lord answered Moses, "Walk on ahead of the people. Take with you some of the elders of Israel and take in your hand the staff with which you struck the Nile, and go. I will stand there before you by the rock at Horeb. Strike the rock, and water will come out of it for the people to drink"* (Exodus 17:2,5,6).

God used Moses to give water to the people of God. Jesus lived in an area which had plenty of water, so he did not miraculously produce physical water, but in answer to the woman at the well who thirsted spiritually, he said,

> *"Everyone who drinks this water will be thirsty again, but whoever drinks the water I give him will never thirst. Indeed, the water I give him will become in him a spring of water welling up to eternal life"* (John 4:13,14).

Naturally, the woman asked Jesus to give her this water. In John 7:37,38 we are instructed that the gift of the Spirit is this water which Jesus will give to all those who believe in him. Continuing the Old/New Testament pattern, the messianic type gave Israel physical water, while the Messiah gives his followers spiritual water to drink.

Parallels Between Moses and Jesus

MOSES	JESUS
Pharaoh tried to kill him	Herod tried to kill him
Called by God to leave Egypt	Carried out of Egypt
Forty years in the wilderness to prepare for his ministry	Forty days in the wilderness to prepare for his ministry
Left his position with the king of Egypt to dwell with the Jews	Left the right hand of the Father to live with the Jews
Led Israel out of slavery in Egypt	Leads Spiritual Israel out of sin
Aaron prepared the way	John the Baptist prepared the way
Baptized Israel in the Red Sea in order to free them	Commands baptism in water for freedom from sin
Gave manna in the wilderness	Gives spiritual bread to all who hunger
Gave water to the people in the desert	Gives spiritual water (Holy Spirit)
Spoke to God on Mt. Sinai	Spoke to God on Mt. Hermon
Offered up his place with God to atone for the people's sin	Offered up his place with God to atone for the people's sin

Moses and Jesus were both mountain climbers. Moses traveled up Mount Sinai where God spoke directly to him. In one case, Moses brought Aaron with him when he talked with God (Exodus 19). Another time Moses spoke to God face to face on the mountain. When he returned his face radiated a brilliant light (Exodus 34:29-35). His face shone so brightly that they put a veil over him so people could look at him. Similarly, Jesus traveled with Peter, James and John *"up a high mountain by themselves. There he (Jesus) was transfigured before them. His face shone like the sun, and his clothes became as white as the light. Just then there appeared before them Moses and Elijah, talking with Jesus"* (Matthew 17:1-3). The mountain they climbed to speak with God was probably Mount Hermon in the Golan Heights. Moses got to see the fulfillment of the prophecy God had acted out through him over fourteen centuries earlier.

Consider one more parallel between Moses and the second Moses—Jesus Christ. While Moses was on Sinai, receiving the Law from God, the people were engaged in revelry and worshipping a golden calf they had built with their own hands. Moses returned from communing with God to face a faithless people indulging in the grossest of sin. Moses was so upset he smashed the two tablets on which God had miraculously inscribed the Ten Commandments. Aaron tried to shift the blame, but Moses did the opposite.

> *The next day Moses said to the people, "You have committed a great sin. But now I will go up to the LORD; perhaps I can make atonement for your sin."*
>
> *So Moses went back to the LORD and said, "Oh what a great sin these people have committed! They have made themselves gods of gold. But now, please forgive their sin—but if not, then blot me out of the book you have written"* (Exodus 32:31-32).

Moses had not sinned in this situation, yet he offered to give up his place in heaven with God to make atonement for the sin of the people. What a sacrificial heart for a people who definitely did not deserve it! Does that remind you of anyone?

Moses is an obvious foreshadow of the Messiah, Jesus Christ. Those who wrote down the details of his life had no idea of the prophecy they were recording. In Moses, God told us that his savior would call people out of sin, would bring baptism for forgiveness of sin, would provide spiritual food and drink, would offer his life to save God's people, and many other things.

V. JOSHUA

Because of Moses' sin of rebellion in the desert,[3] he was not able to lead God's people into the Promised Land. He was unable to complete the messianic foreshadow that God had intended. Nevertheless, God chose to provide a type of the Christ to bring his people into the Promised Land. He chose Moses' second in command, Joshua.

From his name we already have a hint that Joshua is a foreshadow of Jesus. The two saviors of Israel had the same name! *Jeshua* is the Aramaic name by which Jesus was called by his contemporaries. Jesus is the Greek equivalent used in the New Testament. The Aramaic name *Jeshua* is a transliteration of the Hebrew Joshua. The Jewish name Joshua means Yahweh saves. Could there be any more appropriate name for a foreshadow of the Savior of the world?

There are a few parallels between Moses and Joshua as prefigures of the Messiah. As Moses led God's people out of slavery in Egypt, Joshua led Israel into the Promised Land. Jesus Christ leads us into heaven. Hebrews 4:8-11 describes the parallel work of Joshua and Jesus:

> *For if Joshua[4] had given them rest, God would not have spoken later about another day. There remains, then, a Sabbath-rest for the people of God; for anyone who enters God's rest also rests from his own work, just as God did from his. Let us, therefore, make every effort to enter that rest, so that no one will fall by following their example of disobedience.*

The point of the Hebrew writer is that, just as Joshua could not let Israel rest until they entered the Promised Land, so we who are in Christ cannot rest from our work for God until we are safely in the spiritual Promised Land of heaven.

As Moses baptized Israel in the Red Sea in order to lead them out of slavery in Egypt, so Joshua baptized Israel in the Jordan River in order to enter rest in the Promised Land. Similarly, those who follow Jesus are baptized into him to be freed from sin.

In order for them to be identify themselves as God's people, Joshua had all the males of Israel circumcised immediately after crossing the Jordan before they were to be allowed to conquer the land. They could not enter their rest uncircumcised. Similarly, Jesus commanded spiritual circumcision, which is baptism, *"in the putting off of the sinful nature, not with a circumcision done by the hands of men but with the circumcision done by Christ, having been buried with him in baptism and raised with him through your faith in the power of God, who raised him from the dead"* (Colossians 2:11,12). In baptism, a person enters a new life. *"We were therefore buried with him through baptism into death in order that, just as Christ was raised from the dead through the glory of the Father, we too may live a new life"* (Romans 6:4). After Israel was circumcised under Joshua's orders, they too entered a new life with God in Palestine.

As a prefigure of Jesus of Nazareth, Joshua reminds us that the Messiah is to be a savior of God's people and that he will offer us rest from wanderings in the wilderness.

VI. SAMSON

One discernable theme throughout the Old and the New Testament is God's plan to bring salvation to his people. It seems that the people of God were always getting themselves into trouble and needing a "savior." This was especially true during the period in the history of Israel known as the time of the Judges. It has already been stated that the relationship between the nation of Israel and God during the time they were in the Promised Land is a type of our relationship individually with God. If that is so, then the time of the Judges represents a largely negative aspect of our behavior toward God. During the Judges period, Israel was consistently unfaithful. God had worked amazing miracles for Israel under the leadership of the messianic prefigures Moses and Joshua. Despite this, soon after Joshua died, the people of Israel stopped giving God credit for their tremendous blessings.

> *After that whole generation had been gathered to their fathers, another generation grew up, who knew neither the LORD nor what he had done for Israel. Then the Israelites did evil in the eyes of the LORD and served the Baals. They forsook the LORD, the God of their fathers, who had brought them out of Egypt"* (Judges 2:10-12).

There is a clear warning to us here. Remember the words of 1 Corinthians 10:11,12: *"These things happened to them as examples and were written down as warnings for us, on whom the fulfillment of the ages has come. So if you think you are standing firm, be careful that you don't fall!"* From the historical events of the period of the Judges we can learn that its easy to forget God's grace, lose our thankfulness, forget the source of our blessings, and ultimately be overcome by sin again—perhaps ending up worse than before. The pattern in Judges is that when Israel forgot to give thanks to God, they soon returned to idols and God allowed them to be enslaved once again by the peoples around them.

> *In his anger against Israel the LORD handed them over to raiders who plundered them. He sold them to their enemies all around whom they were no longer able to resist. Whenever Israel went out to fight, the hand of the LORD was against them to defeat them, just as he had sworn to them.[5] They were in great distress* (Judges 2:14,15).

The situation for Israel rapidly became desperate. The type is Israel, the antitype is us. When someone who has made a commitment to God turns his back on God, He will allow that person to be enslaved to sin once again. Israel became enslaved to their enemies over and over again. We too can become enslaved to the same sin we repented of when we first entered our relationship with God.

But that is not the main point of this chapter. The point is that when God's people got themselves in trouble, and when in their misery they cried out to their Father, God always sent a savior—a prefigure of the Messiah—to save them out of their slavery to sin.

> *"Then the LORD raised up judges, who saved them out of the hands of these raiders...Whenever the LORD raised up a judge* (a prefigure of the Messiah) *for them, he was with the judge and saved them out of the hands of their enemies as long as the judge lived; for the LORD had compassion on them as they groaned under those who oppressed and afflicted them"* (Judges 2:16-18).

God is deeply pained when he sees us enslaved to sin, as was Israel. His response is to send a savior. The symbolism of the Judges of Israel is fairly plain to see.

Consider Gideon. *"Again, the Israelites did evil in the eyes of the LORD, and for seven years he gave them into the hands of the Midianites* (Judges 6:1). God sent Gideon to save his people. *"The Lord is with you mighty warrior." "Go in the strength you have and save Israel out of Midian's hand. Am I not sending you?"* (Judges 6:12,14). Then there was Jephthah who saved Israel from slavery to the Ammonites (Judges 11:1-12:7). And yes, Deborah, too, is a type of the Messiah. No male leader could be found to save Israel from the hands of Jabin, a Canaanite King. God wanted to save his people, so he chose Deborah as a type of Christ.

Samson is the most well known of the messianic types in Judges. Several parallels between Samson and Jesus can be noted. Most famously, Samson saved Israel from the Philistine enemy who had enslaved them. In fact, in his final act, Samson gave his life to save Israel from their Philistine enemies.

> *Samson said, "Let me die with the Philistines!" Then he pushed with all his might, and down came the temple on the rulers and all the people in it. Thus he killed many more when he died than while he lived* (Judges 16:30).

Of course, Samson was unaware of the messianic symbolism when he willingly offered up his life to save his people from their humiliating slavery to the Philistines.

VII. SAMUEL

Parallels between Samuel and Jesus can be found from the time of their birth. Hannah had been barren for many years. She cried out to God at the temple, vowing to devote her son to God. *"O LORD Almighty, if you will only look upon your servant's misery and remember me, and not forget your servant but give her a son, then I will give him to the LORD for all the days of his life, and no razor will ever be used on his head"* (1 Samuel 1:11). God granted her wish and despite being barren for years she miraculously bore a child. Both Samson and Jesus were born from their mothers by the miraculous work of God. Mary was not barren, but the birth of her son was miraculous. She devoted her son to God from birth. Like Samson (and symbolically, like Jesus) Samuel was a Nazirite, devoted to God from birth.

As previously stated, in Jesus, God combined the biblical roles of priest, prophet and king. Samuel was a prophet: *"And all Israel from Dan to Beersheba recognized that Samuel was attested as prophet of the LORD"* (1 Samuel 3:20). He was also a priest: *"The boy Samuel ministered before the LORD under Eli"* (1 Samuel 3:1). Samuel also served as a judge and governor, the closest equivalent to a king Israel had at that time: *"And Samuel was leader* (Judge) *of Israel at Mizpah"* (1 Samuel 7:6). As a prophet, Samuel, like Jesus, spoke the words of God to Israel. As an anointed priest, Samuel, like Jesus, made intercession for the people of God, except in an earthly tabernacle, not the heavenly one in which Jesus serves. As a Judge, Samuel led Israel and rescued them from the nations which enslaved them.

VIII. DAVID

If it were possible to go back in time to the century before Jesus was born and ask either a common Jew or one of their teachers who God used as a foreshadow of the Messiah in the Bible, most if not all would have answered that King David would be God's model for the Anointed One. To the Jew, David represented the personification of the Messiah as anointed King of Israel. The Hebrew word for anointed one is *mashiah,* from which we get the Greek word *christos,* or anointed one. When the Jews saw Jesus working stupendous miracles, they asked what would be only natural to a Jew, *"Could this be the son of David?"* (Matthew 12:23). In other words, they were asking if Jesus could be the Messiah—the promised Son of David.

In order to verify the claim that the Jews would consider David as the model/type of the Messiah, consider Ezekiel 37:24,25:

> *"My servant David will be king over them, and they will all have one shepherd. They will follow my laws and be careful to keep my decrees. They will live in the land I gave to my servant Jacob, the land where your fathers lived. They and their children's children will live there forever, and David my servant will be their prince forever."*

The prophet Ezekiel was not talking about the King David who had ruled over four hundred years before he wrote down this prophecy.

He was talking about the Son of David: Jesus Christ, who will be prince over spiritual Israel forever in a heavenly kingdom.

Ezekiel described the antitype to David, the Messiah, as a shepherd. Of course, David was a shepherd. He laid down his life for his sheep. *"When a lion or bear came and carried off a sheep from the flock, I went after it struck it down and rescued the sheep from its mouth"* (1 Samuel 17:34). Jesus said: *"I am the good shepherd. The good shepherd lays down his life for his sheep"* (John 10:14). Both David and Jesus laid down their lives for their sheep.

David was born in Bethlehem. Jesus was born in Bethlehem as well. This parallel between Jesus and David should not be a great surprise, as the Messiah is called the Son of David in the Old Testament. Descendants of David tended to be born in the ancestral home of Jesse, which was Bethlehem (although God had to arrange for Augustus to call a census in order to make sure Jesus was born in Bethlehem). David was the son of Jesse. Jesus, the Messiah is called the root of Jesse (Isaiah 11:10). He was a direct descendant of David.

Like Jesus, David was set apart and anointed by God from a very young age: *"the LORD has sought out a man after his own heart and appointed him leader of his people"* (1 Samuel 13:14). As a youth, David was anointed as king of Israel by Samuel. He was literally the anointed one, or Messiah of Israel. *"So Samuel took the horn of oil and anointed him in the presence of his brothers, and from that day on the Spirit of the LORD came upon David in power"* (1 Samuel 16:13). The Spirit descended on David when he was anointed. Similarly, the Spirit descended on Jesus when he was baptized in the Jordan by John the Baptist. *"Then John gave this testimony: "I saw the Spirit come down from heaven as a dove and remain on him"'* (John 1:32).

Of course, any messianic prefigure would have saved Israel. David did this more than once. The most well known is when as a mere youth, he slayed Goliath and delivered Israel from the armies of the Philistines.

> *"This day the LORD will hand you (Goliath) over to me, and I'll strike you down and cut off your head. Today I will give the carcasses of the Philistine army to the birds of the air and the beasts of the earth, and the whole world will know that there is a God in Israel. All those gathered here will know that*

it is not by sword or spear that the LORD saves; for the battle is the LORD'S, and he will give all of you into our hands" (1 Samuel 17:46,47).

One more time, God sends his Messiah, his savior, to Israel. Here we see repeated the pattern that God uses a prefigure of the Messiah in the Old Testament to save Israel from her enemies. The pattern is preparing the reader of the New Testament to understand that the Messiah will save God's people from their spiritual enemies: the forces of evil and the consequences of sin.

This was not the only time David "saved" Israel. Another is recorded in 2 Samuel 24. Due to David's own pride and lack of faith, he had called a census of Israel. This personal sin of David by not trusting God brought down on Jerusalem an avenging angel and a plague broke out in Jerusalem. When the angel was about to destroy Jerusalem, David intervened, offering up a sacrifice at the threshing floor of Araunah. This sacrifice was offered on the site where the temple was eventually built. It was the same mountain on which Abraham offered Isaac as a sacrifice. When David was offered a gift of oxen to make a sacrifice, David replied, *"I will not sacrifice to the LORD my God burnt offerings that cost me nothing"* (2 Samuel 24:24). David offered up a sacrifice which saved Israel from destruction, and so did his antitype.

David was king of physical Israel, Jesus is king of spiritual Israel. David conquered and entered Jerusalem as a king. Jesus entered Jerusalem as a king, riding on a donkey. David went out from Jerusalem and conquered all of Israel's enemies. Jesus' earthly kingdom began in Jerusalem. As Jesus told his apostles, *"...repentance and forgiveness of sins will be preached in his name to all nations, beginning at Jerusalem"* (Luke 24:47) and *"...you will be my witnesses in Jerusalem, and in all Judea and Samaria, and to the ends of the earth"* (Acts 1:8).

David was clearly blessed by God. Unfortunately, not everyone appreciated this fact. Out of jealousy, Saul persecuted David and tried to kill him. Many of David's descriptions of his persecution sounds so much like what Jesus went through that it is hard to decide, at times, if David was writing about himself or if he was prophesying the future sufferings of his antitype, Jesus Christ. In fact there is a double meaning in many of these descriptions of David's travails.

> "Why do the nations conspire
>   and the peoples plot in vain?
> The kings of the earth take their stand
>   and the rulers gather together against the Lord
>   and against his Anointed One" (Psalms 2:1,2).

Is the Psalmist talking about David's persecutions or about the suffering of his antitype, Jesus, Son of David?

Psalms twenty-two starts out with David describing his sufferings and persecutions, presumably at the hands of Saul, but his description morphs into a description of the sufferings of Jesus.

> *My God, my God, why have you forsaken me?*
> *Why are you so far from saving me,*
>   *so far from the words of my groaning?*
> *O my God, I cry out by day, but you do not answer,*
>   *by night, and am not silent....*
> *All who see me mock me;*
>   *they hurl insults, shaking their heads:*
> *"He trusts in the* LORD;
>   *let him deliver him,*
>   *since he delights in him...."*
> *Dogs have surrounded me;*
>   *a band of evil men has encircled me,*
>   *they have pierced my hands and my feet*
> (Psalms 22:1,2,7,8,16).

We can see the similarity between David and the Messiah in their suffering and persecution. King Saul tried to kill King David. King Herod tried to kill King Jesus.

We learn something about the Messiah from each of those who prefigured him. From David we learn that the Messiah is a powerful king, ruling from spiritual Jerusalem. *"I saw the Holy City, the new Jerusalem, coming down out of heaven from God"* (Revelation 21:2). Having David reigning as king in the old Jerusalem brought great joy and blessing to Israel. Dwelling with Jesus in the New Jerusalem will be an even greater blessing.

IX. SOLOMON, DANIEL, CYRUS, EZRA, JOSHUA THE PRIEST...

The list of those who God used as prefigures of Christ is extensive. Solomon was the son of David, as the Messiah is the son of David. When one reads God's prophecy to David concerning his son, it is hard to know if he is talking about Solomon or Jesus Christ:

> *"I will raise up your offspring to succeed you, who will come from your own body, and I will establish his kindom. He is the one who will build a house for my Name, and I will establish the throne of his kingdom forever. I will be his father, and he will be my son...Your house and your kingdom will endure forever before me; your throne will be established forever"* (2 Samuel 7:12-14,16).

God established David's son Solomon over his kingdom. God also established a kingdom which will endure forever in his son Jesus Christ.

Solomon built the temple in which God dwelt among men. *"I have built a magnificent temple for you, a place for you to dwell..." "But will God really dwell on earth with men? The heavens, even the highest heavens, cannot contain you. How much less this temple I have built!"* (2 Chronicles 6:2,18). Solomon built the temple so that God could dwell among his people. When Jesus walked the earth, God dwelt among the people of God.

Even more than David, Solomon defeated all the enemies of Israel. His kingdom extended from the border of Egypt all the way to the Euphrates River, encompassing all of the Promised Land. Solomon saved the people of God from their enemies, bringing peace to the Israel for the first time in their history. Jesus saves his people and he is the Prince of Peace (Isaiah 9:6).

There are a number of parallels between the kingdom under Solomon and the messianic kingdom. For example, when the Queen of Sheba came to offer gifts/tribute to King Solomon (2 Chronicles 9:1-12), one is reminded of the magi from the East who brought gifts to King Jesus. The honor the Queen of Sheba paid to Solomon is symbolic of the Gentiles coming to honor God in the spiritual Jerusalem which is the kingdom of God.

God also used Daniel as a prefigure of the Messiah. Daniel was taken as a very young child from Israel. So was Jesus. Jesus was taken to Egypt and Daniel was taken to Babylon. Daniel was a righteous man who prayed for Israel. He was able to proclaim salvation for the people of God and their release from captivity

(Daniel 9:1-3). Daniel was a prophet, as was Jesus. Interesting about the ministry of Daniel is that he served as a prophet to the Gentiles, serving under Nebuchadnezzar and Cyrus. Daniel's ministry was a hint that the Messiah's ministry also would begin with Israel but spread to the Gentiles. Daniel began his life in a powerful family, but later became a captive and a slave in Babylon, but was raised to be offered the second position in the kingdom of Babylon. Similarly, Jesus left a position of power to be born a lowly peasant in a barn, but was raised to the God's right hand.

Perhaps most astounding of all, God even used a Gentile king as a prefigure of Christ! When Judah went into captivity, God prophesied through Jeremiah that the captivity would last for seventy years:

> *"This whole country* (Judah) *will become a desolate wasteland, and these nations will serve the king of Babylon seventy years.*
> *But when the seventy years are fulfilled, I will punish the king of Babylon and his nation, the land of the Babylonians, for their guilt declares the Lord"* (Jeremiah 25:11,12).

By now, it will not be surprising that God sent a prefigure of the Messiah to save Israel from their captivity in Babylon. What is striking is that he used Cyrus, the king of Persia/Media. Cyrus conquered Babylon in 538 B.C., fulfilling the prophecy of Jeremiah that God would punish Babylon. After conquering this great city, Cyrus instituted a policy which was unprecedented. He allowed captive peoples to return to their homeland to reestablish residence and begin worshipping their gods. Specifically, he decreed that Israel could return to Jerusalem and rebuild the temple. In a very real sense, Israel was saved by Cyrus, because thanks to him, they were able to reinstitute the sacrifices which brought forgiveness to the Jews.

Interestingly, God made it clear that he saw Cyrus as a savior of Israel in a prophecy of Isaiah written almost two hundred years before the event.

> *...who says of Cyrus, "He is my shepherd*
> *and will accomplish all that I please;*
> *he will say of Jerusalem, "Let it be rebuilt,"*
> *and of the temple, "Let its foundation be laid"'* (Isaiah 44:28).
>
> *This is what the LORD says to his anointed,*

> to Cyrus, whose right hand I take hold of
> to subdue nations before him
> > and to strip kings of their armor,... (Isaiah 45:1).
>
> "I will raise up Cyrus in my righteousness:
> > I will make all his ways straight.
>
> He will rebuild my city
> > and set my exiles free,
>
> but not for a price or reward,
> > says the LORD Almighty" (Isaiah 45:13).

If one were to substitute Christ or Messiah for Cyrus in this passage it would fit the context remarkably well. Cyrus, pagan king of a pagan nation, was God's anointed one to save Israel, rebuild Jerusalem and lay the foundation of the temple. God calls him his shepherd. Remember that the Hebrew word translated as anointed in this passage is *masiah* or Messiah. Through Isaiah, writing two hundred years beforehand, God told Israel that he would send a Messiah, Cyrus, to save his people.

Let us look at a final prefigure of the Messiah. In the book of Zechariah, God made the high priest Joshua to be a visible, physical prophecy of the coming Messiah. This is not the same Joshua who, almost a thousand years earlier, saved Israel and led them into the Promised Land. This is the high priest Joshua who served Israel in the late 500s B.C. after their restoration to the Promised Land. Joshua was the high priest who oversaw the rebuilding of the Temple. Being a high priest as is Jesus, having the name Joshua (Jeshua, Jesus), rebuilding the temple, the house of God in Israel, would qualify Joshua as a foreshadow of the Messiah. Listen to how God, through Zechariah describes Joshua:

> Then he showed me Joshua the high priest standing before the angel of the LORD and Satan standing at his right side to accuse him. The LORD said to Satan, "The Lord rebuke you, Satan! The LORD, who has chosen Jerusalem, rebuke you!"
>
> "Listen, O high priest Joshua and your associates seated before you, who are men symbolic of things to come: I am going to bring my servant, the Branch. See, the stone I have set in front of Joshua! There are seven eyes on that one stone, and I will engrave an inscription on it," says the LORD Almighty, "And I will remove the sin of this land in a single day" (Zechariah 3: 1,2,8,9).

In the vision, Joshua is tempted by Satan as was Jesus in his forty day wilderness experience. God uses Joshua as a visual representation of the coming Messiah, the Branch, who will remove the sin of the land in a single day.

The list of messianic prefigures could be expanded to include Abraham, Isaac, Jacob, Hezekiah, Ezra, Nehemiah and Esther, but the point is clear. This chapter began with the thesis that given the theme of the Old Testament, the Messiah is coming, and given that the Old Testament is full of prefigures which find their fulfillment in the New, there ought to be many prefigures of the Messiah in the Old Testament. When one looks, one is not disappointed. Any single isolated parallel between Melchizedek, Joshua or David and the life and ministry of Jesus could be dismissed as a coincidence. However, given the seemingly unlimited number of amazing parallels between these people and their fulfillment in Jesus, one is left with only one conceivable explanation. The Bible is the word of God and God has a message for us. The suffering Messiah, the savior of the world, prophet, priest and king, is coming.

Endnotes

1 Leonard Goppelt, *Typos* (Eerdman's Publishing Company, Grand Rapids, Michigan, 1982), p 129.

2 This is what the Lord says: Israel is my firstborn son, and I told you, "Let my son go, so he may worship me" (Exodus 4:22,23). Here God calls the nation of Israel his son.

3 Described in Numbers 20:8-12. God commanded Moses to speak to the rock. Instead, Moses struck the rock at Meribah twice. Graciously, God provided water, but Moses had not obeyed God's command.

4 It is interesting to note that the King James Version uses Jesus instead of Joshua in Hebrews 4:8. This mistake was caused both because the names are essentially identical and because the work of Joshua and Jesus in saving God's people are parallel.

5 Deuteronomy 28:15-35.

The Earthly Tabernacle and the Heavenly Tabernacle

It was necessary, then, for the copies of the heavenly things to be purified with these sacrifices, but the heavenly things themselves with better sacrifices than these. For Christ did not enter a man-made sanctuary that was only a copy of the true one; he entered heaven itself, now to appear for us in God's presence.

Hebrews 9:23

The billowing smoke of burning incense, the blood of a goat splattered on the furniture and the curtains, the mystery of it all... What lies behind the curtain? The daily supply of showbread, the inner court, the outer court, the court of the gentiles, the Holy of Holies...The gold, the blue, purple and scarlet cloth, pomegranates, lampstands, priests going through ritual motions which are hundreds of years old...To the modern, Western mind, the religious ceremony performed in the tabernacle in the wilderness, and later in the temple in Jerusalem seems to have more in common with a pagan religion than with the stark simplicity of Christian worship. What does all this teach us?

Nothing had more importance to the Jews and to Judaism than the ceremony, the symbolism and the sacrifices involved in worship at the temple in Jerusalem. The temple was the place where God dwelt among his people. The temple was the place where sacrifice for sins were made. It was the heart of what made a Jew a Jew. The pilgrimage to the temple at Jerusalem on *Yom Kippur* or one of the other festivals was the highlight of the religious year; indeed it was the highlight of the entire religious life of most Jews. When Jews wanted to reassure themselves that they were truly the people of God, they would say the mantra, *"This is the temple of the* LORD, *the temple of the* LORD, *the temple of the* LORD" (Jeremiah 7:4). To their shame, many Jews came to rely on the mere presence of the temple in Jerusalem to make them right with God, rather than maintaining a righteous life. As long as the temple stood in Jerusalem, the Jews rationalized that God had not abandoned them.

It is also hard to overstate the devastation to the Jews when the temple was destroyed for seventy years beginning in 586 B.C., under the Babylonian King Nebuchadnezzar and again in A.D. 70, by the Roman general Titus. For a person operating under the Old Covenant, taking temple sacrifice and worship out of Judaism would be analogous to taking the gospel out of Christianity. Absent forgiveness of sin, salvation and a prayer life, the Christian religion would still maintain a shell of good moral teaching, with advice about how to live a good life, and some nice ceremony, but it would have been gutted of its core meaning to say the least. What is Christianity without salvation in the blood of Jesus Christ? Judaism as practiced today is in an analogous position. Without the temple, there is no more presence of God with his people, no more forgiveness of sins, no more unifying religious ceremony as revealed in the Old Testament.

As the Hebrew writer said, probably some time in the 60s A.D., *"By calling this covenant 'new,' he has made the first one obsolete; and what is obsolete and aging will soon disappear"* (Hebrews 8:13). When Jesus Christ came, not to abolish the Law or the Prophets, but to fulfill them (paraphrasing Matthew 5:17), the ceremonies performed at the temple turned from a foreshadow of the amazing things we have in Christ to a shadow of former things. The prophecy of Hebrews 8:13 was fulfilled shortly after it was written. In A.D. 70, when the temple was destroyed, temple worship and sacrifice came to a permanent end. What was old and obsolete did indeed disappear forever.

The worship and sacrifice performed at the tabernacle, and later in the temple of Solomon and its reconstruction under Zerubbabel, was the heart of Judaism. Every part of the daily and weekly ceremony as well as the annual *Yom Kippur* (Day of Atonement) sacrifice held great significance to the Jews. As great a significance as these ceremonies carried for the Jews, their depth of meaning to those under the New Covenant is still greater. Every aspect of the physical worship at the temple was a foreshadow of a greater spiritual reality which finds its fulfillment in Jesus Christ. For fourteen centuries, the levitical priests carried out both daily ceremony and yearly sacrifice in the temple and tabernacle. The deepest meaning of their actions were a mystery to them. They were unaware that their actions were a foreshadowing play of the greater reality found in Jesus Christ and the New Covenant which was sealed by his blood. As the Hebrew writer put it:

> *It was necessary, then, for the copies of the heavenly things to be purified with these sacrifices, but the heavenly things themselves with better sacrifices than these. For Christ did not enter a man-made sanctuary that was only a copy of the true one; he entered heaven itself, now to appear for us in God's presence* (Hebrews 9:23,24).

This passage clearly spells it out. The tabernacle and temple were a copy of a reality which is found in the spiritual tabernacle in heaven. Each item in the physical tabernacle, set up by human hands under very specific instructions by God, will prove to be a wonderful symbol of a major aspect of our relationship with God. The Old Covenant tabernacle will foreshadow our relationship with God under the New Covenant. It also remains as a foreshadow of what we will have in the New Jerusalem—in the tabernacle in heaven where we will stand face to face with God. What are these great realities symbolized in the earthly tabernacle?

I. THE TABERNACLE AND THE TEMPLE

First, let us consider in some detail the actual layout, both of the portable tabernacle which was carried by the Levites during the wanderings in the desert, and of the more palatial temple in Jerusalem.

God gave the instructions for building the tabernacle through Moses, as recorded in Exodus chapters twenty-five through twenty-seven and chapter thirty.

"Then have them make a sanctuary for me, and I will dwell

> among them. Make this tabernacle and all its furnishings exactly like the pattern I will show you" (Exodus 25:8,9).

The purpose for the building of the tabernacle was so that God could dwell among his people without them seeing him directly, because for anyone to see God face-to-face would mean death. *"You cannot see my face, for no one may see me and live"* (Exodus 33:20). Once the tabernacle was set up, God's presence was seen as a pillar of cloud by day, and a pillar of fire by night which stood over the tent (Numbers 14:14). Not surprisingly, the Jews took God dwelling with them quite literally.

The tabernacle was surrounded by a large outer curtain which made a courtyard. The outer courtyard was rectangular; one hundred cubits by fifty cubits (about 150 feet by 75 feet). There was an entrance on the east side which was twenty cubits (about thirty feet) long. The curtain was made of blue, purple and scarlet yarn. The Jews were not allowed into the courtyard. Only the Levitical priests were allowed there. Even among the Levites, only one designated priest was allowed into the Holy Place to perform ceremonies on any given day. That priest was definitely not allowed into the Most Holy Place. The two main objects in the courtyard outside the Holy Place were the bronze altar and the laver.

The bronze altar was a platform five cubits (about 8 feet) on a side and three cubits (about 5 feet) tall. It was made of acacia wood and was overlaid with bronze. The altar was for the burnt sacrifice of animals, grain and so forth. As one passed the altar, one came to a large basin, sometimes known as the laver. The laver was made of solid bronze. It was definitely nothing like a bird bath. The laver in the temple (2 Chronicles 4:2-6) held around 15,000 gallons. It was also known as the Sea. The priests were required to wash in the laver before they could enter the tabernacle itself. *"Whenever they enter the Tent of Meeting, they shall wash with water so that they will not die"* (Exodus 30:20). The New Testament symbolism of the laver will be important, but even for the Jews, the symbolism should have been obvious. God wanted his people to be ceremonially clean when they came into his presence.

The actual tabernacle was surrounded by an inner curtain ten cubits (about 15 feet) by thirty cubits (about 45 feet). The tabernacle was divided into the Holy Place, which was ten cubits by twenty cubits and the Holy of Holies or Most Holy Place, which was ten cubits square. There was an additional curtain separating the Holy Place from the Holy of Holies. When one entered into the Holy Place (and one better be a priest or one might be killed), one saw a table inlaid with gold, with twelve large round loaves of bread, sometimes known as the show bread. The bread was replaced daily by the designated priest. On the left wall was a lampstand of solid gold. The lampstand was constructed as a stand with seven branches, each topped with a lamp. The lamps were lit whenever the tabernacle was erected. At the back of the Holy Place stood a golden altar for burning incense which stood up against the curtain which led to the innermost sanctuary.

Behind this curtain was the Holy of Holies. Here stood the Ark of the Covenant. The ark was constructed of acacia wood, inlaid with pure gold. Contained inside the ark was contained a gold jar of manna, and the tablets (the engraved Ten Commandments) Moses received from God on Mount Sinai. Also in the ark was Aaron's rod. The lid of the ark was made of pure gold. It was engraved with elaborate detail. The lid was called the atonement cover or the mercy seat. Two golden cherubim stood at either end of the atonement cover, with their wings spread upward, overshadowing the ark. Other than Moses, only the high priest was allowed into the Holy of Holies. Even the high priest was allowed into the Most Holy Place only once a year, on the Day of Atonement, and only after first sprinkling the blood of a goat and a bull slain on that day. We will see that every aspect of the tabernacle will be a foreshadow of a very important aspect of the New Covenant. Before we get to that, let us consider the temple in Jerusalem.

Before entering the Promised Land, God promised the people that he would establish a permanent place for his presence and for the people to worship him in the Holy Land (Deuteronomy 12:4-7). This promise was delayed for over three hundred years during the chaotic time of the judges. During this time the tabernacle was set up at Shiloh (Joshua 18:1). The ark did not spend all its time at Shiloh, but that interesting story is outside the subject matter of this book.

Finally, King David conquered Jerusalem, the city formerly known as Salem, where Melchizedek had ruled. The mountain of Moriah, where Abraham had offered up Isaac was at the site of Jerusalem. Significantly, Mount Moriah became the site for the temple of God. After establishing Jerusalem as his capital, David wanted to build the temple. Despite his sincere desire, the task fell to his son Solomon because there was too much blood on David's hands. Solomon built a grand temple with a Holy Place and a Most Holy Place constructed almost exactly on the plan of the tabernacle, except on a larger scale. When the ark was finally brought into the inner sanctuary God caused a conspicuous grand opening:

> When the priests withdrew from the Holy Place, the cloud filled the temple of the LORD. And the priests could not perform their service because of the cloud, for the glory of the LORD filled the temple (1 Kings 8:10,11).

Here, God provided powerful evidence that he was dwelling in his temple in Jerusalem!

Solomon's temple was different from the tabernacle in that it provided several different courtyards. The Holy Place was surrounded by an inner area, known as the courtyard of the priests. The sacrificial altar and the laver were in the courtyard for the priests. It would be more accurate to say the lavers (plural). Due to the volume of sacrifices on special feast days, there were ten basins set up in the courtyard of the priests. Outside this courtyard was the courtyard of Israel, where Jewish men who were not priests were allowed. In front of this, on the eastern end of the temple was the courtyard of women where Hebrew women were allowed to enter. Still further from the sanctuary was an even larger courtyard reserved for the Gentiles. The Jews saw this as an arrangement of those closer to and farther from the presence of God. However, there is no command in the Bible to build separate courts for men and women, so it is questionable to assume that God saw the distinction between male and female as the Jews did.

Solomon's temple was completed sometime after 970 B.C. It survived, with some renovations, until its destruction by Nebuchadnezzar's army in 586 B.C. By 516 B.C., after the return from the exile, a second, smaller temple was built under Zerubbabel along a pattern similar to Solomon's temple. This temple stood until it was completely rebuilt under King Herod. Herod's temple was begun in 20 B.C. It was still being constructed during the life of Jesus Christ, finally being finished in A.D. 64. Herod's temple was destroyed only a few years later in A.D. 70, bringing to an end the sacrificial form of worship of Yahweh.

Schematic Plan of the Temple

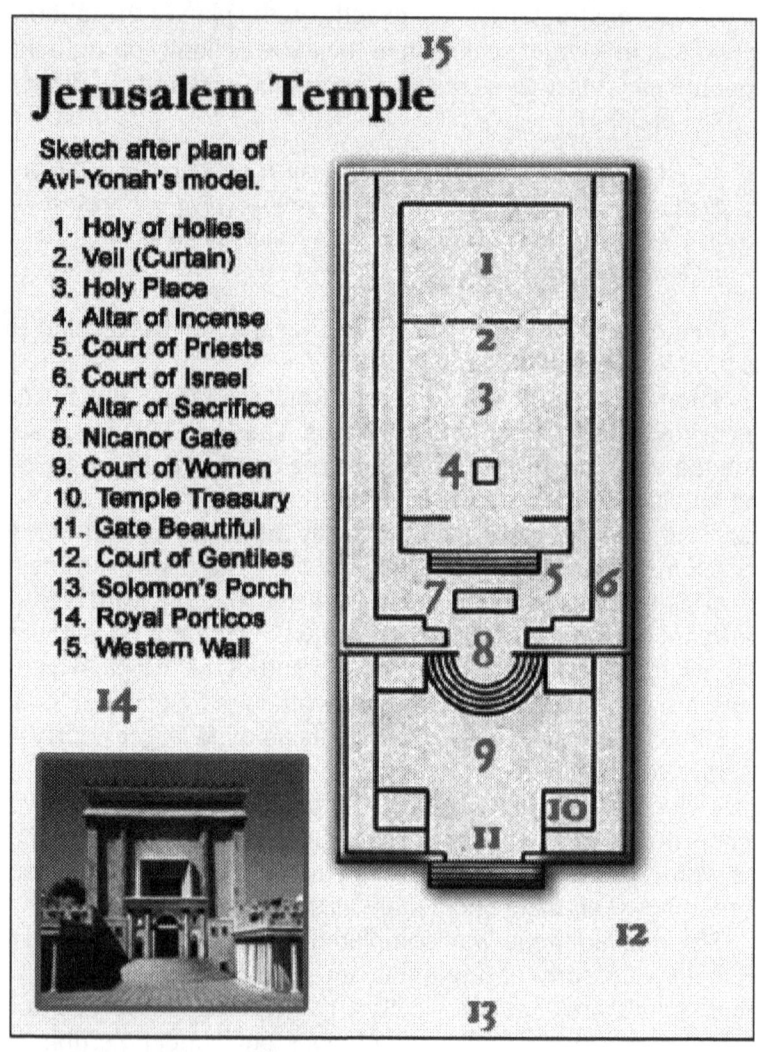

II. FORESHADOWS

The tabernacle, and later the temple, were the centers of worship for the entire Hebrew nation. If the tabernacle was the place where God dwelt among his people, then one could argue that the focus of the Old Covenant worship was to establish a way to be in fellowship with God and to come into his presence. This, too, is the focus of the New Covenant. How are we to come into a relationship with God? The earthly tabernacle gives us many hints.

The setup of the tabernacle in the Old Testament tells us that only a person who is free of sin can enter into the presence of God. Only the high priest could enter the presence of the Lord behind the curtain, only once a year, and even then, only after the blood of a goat and a bull was splattered on the atonement cover of the ark to atone for his sins.

There is a sense in which this remains true under the New Covenant as well. Only a perfect person can come into the presence of God. However, when Jesus came to dwell on the earth, he did something amazing. In John 1:14, we read, *"The Word became flesh and made his dwelling among us."* The phrase translated in the NIV as *dwelling among us* in the Greek means literally, he came and *tabernacled among us*. In Jesus, we see God face-to-face. When Jesus stepped into Jerusalem, the Jews were still going through the motions of the sacrificial system so that the high priest could go before God once a year to represent them. While they were going through this symbolic ceremony, God was tabernacling among them in the form of Jesus Christ. God had truly come to Jerusalem.

But Jesus has gone back into heaven to be at the right hand of God. How are we to come into the presence of God now?

> *Every high priest is appointed to offer both gifts and sacrifices, and so it was necessary for this one* (i.e. the high priest Jesus) *also to have something to offer. If he were on earth, he would not be a priest, for there are already men who offer the gifts prescribed by the law.* **They serve at a sanctuary that is a copy and a shadow of what is in heaven.** *This is why Moses was warned when he was about to build the tabernacle: "See to it that you make everything according to the pattern shown you on the mountain." But the ministry Jesus has received is as superior to theirs as the covenant of which he is a mediator is superior to the old one, and is founded on better promises* (Hebrews 8:3-6).

During the time Jesus was on the earth he did not enter into the Holy of Holies in the temple at Jerusalem. Instead, when he died and was raised, he entered the perfect heavenly tabernacle to offer gifts and sacrifices there for us directly before God. That is the meaning of the phrase, "if he were here on earth." Although Jesus walked into the temple precincts while here on the earth, he did not enter into the Holy of Holies. He did not need to. He entered the heavenly tabernacle—the reality of which the physical tabernacle is merely a copy.

The tabernacle itself, then, represents the presence of God with his people. In the heavenly tabernacle, those who are saved by the blood of Jesus will dwell with God forever.

> And I heard a loud voice from the throne saying, "Now the dwelling of God is with men and he will live with them. They will be his people and God himself will be with them and be their God" (Revelation 21:3).

Again, the Greek word translated as dwelling in this passage is literally tabernacling. In heaven, God will tabernacle with us as he tabernacled with us when Jesus came to the earth as God in the flesh.

Actually, for those who are in Christ, God is dwelling with and in them right now. *"Don't you understand that you yourselves are God's temple and that God's spirit lives in you?"* (1 Corinthians 3:16). What an awesome reality! At least in a sense, the antitype to the Jewish temple is the bodies of those who have been baptized into Christ, receiving the promised Holy Spirit to dwell in them (Acts 2:38). God is tabernacling with his people. No wonder God allowed the temple in Jerusalem to be destroyed in A.D. 70. Because of the New Covenant, it was no longer needed.

III. THE BRONZE ALTAR

Let us look at the individual items in the tabernacle as foreshadows of things to come. When one entered the tabernacle, one came to the sacrificial altar. This is where the fellowship offering, the peace offering, the sin offering and so forth were laid out and burned in the presence of God. We will spend an entire chapter considering the significance of each of the offerings prescribed in Leviticus, so let's keep it simple for now. What we learn from the presence of the bronze altar in the courtyard is that in order to come before God, a sacrifice is needed. This sacrifice involves the shedding of blood. Coming into fellowship with God has always required the shedding of blood. Jesus entered the heavenly tabernacle for us by virtue of his own blood. Consider Hebrews 9:23-26, for this passage makes the concept clear.

> *It was necessary, then, for the* **copies of the heavenly things** *to be purified with these sacrifices but the heavenly things themselves with better sacrifices than these. For Christ did not enter a man-made sanctuary that was only a copy of the true one; he entered heaven itself, now to appear for us in God's presence. Nor did he enter heaven to offer himself again and again, the way the high priest enters the Most Holy Place every year with blood that is not his own. Then Christ would have had to suffer many times since the creation of the world. But now he has appeared once for all at the end of the ages to do away with sin by the sacrifice of himself.*

The presence of the bronze altar in the tabernacle was a constant reminder for the Jews of the continuing need for sacrifice in order to have fellowship with God. The antitype of the tabernacle sacrifices is the sacrifice of Jesus Christ. As blood sacrifice on the altar was required for the priests of Aaron to enter the Holy Place, so the blood of Jesus, sacrificed on the cross, allows us to come into the presence of the Most High God—to enter the spiritual tabernacle in Heaven. Daily, weekly, yearly sacrifice is no longer needed in the New Covenant.

> *When Christ came as a high priest of the good things that are already here,* **he went through the greater and more perfect tabernacle that is not man-made**, *that is to say, not a part of this creation. He did not enter by means of the blood of goats and calves; but he entered the Most Holy Place once for all by his own blood, having obtained eternal redemption. The blood of goats and bulls and the ashes of a heifer sprinkled on those who are ceremonially unclean sanctify them so that they are outwardly clean. How much more, then, will the blood of Christ, who through the eternal Spirit offered himself unblemished to God, cleanse our consciences from acts that lead to death, so that we may serve the living God!* (Hebrews 9:11-14).

Imagine the number of goats, sheep, calves, doves and other animals sacrificed on the altar at the tabernacle or at the temple in Jerusalem over the fourteen centuries of their existence! On the great feast days, the brook of Kidron in Jerusalem ran red with the blood. All of these sacrifices were foreshadows, copies, reminders of the one great sacrifice of Jesus' blood on the cross. Could God have created a more graphic illustration of the problem of sin and its solution?

IV. THE LAVER

Let us draw closer to the inner sanctuary. What do we come to next? We come to the laver. Before the priests could enter the sanctuary to offer their daily service before God, they were required to bathe: *"They shall wash their hands and feet so that they will not die"* (Exodus 30:20). A sacrifice for sins is required in order to come into the presence of God. Is anything else required? Apparently, yes. It is not hard to recognize what God intended the washing in the laver to foreshadow. We have already seen the Hebrew writer declare the things in the tabernacle to be copies of things to come. The requirement that the priests to be washed in water in the basin is clearly a foreshadow of the command in the New Testament to be washed in the water of baptism.

> *"...and this water symbolizes baptism that now saves you also— not the removal of dirt from the body, but the pledge of a good conscience toward God"* (1 Peter 3:21).

In 1 Peter 3:21, Peter explains that the water of Noah's flood is a foreshadow of the cleansing water of baptism. He could just as easily have said that the water in the laver is a symbol (foreshadow) of New Testament baptism. The water in the laver removed dirt from the bodies of the priests, but it also made them ceremonially clean so that they could serve the living God. Similarly, the water of baptism makes those who come to Jesus clean, so that they may serve God.

From the presence of the laver in the courtyard, outside the actual tabernacle, we learn that baptism in water is required in order to come into the presence of God. So much for those who teach that baptism is simply a ceremony reminding us of something which had already happened. What happened to the priests who forgot to wash their hands and their feet before they entered the sanctuary? *"They shall wash their hands and feet so that they will not die."* There is water in God's plan for us to come to him. It has been so since the beginning.

After repenting and being baptized (Acts 2:38), after the sacrifice of Jesus' blood has been applied to us, *"through faith in his blood"* (Romans 3:25), we can come into the sanctuary—into the place where God dwells with his people. Let us visualize in our minds entering into the Holy Place. What do we find there? We find symbols of our relationship with God.

V. THE SHOW BREAD, THE LAMP AND THE ALTAR OF INCENSE

On the right as one came into the Holy Place sat a gold-inlaid table with twelve large round loaves placed on the top. The loaves were baked fresh and replaced daily by the priest on duty. The twelve loaves were symbolic of the twelve sons of Israel and of the twelve tribes descended from them. The antitype of the twelve tribes in the Old Testament is the twelve apostles in the New. The significance of the twelve loaves is that there is sufficient spiritual food for all of God's people. It does not seem to be a coincidence that when Jesus fed the five thousand in the wilderness (John 6:1-15) there were twelve basketfuls of bread left over. The bread in the tabernacle, traditionally known as the show bread, was a foreshadow of the spiritual food we have in Christ. Jesus did not leave us in much doubt about the significance of the bread in the sanctuary. *"I am the bread of life. He who comes to me will never go hungry..."* (John 6:35). When Jesus made this statement, soon after miraculously providing bread to the five thousand in the wilderness, his hearers thought both of the manna in the wilderness and of the bread in the sanctuary. Jesus is spiritual food. He is also known as the Word of God. Jesus said, *"I am the way, the truth and the life."* The bread then is spiritual food. It is the truth and it is the Word of God. As people in fellowship with God through the blood of Jesus, we have daily access to this food by reading the Word of God and by experiencing a relationship with Jesus.

There is a somewhat obscure event in the life of King David which takes on added meaning in this light. Although David had been anointed king, Saul was still officially King of Israel. Saul was persecuting David, chasing him throughout Palestine. One day

David came to the tabernacle. He and his men were famished. David asked the priest for bread. Because there was no other bread available, God moved the heart of the priest Ahimelech to do something which would normally have been inconceivable. He gave David some of the consecrated show bread which had been removed from the tabernacle that day. King David, the type, ate the bread of the sanctuary which was a forshadow of the antitype, his "son," Jesus Christ.

On the left side of the outer sanctuary as one entered from the east was the golden lampstand. This lampstand had seven branches, seven being the symbolic number of God and of the Spirit of God.[1] Each of the branches had a bowl at its end with oil in the bowl. The lamps were kept burning, unless the people of God were moving the tabernacle through the desert. Of course, every detail in the tabernacle is a copy or foreshadow of something we have in Christ. What is the significance of the lamps?

A number of Bible passages could help answer this question. Consider one of the visions given to Zechariah:

> Then the angel who talked with me returned and wakened me, as a man is wakened from his sleep. He asked me, "What do you see?"
>
> I answered, "I see a solid gold lampstand with a bowl at the top and seven lights on it, with seven channels to the lights. Also there are two olive trees by it, one on the right of the bowl and the other on its left."
>
> I asked the angel who talked with me, "What are these, my lord?"
>
> He answered, "Do you not know what these are?"
>
> "No, my lord," I replied.
>
> So he said to me, "This is the word of the LORD to Zerubbabel: 'Not by might nor by power, but by my Spirit,' says the LORD Almighty" (Zechariah 4:1-6).

The lamps represented the Holy Spirit of God! On the right side of the Holy Place one had a foreshadow of the Son of God in his work as our provider. On the left of the outer sanctuary was a foreshadow of the sustaining power of the Holy Spirit.

The significance of the olive trees and the seven channels to the seven lamps in this vision was that the lamp will never run out of oil. Similarly, the lamps in the tabernacle and later in the temple were left burning. This is a foreshadow of the nature of the Holy Spirit in the New Covenant. In Acts 2:38,39 the apostle Peter describes the working of the Holy Spirit in those who repent and are baptized into Christ as a promised gift to all who accepted his message.

God had made the Holy Spirit available in certain special situations in the Old Testament. David prayed to God, *"Do not cast me from your presence or take your Holy Spirit from me"* (Psalms 51:11). We have already seen that David received the Spirit when he was anointed by Samuel. David feared being cast from the presence of God and having the Holy Spirit taken from him. The foreshadow of the lamp in the tabernacle tells us that those who come to God through Jesus Christ will receive a gift of the Holy Spirit which will never be snuffed out.

> *"If anyone is thirsty, let him come to me and drink. Whoever believes in me, as the Scripture has said, streams of living water will flow from within him." By this he meant the Spirit, whom those who believed in him were later to receive"* (John 7:37-39).

Praise God that the Christian does not have to cry out with David, *"Take not your Holy Spirit from me."* As long as we are faithful, our lamp will never go out, although followers of Jesus are admonished, *"do not put out the Spirit's fire"* (1 Thessalonians 5:19).

It is difficult to leave Zechariah four without noting a further foreshadow. Zechariah asked about the two olive trees on the right and the left of the lampstand with the pipes, which poured out an unending supply of golden oil. When asked, the angel explained the typology of the two trees, *"These are the two who are anointed to serve the LORD of all."* The two who are anointed are a reference to the high priest Joshua and the governor Zerubabbel, both of whom were foreshadows of the anointed one: the Messiah.

Other references to the connection between the lamp and oil in the sanctuary and the anointing of the Holy Spirit should be mentioned. In 1 Samuel 16:13, David, a type of Christ was anointed by Samuel with oil—setting him apart as King of Israel; *"from that day on the Spirit of the LORD came upon David in power."* Similarly, King Saul was anointed and at the same time received an outpouring of the Spirit in 1 Samuel 10:1,9,10.

The last item in the Holy Place was the golden altar of incense which stood in front of the curtain which led to the Holy of Holies. This, too, represents a major aspect of the spiritual life of those who are in Christ.

> *"Aaron must burn fragrant incense on the altar every morning when he tends the lamps. He must burn incense again when he lights the lamps at twilight so incense will burn regularly before the L*ORD *for the generations to come. Do not offer on this altar any other incense or any burnt offering or grain offering, and do not pour a drink offering on it"* (Exodus 30:7-9).

This altar was never used for offerings (although it, with all the other items in the Holy Place, was sprinkled with blood on the Day of Atonement).

What is the significance of this golden altar and of the incense? In a scene set in heaven in the book of Revelation, one finds the interesting passage, *"Each one had a harp and they were holding golden bowls full of incense, which are the prayers of the saints"* (Revelation 5:8). The incense burned right in front of the Holy of Holies was a foreshadow representing the prayers of the saints. The prayers of his people smell beautiful to God. Notice that the priests were required to offer up incense, which is a foreshadow of our prayer every day, both morning and night. We would do well to consistently offer up prayers to God.

What a beautiful picture we have in the outer sanctuary of our relationship with God in the New Covenant. These copies of the greater, heavenly realities create a wonderful picture of the security, power and the intimacy of our relationship with God. When we walk before God, we always have the sustaining strength of the Son of God in our right hand, and the ever-burning power of the Holy Spirit in our left, with our offerings of prayer to God ever before him. With the Son on the right and the Holy Spirit on the left, guess who is right in front of us as we enter the Holy Place!

VI. THE CURTAIN

Now we come to the curtain. The curtain which separated the Holy Place from the Holy of Holies was made of twined blue, purple and scarlet yarn. It was behind this curtain that God dwelt between the wings of the cherubim. The blue represents heaven where God resides. The purple has always been the color of royalty. It stands for God, the King of kings. The scarlet yarn in the curtain stands for the blood which is required to purify all the items in the sanctuary.

For the Jew, the curtain which separated the Holy Place from the Most Holy inner sanctuary offered a great lesson about the Holiness of God. They were reminded that to see God face to face was fatal. The typical Jew did not generally think of God as someone with whom to have an intimate relationship. (The life of David and the Psalms he and others wrote are a notable exception to this rule). To the Jew, God took care of his people, but from a distance. He was to be feared and was not to be approached directly. All the items in the sanctuary were carried by the Levites using poles through rings on the sides so that they did not have to touch the holy items.

It is unlikely the Jews forgot the time Uzzah had touched the ark of God. David had ordered the ark to be moved to Jerusalem so that God could be worshipped there.

> *David again brought together out of Israel chosen men...to bring up from there the ark of God, which is called by the Name, the name of the Lord Almighty who is enthroned between the cherubim that are on the ark....*
>
> *When they came to the threshing floor of Nacon, Uzzah reached out and took hold of the ark of God, because the oxen stumbled. The LORD'S anger burned against Uzzah because of his irreverent act; therefore God struck him down and he died there beside the ark of God* (2 Samuel 6:1,2,6,7).

It seems hard to fault Uzzah for trying to save the ark from damage as it was about to slip from the wagon, but God struck him down. Those who would touch the ark of God, even for apparently good reason, forfeited their life. No wonder the Jews viewed God with awe and fear.

The curtain which led to the Holy of Holies represented for the Jews their separation from God. Because of the curtain, none could see God. None of them could come into the presence of God except the high priest, one day a year, only after the sprinkling of much blood. The day on which this happened was the Day of Atonement (detailed in chapter seven). The awesome thing about the curtain as a foreshadow is that it does not exist in the greater tabernacle in heaven. The day Jesus was crucified a wonderful thing happened in Herod's temple which probably went unnoticed by most that day.

> *And when Jesus had cried out again in a loud voice, he gave up his spirit.*
> *At that moment the curtain of the temple was torn in two from top to bottom..."* (Matthew 27:50,51).

At the time Jesus died, the curtain in front of the Most Holy Place where the priests ministered (and where we minister in our priestly relationship with God) was ripped in two from top to bottom. What a breath-taking portent. Bad news for the Jews, or at least for those under the Old Covenant. God had left his temple. God was no longer dwelling among men in a physical temple. *"By calling this covenant "new," he has made the first one obsolete; and what is obsolete and aging will soon disappear"* (Hebrews 8:13). From this moment forward the Old Covenant was obsolete. Forty years later (when Titus destroyed the temple in A.D. 70) animal sacrifice ended.

Bad news, but only for those Jews who would not come into a New Covenant relationship with God. In the heavenly tabernacle where Jesus entered by virtue of his own blood, there is no curtain blocking our view of God. Figuratively, it has been ripped in two. There is no separation between God and man. Our high priest has gone in to the Most Holy Place and called us to come right in behind him. What a great picture we are given in the earthly tabernacle, and what an inspiring foreshadowing we have of our relationship with God. Listen to this great news:

> *Therefore, brothers, since we have confidence to enter the Most Holy Place by the blood of Jesus,* **by a new and living way opened for us through the curtain,** *that is his body, and since we have a great priest over the house of God, let us draw near to God with a sincere heart in full assurance of faith, having our hearts sprinkled to cleanse us from a guilty conscience and having our bodies washed with pure water"* (Hebrews 10:19-22).

When the curtain was torn in two, everything changed. Those who come to God through the sacrifice on the altar and the water in the laver—prefigures of the blood of Christ and of baptism into Christ—come straight into the presence of God. There is no longer a separation between the Holy Place and the Most Holy Place. We no longer need a human intercessor. Thanks to Jesus, we come straight to the throne room with our prayers, even though there is still sin in our lives.

VII. THE ARK, THE MERCY SEAT AND THE CHERUBIM

The significance of the items in the Holy of Holies has already been hinted at. *"Then the cloud covered the Tent of Meeting, and the glory of the LORD filled the tabernacle. Moses could not enter the Tent of Meeting because the cloud had settled upon it, and the glory of the LORD filled the tabernacle"* (Exodus 40:34,35). The LORD Almighty, Yahweh God actually dwelled between the cherubim on the ark! This is not a fairy tale. Ask Uzzah. No wonder the Jews were tempted to rely on the mantra, *"the temple of the LORD, the temple of the LORD."* Given the billowing smoke and the blinding light which were seen when the temple was consecrated, it is easy to understand what the ark, mercy seat and cherubim represent: the presence of God with his people.

For the Jews, the items behind the curtain were a mystery. They had heard their whole lives about the manna, the tablets and Aaron's rod being in the ark and about the cherubim standing over the ark. For them, however, the idea of actually seeing these awesome portents was beyond any possibility. All this is changed for those who are in Christ. When Moses came out from being face to face with God in the Holy of Holies, his face was so brilliant with light that they had to cover him with a veil so that the people would not be blinded by the light. The veil on Moses's head was symbolic of the curtain in front of the Holy of Holies which kept the Israelites from the presence of God. Not so with those who are in Christ:

> *Therefore, since we have such a hope, we are very bold. We are not like Moses, who would put a veil over his face to keep the Israelites from gazing at it while the radiance was fading away. But their minds were made dull, for to this day, the same veil remains when the old covenant is read. It has not*

ITEM IN THE TABERNACLE OR TEMPLE	ANTITYPE IN THE NEW COVENANT	SCRIPTURE REFERENCE
The tabernacle itself	God dwelling with his people	John 14: 1-3, John 1: 14, Rev 1: 13
The bronze altar of sacrifice	The sacrifice of Jesus for sins	Hebrews 9: 14
The basin/laver	Baptism	Titus 3: 5
The show bread	The bread of life, Jesus Christ	John 6: 48-51
The lampstand	The Holy Spirit	Zechariah 4: 1-6
The altar of incense	The prayers of the saints	Revelation 5: 8
The blue, purple and scarlet yarn	The heavens, the kingship of God, the blood of Jesus	
The curtain	Separation from God	Matthew 27: 51
The ark of the covenant	The presence of God	Psalm 132: 7,8
The Mercy Seat	The grace of God	
The Cherubim	The angels in heaven	Ezekiel 10: 15-22

been removed, because only in Christ is it taken away. Even to this day when Moses is read, a veil covers their hearts. But whenever anyone turns to the Lord, the veil is taken away (2 Corinthians 3:12-16).

When the curtain was rent at the moment of Jesus' death, a way was opened for us to look right into the Holy of Holies. The veil has been removed for those who are in Christ. We see God more clearly. When the "Old Covenant" (the Old Testament) is read, we understand it more fully. We can come, as priests, directly to God to offer our sacrifices to him.

Those who pulled back the curtain and came into the Holy

of Holies, would be drawn first to the cherubim. To the Jew, the golden cherubim were something to be feared. Cherubim were the spiritual equivalent of armed guards. When God placed Adam and Eve in the Garden of Eden, they were in an intimate relationship with him, actually being able to "walk with God" in the garden. God had always intended for mankind to be in a close relationship with him. Unfortunately, sin entered the scene, and thus the separation.

> *After he drove the man out, he placed on the east side of the Garden of Eden cherubim and a flaming sword flashing back and forth to guard the way to the tree of life* (Genesis 3:24).

These cherubim were not the cute, pudgy angels of artistic fantasy. Adam and Eve were kept from the presence of God upon pain of death. It is the same with the cherubim in the Holy of Holies.

If the cherubim are a type, (and everything in the tabernacle is a copy of a heavenly thing, so they must be a type) then what is the antitype? The golden statues of cherubim above the ark are types of the real cherubim in heaven. The antitype to the Holy of Holies is the heavenly tabernacle—the throne room of the Almighty God. Revelation chapter five describes a scene in this room: *"Then I looked and heard the voice of many angels, numbering thousands upon thousands, and ten thousand times ten thousand. They encircled the throne and the living creatures and the elders. In a loud voice they sang: 'Worthy is the Lamb who was slain...'"* (Revelation 5:11,12).

The difference between the type and the antitype is that for the Jew, the cherubim were a cause for abject fear. They were God's guardians barring them from his presence because of their sin. For those who are in Christ, the cherubim represent something very different. They represent God's holy angels with whom we will worship day and night forever before the throne of God.

The objects inside the ark were types as well. The tablets which God had given to Moses were there. They had obvious significance. They represented the Law of Moses and the covenant given at Mount Sinai. The antitype to the covenant at Sinai is the New Covenant, which was sealed in the blood of Jesus. The prophetic relationship between the covenants will be discussed in chapter five.

Also in the ark was Aaron's rod. This was the same rod which Moses had placed in the Tent of the Testimony (the tabernacle). The next day, the rod had budded, blossomed and produced almonds (Numbers 17:6-13). For the Israelites, the rod was something to fear.

> The LORD said to Moses, "Put back Aaron's staff in front of the Testimony, to be kept as a sign to the rebellious. This will put an end to their grumbling against me so that they will not die..."
> Then the Israelites said to Moses, "We will die! We are lost, we are all lost! Anyone who even comes near the tabernacle of the LORD will die. Are we all going to die?" (Numbers 17:10-13).

The type represents something to fear for the Israelites, but not for us. *"Perfect* (i.e., complete, fully realized) *love drives out fear"* (1 John 4:18). The budding of Aaron's rod is a prefigure of God taking things which are dead and making them alive. Most specifically, it is a foreshadow of the resurrection of Jesus from the dead.

The last item in the Holy of Holies which needs mentioning is the Mercy Seat—the solid gold lid on the ark. This was the place where blood was splattered to make atonement for the people on *Yom Kippur*, the Day of Atonement. The Mercy Seat was also known as the Atonement Cover. To the Jews, the Mercy Seat was the throne of God. For them to come into the Most Holy Place, before the throne of God, meant death.

In the New Testament this seat symbolizes the grace of God. It is where we go to receive mercy from God, based not on the blood of a bull or a goat, but based on the blood of Jesus Christ. As with the cherubim, the type can represent something to fear under the Old Covenant, but the antitype represents something to be joyful about in the New Covenant. When all appear before the judgment seat of God, as mentioned in Romans 14:10 and as described in Revelation 20:11-14, for some it will be an Old Covenant experience: fear and judgment will be involved. For others, those whose names are written in the Lamb's book of life, the Mercy Seat will be a place to experience mercy and grace. Great joy will result.

SUMMARY

For well over a millennium the Levitical priests offered regular service, either in the tabernacle or in the temple. The tabernacle had a real and great significance to the Jews—it represented the presence of God among his people. As God had said to Moses, *"Then have them make a sanctuary for me, and I will dwell among them. Make this tabernacle and all its furnishings exactly like the pattern I will show you"* (Exodus 25:8,9). As the participants fulfilled their religious duty, little did they know that, *"They serve at a sanctuary that is a copy and a shadow of what is in heaven"* (Hebrews 8:5). For the Jews, the items inside the Holy of Holies were a mystery. For us, the mystery is solved by Jesus Christ.

Every detail of the design and the furnishings in the tabernacle was given by God to his people as a foreshadow of the New Covenant he would establish by the blood of Jesus. Surely we can say with Sir Robert Anderson,

> *"No one who reads Hebrews in the light of the Pentateuchal types could be deluded by the profane figment that the Books of Moses are literary forgeries concocted by the apostate priests of the exilic era. For the typology answers to the New Testament revelation of Christ as exactly as a key fits the lock it is intended to open."*[2]

Truly we have here impressive evidence of the inspiration of the Bible. We have clear cut evidence that God had the plan of salvation in mind from the beginning. This was no afterthought. The only real question for us is whether we will respond to that plan and come into the presence of the one, true, living God in the heavenly tabernacle, following in the wake of our great high priest, Jesus Christ. As Paul says in 2 Corinthians 6:16, *"For we are the temple of the living God. As God has said: 'I will live among them and walk among them and I will be their God and they will be my people.'"*

Endnotes

1 Revelation 1:12-16 is one of many passages which support this claim.
2 Sir Robert Anderson, *Types in Hebrews* (Kregel Publications, Grand Rapids, Michigan,1978), p. 153.

The Old Covenant Priesthood Foreshadows the Priesthood of the New Covenant

The point of what we are saying is this: We do have such a high priest, who sat down at the right hand of the throne of the Majesty in heaven, and who serves in the sanctuary, the true tabernacle set up by the Lord, not by man.

Hebrews 8:1,2

If an Israelite high priest were to come into the fellowship of a Christian gathering today, dressed in his linen tunic, ephod, breastplate, turban, and Urim and Thummim, he would certainly create a stir. When one reads Exodus and Leviticus, it can be a daunting task to try to relate to all the ceremony, regulations, special clothing, and the different orders associated with the Jewish priesthood. If one will bear in mind that in all this, God had a plan to reveal the mystery of the ministry of Jesus Christ and his church, what is for us a confusing array of information will begin to make sense. In trying to understand the Old Covenant priesthood and the foreshadows in all these regulations, we will find further evidence to support the claim that the theme of the Old Testament is The Messiah is coming, bringing salvation.

Under the Old Covenant, the tabernacle and the temple would not have counted for much without priests to serve there. Who were the priests? What did they do, and specifically what does all this foreshadow in the New Testament? That is the subject of this chapter.

THE PRIESTHOOD

First, let us take a primer on the Jewish priesthood. Sometimes the priesthood in the Mosaic Law is called the Levitical priesthood. This is somewhat a misnomer. All priests were Levites, but not all Levites were priests. The Levites were the sons of Levi, one of the twelve sons of Israel. God designated the Levites to serve at the tabernacle and the temple. The Levites were, in a sense, the "tithe" of God's people—devoted to the ministry of God. However, only a small portion of the Levites were actually designated priests. *"The LORD said to Moses, 'Speak to the priests, the sons of Aaron...'"* (Leviticus 21:1). Only the sons of Aaron were accepted as priests to actually serve in the sanctuary, making sacrifices, keeping the lamps lit, replacing the bread and so forth.

The rest of the Levites were designated for such tasks as moving the tabernacle, singing at the temple and so forth.

> *Their fellow Levites were assigned to all the other duties of the tabernacle, the house of God. But Aaron and his descendants were the ones who presented offerings on the altar of burnt offering and on the altar of incense in connection with all that was done in the Most Holy Place, making atonement for Israel, in accordance with all that Moses the servant of God had commanded"* (1 Chronicles 6:48,49).

There were many special regulations in the Law of Moses requiring the sons of Aaron, the priests, to keep ceremonially clean. They could not touch a dead body, shave their head or marry women who had been prostitutes and so forth.*"They must be holy to their God and must not profane the name of their God. Because they present the offerings made to the LORD by fire, the food of their God, they are to be holy"* (Leviticus 21:6). No son of Aaron with any physical deformity was allowed to serve in the sanctuary. To us, this might seem a bit prejudiced against the physically disabled, but all these restrictions have meaning in the antitype to the priesthood in the New Testament. The point of all these restrictions was so that priests would be more "holy" than the other Israelites. The word holy in the Hebrew means one specially designated, set apart, or pure. This will have great significance in the antitype to the priesthood in the New Testament.

Among the priests, there was one specially designated as high priest. The office of high priest was of great significance to the entire system of atonement instituted by God through Moses. The High Priest, obviously, had to be a descendant of Aaron. In fact, Aaron was the first high priest. The high priest was designated so by anointing with oil. There were even more stringent rules of holiness for the high priest than for the other sons of Aaron.

> *The high priest, the one among his brothers who has had the anointing oil poured on his head and who has been ordained to wear the priestly garments, must not let his hair become unkempt or tear his clothes. He must not enter a place where there is a dead body. He must not make himself unclean, even for his father or mother, nor leave the sanctuary of his God or desecrate it, because he has been dedicated by anointing oil of his God. I am the LORD"* (Leviticus 21:10-12).

The high priest could not even be in the room with a dead body, much less touch one. He was not allowed to leave the sanctuary grounds during his entire term of office. This must have been a particularly onerous requirement. Another aspect of the office of high priest which stands out when one reads the Pentateuch is the high priestly garments. These are described in detail in Exodus chapter twenty-eight. These garments worn by the high priest included a woven tunic, turban and sash of fine, white linen, and an ephod of gold, blue, purple and scarlet thread, with twelve different prescious stones woven into the shoulder pieces. Also included was a breastpiece of the same materials as the ephod. *"Fasten a breastpiece for making decisions...It is to be square..."* (Exodus 28:15,16). The breastpiece, like the ephod, contained twelve different precious stones, one to represent each of the twelve tribes of Israel. This breastpiece was to be worn when the high priest made decisions in his role as judge. Lastly, the Urim and Thummim were attached to the breastpiece. These were apparently two larger precious stones which were to be involved in the high priest's role of decision-making as judge. The word Urim is derived from the Hebrew *ur,* which means "light", or "to give light", and Thummim derives from the Hebrew word *tummim* which means "completeness", "perfection", or "innocence".

The high priest had many important functions, but his most important role was to carry out the annual sacrifice on *Yom*

Kippur, the Day of Atonement. Only he was allowed to enter the Most Holy Place on that day, and only after a liberal sprinkling of the blood of a goat and a bull, offering a sacrifice of atonement for the sins committed by all the people that year. Bottom line, only the High priest was allowed into the presence of the Almighty God.

THE SONS OF AARON

What is the meaning of all this for those under the New Covenant? Why should we plow through all this arcane detail in Exodus and Leviticus which seems unnecessary for a follower of Jesus to understand? The priesthood of the sons of Aaron can teach us much about our relationship with God. Even though all of Israel were chosen as God's special people, and even though one of the twelve tribes, the Levites, were chosen and specially dedicated to the service of the Lord, it was only a very small proportion of the people, the sons of Aaron, who were holy enough to serve in the presence of God, ministering in the temple or tabernacle.

What is the antitype to the priests in the Old Testament? It is anyone who is saved under the New Covenant. All Christians are a royal priesthood, dedicated to serving God in his spiritual temple, the heavenly tabernacle. This should speak volumes to us about how blessed we are to serve God under the lordship of Jesus.

> But you are a chosen people, a royal priesthood, a holy nation, a people belonging to God, that you may declare the praises of him who called you out of darkness into his wonderful light (1 Peter 2:9).

Through the sacrifice of Jesus Christ, those who are sanctified through him are made a royal priesthood. When Peter says *"a chosen people, a royal priesthood"* he is not repeating himself. He is saying that if you are made holy by the blood of Christ, you are more than a chosen people (as was all Israel), you are that very small portion of the chosen people, those holy enough to be declared priests to serve before God. The astonishing thing about this is that, unlike the sons of Aaron, we serve in a temple where the curtain has been removed. Thanks to Jesus, as priests we serve in a tabernacle where there is absolutely no restriction to direct access to the throne of the Father in Heaven.

If those who are in Christ are priests, then what does the type say about the antitype?

> ...you also like living stones, are being built into a spiritual house to be a holy priesthood, offering spiritual sacrifices acceptable to God through Jesus Christ (1 Peter 2:5).

The priests under the Old Covenant were not expected to relax, or have others do the work. They were expected to actually offer sacrifices. That is what God expects of all his priests today. The Christian life is about offering spiritual sacrifices, not in order to become holy, but because we are holy. Are these sacrifices required to become a priest? No! They are vital because we are priests. That is our role. If you are a follower of Jesus, are you offering these sacrifices through your life right now? Jesus as high priest offered up as a sacrifice his very self. He expects no less of us as his priests. *"If anyone would come after me, he must deny himself and take up his cross daily and follow me"* (Luke 9:23). The next chapter will give additional detail about the kinds of sacrifices God expects of his priests.

There is more to the type and to the antitype. The priests were to have their lives devoted to God.

> He ordered the people living in Jerusalem to give the portion due the priests and Levites so they could devote themselves to the Law of the LORD (2 Chronicles 31:4).

The people of Israel were to supply the physical needs of the Levites and the priests so that they could have their lives totally devoted to the service of the Lord. It is tempting to see this as analogous to members of a church giving their "tithe" so that the paid "ministers" can devote their time to serving God and the church. This would be an absolutely false application of this passage. All of those who are in Christ are priests, and all are to be, as the priest in the Old Covenant, completely devoted to the service of God. We live in a world where we must earn a living so that we can supply our own needs and the needs of others. The world gives us a job and a place to live (based on our hard work of course) and we, in turn, minister to them the message of reconciliation. There is absolutely no clergy/laity implied in the

New Covenant priesthood of believers. If anything, the "clergy" is all the saints (and all Christians are saints), and the "laity" are those who are not yet saints.

We learn from the Levites and the priests that those who are in Christ are to be dedicated to their work of ministry before God. This is reminiscent of the challenge of Jesus to all who would come after him. *"In the same way, any of you who does not give up everything he has cannot be my disciple."* If the relation between the type and the antitype is correct, there are not two standards of devotion. A priest of Christ is devoted to him—totally!

There is more still to this New Covenant priesthood.

> *To him who loves us and has freed us from our sins by his blood, and has made us to be a kingdom and priests to serve his God and Father—to him be glory and power for ever and ever!* (Revelation 1:5,6).

> *"...because you* (i.e., Jesus) *were slain, and with your blood you purchased men for God from every tribe and language and people and nation. You have made them to be a kingdom and priests to serve our God, and they will reign on earth"* (Revelation 5:9,10).

> *Blessed and holy are those who have a part in the first resurrection. The second death has no power over them, but they will be priests of God and of Christ and will reign with him for a thousand years* (Revelation 20:6).

From Revelation 20:6 and 1 Peter 2:9 we see that we are blessed as priests, and that we are also made holy. We are holy, set apart, pure, saints, both because we are declared to be holy by God and because we dedicate ourselves to remain holy. If a priest under the Old Covenant defiled himself by commiting a sin or some sort of act which made him ceremonially unclean, he was disqualified from service—in certain cases for a certain set period; in others, forever. In Christ, we are priests, holy and acceptable to God, not based on maintaining perfect holiness in our own life but by the blood of Jesus. Nevertheless, it is the duty of all New Testament priests to remain as holy as they possibly can. God said to Israel, *"Be holy because I am holy"* (Leviticus 11:45). Is the call to make every effort to maintain holy living any less a relevant teaching for those who follow Christ?

One New Testament passage which makes this point clear is 1 Corinthians 1:2. Here Paul says, *"To the church of God in Corinth, to those sanctified in Christ Jesus and called to be holy..."* The Greek word for sanctified and holy are the same in this passage. Paul is telling the Christians at Corinth that they are already holy, but that they should strive to live in a holy way. All who would be priests of God must make every effort to abstain from sin. We should strive to maintain the holiness which we already have in Christ. Being declared a holy priest is no excuse for failing to make every effort to stay holy. That is the message of Paul, and that is the message of the Old Testament type—the priesthood of Aaron.

The purpose of the priests under the Old Covenant was to make intercession for Israel. In a sense they were to make up for the lack of holiness of the people of God through their ministry of sacrifice before God. If this is the type, then what is implied about the antitype—Christians? Every follower of Jesus is a priest and therefore is a minister as well. Is that not what is taught in 2 Corinthians 5:18-20?

> *All this is from God, who has reconciled us to himself through Christ and gave us **the ministry of reconciliation:** that God was reconciling the world to himself in Christ, not counting men's sins against them. And he has committed to us the message of reconciliation. We are therefore Christ's ambassadors, as though God were making his appeal through us.*

Those who are in Christ are priests and they are ministers, ministers of reconciliation. Every Christian is a priest and a minister to bring those in the world into the priesthood! Ministry to the lost world is an automatic part of the job description of a New Covenant priest.

Another passage which illustrates this point is found in Romans 15:15,16:

> *I have written you...because of the grace God gave me to be a minister of Christ Jesus to the Gentiles with the priestly duty of proclaiming the gospel of God, so that the Gentiles might become an offering acceptable to God, sanctified by the Holy Spirit.*

Paul makes the connection between being a New Covenant priest and a minister. One of our priestly duties is to proclaim the gospel of Jesus Christ to the lost so that they may become an offering, acceptable to God. As was the case with Paul, Christians proclaim the gospel, not to become priests but because they are priests, making intercession for the lost.

To summarize, all those who are saved by the blood of Jesus become New Covenant priests. They are made holy, and therefore they strive to be holy. They are devoted to God, not to the pursuits of the world. They serve in a temple not made with human hands. They have direct access to the living God in his holy tabernacle. They are ministers of reconciliation to those in the world who are not yet priests. If you are a priest of God, how is your ministry going?

THE HIGH PRIEST

The priesthood of the sons of Aaron is a type, while the the priesthood of all believers who are in Christ are the antitype. The former served in a physical tabernacle, the latter in a heavenly tabernacle. What are we to make of the role of the high priest? The plain white linen garments, worn by all the priests when they served at the sanctuary are mirrored by (are foreshadows of) those in white robes in Revelation:

> Then one of the elders asked me, "Those in white (priestly) robes—who are they and where did they come from?"
> I answered, "Sir, you know."
> And he said, "These are they who have come out of the great tribulation; they have washed their robes and made them white in the blood of the Lamb" (Revelation 7:13,14).

But what of the high priest, with his beautiful, colorful garments—perhaps even gaudy by modern standards?

The antitype to the high priest in the Mosaic dispensation is Jesus Christ himself. Like the high priest of old, he is the one who has gone into the spiritual Most Holy Place to make intercession for us. Hebrews makes this fact abundantly clear.

> Therefore, since we have a great high priest who has gone through the heavens, Jesus the Son of God, let us hold firmly to the faith we profess. For we do not have a high priest who is unable to sympathize with our weaknesses, but we have one who has been tempted in every way, just as we are—yet was without

sin. *Let us then approach the throne of grace with confidence, so that we may receive mercy and find grace to help us in our time of need* (Hebrews 4:14-16).

The high priest could relate to the people they represented because they suffered the same temptations as those for whom they were making intercession, but so can Jesus Christ! He, too, was tempted in every way we are, yet he did not stumble. The high priest of Israel went through the curtain into the Holy of Holies once a year, by virtue of the blood of a goat and a bull, to make intercession for the people. Jesus has gone into the heavenly equivalent by virtue of his own blood to make intercession for us. The high priest was able to approach the throne of God—the Mercy Seat—once a year. Through Jesus, our high priest, we can approach the throne of God directly every day of our lives. The curtain has been ripped in two! What a great high priest we have in Jesus. The antitype goes very far beyond the type indeed.

Where would Israel have been without the ministry of their chosen high priest? They could not approach God directly, but,

> *Every high priest is selected from among men and is appointed to represent them in matters related to God, to offer gifts and sacrifices for sins* (Hebrews 5:1).

Where would Judaism be without the high priest? Where would forgiveness of sins be found? The problem is that under the covenant at Sinai, there was no forgiveness without the ministry of the high priest. Judaism today is in at least a sense an empty shell in that it does not offer access to the presence of God. The entire sacrificial system, along with its priests and the high priest disappeared almost two thousand years ago, exactly as prophesied by Daniel (Daniel 9:26,27), Jesus (Luke 21:20-24) and the Hebrew writer (Hebrews 8:13).

The high priest had an honored position, but he was not without his problems. First of all, he was a sinner. Jesus, on the other hand, was sinless. Second, the person selected as high priest had a way of dying on a regular basis: *"...but because Jesus lives forever, he has a permanent priesthood. Therefore he is able to save completely those who come to God through him, because he always lives to intercede for them"* (Hebrews 7:24,25). No more getting used to a new high priest. No more revolving door involved. Our high priest is a priest forever.

> *Such a high priest meets our need—one who is holy, blameless, pure, set apart from sinners, exalted above the heavens. Unlike the other high priests, he does not need to offer sacrifices day after day, first for his own sins, and then for the sins of the people. He sacrificed for their sins once for all when he offered himself. For the law appoints as high priests men who are weak; but the oath, which came after the law, appointed the Son, who has been made perfect forever* (Hebrews 7:26-28).

Jesus has done it. He has arrived in the heavenly temple forever. No more daily sacrifice. No more cringing, hoping we do not somehow violate some minor aspect of the law as did Uzzah, when he was struck dead. The ministry of Jesus may be the antitype of the ministry of the high priest, but his ministry is so much superior! The earthly sanctuary where the old high priests served was just a copy. When someone who comes into the sanctuary on the coattails of Jesus, that person is coming into the genuine presence of God. We do not need priests to intercede for us: we are priests! And we have a personal relationship with the head guy in the priesthood—high priest Jesus Christ. *"The throne of God* (the mercy seat) *and of the Lamb* (high priest Jesus) *will be in the city, and his servants* (us as priests) *will serve him. They will see his face, and his name will be on their foreheads"* (Revelation 22:3,4). The high priest offered incense at the golden altar, we offer the antitype to incense, prayer, right there at the feet of the throne. What an honor and a privilege! Do we really appreciate this fact?

> *The point of what we are saying is this: We do have a high priest who sat down at the right hand of the throne of the Majesty in heaven, and who serves in the sanctuary, the true tabernacle set up by the Lord, not my man..*
>
> *Every high priest is appointed to offer both gifts and sacrifices, and so it was necessary for this one also to have something to offer...They serve at a sanctuary that is a copy and a shadow of what is in heaven...But the ministry Jesus has received is as superior to theirs as the covenant of which he is a mediator is superior to the old one, and is founded on better promises* (Hebrews 8:1-6).

More will be said on the superiority of the New Covenant in the next chapter.

Consider some of the details of the Old Testament description of the ministry of the high priest, and their application to the antitype, Jesus Christ. *"He must not enter a place where there is a dead body"* (Leviticus 21:11). The priests could not touch a dead body and the high priest could not even be in the same room with a dead person. This is a foreshadowing of the spiritual high priest who serves in a sanctuary where there is no more death and no more tears.

"He must not make himself unclean, even for his father or mother, nor leave the sanctuary of his God or desecrate it, because he has been dedicated by the anointing oil of his God" (Leviticus 21:11,12). The high priest was kept very pure through a seemingly endless list of rules for keeping ceremonially clean. Jesus, our high priest, was pure throughout his life. He never sinned at all. He asked the crowd, *"Can any of you prove me guilty of sin?"* (John 8:46). His accusers were silent.

Notice that Leviticus 21:12 states that the high priest was not allowed to leave the sanctuary for the entire duration of their office for any reason. This was a very tough restriction. Perhaps the high priest was tempted to think his office was not such a great privilege. What a great foreshadow of the ministry of Jesus, who has gone into the heavenly tabernacle. *"The LORD has sworn and will not change his mind: 'You are a priest forever, in the order of Melchizedek'"* (Psalm 110:4). Jesus never leaves the heavenly sanctuary either. He is at the right hand of the throne forever.

No one with a physical defect was allowed to serve as high priest. *"No descendant of Aaron the priest who has any defect is to come near to present the offerings made to the LORD by fire"* (Levitics 21:21). This was not a sign of Judaism's insensitivity to the physically challenged. It is a foreshadow of the lamb without defect; Jesus Christ.

And what about the really strange garments the high priest wore: the tunic and sash, the ephod, the breastplate and the Urim and Thummim? Of course these served their purpose for the Jews in order to mark out the significance of the office of high priest. One can imagine the Jews loving the pomp and circumstance of the office of high priest. However, one should bear in mind that all these things serve as foreshadows of the work of the antitype—the high priest Jesus Christ. The apostle John saw a vision of high priest Jesus on the island of Patmos, including his brilliant white robe and golden sash (Revelation 1:13). Like Moses when he went into the Most Holy Place, Jesus' face shines with an intense brilliance.

The twelve different precious stones on the ephod and on the breastplate of the high priest stand for the twelve tribes of Israel, but also are prefigures of the twelve apostles chosen by the greater high priest, Jesus Christ. The twelve precious stones in the high priestly garment also prefigure the twelve gates, the twelve angels and the twelve foundations in the heavenly city where Jesus Christ rules:

> *And he carried me away in the Spirit to a mountain great and high, and showed me the Holy City, Jerusalem, coming down out of heaven from God. It shone with the glory of God, and its brilliance was like that of a very precious jewel, like jasper, clear as crystal. It had a great, high wall with twelve gates, and with twelve angels at the gates. On the gates were written the names of the twelve tribes of Israel. There were three gates on the east, three on the north, three on the south and three on the west. The wall of the city had twelve foundations, and on them were the names of the twelve apostles of the Lamb.... The foundations of the city walls were decorated with every kind of precious stone. The first foundation was jasper, the second sapphire, the third chalcedony, the fourth emerald...and the twelfth amethyst"* (Revelation 21:10-14, 19,20).

Some claim that the Pentateuch does not teach about heaven. It is true that the earliest books of the Old Testament do not speak to the afterlife in detail, but one certainly finds many foreshadowings of heaven there.

Remember that the high priest wore the breastpiece and the Urim and Thummim when he was in the role of judge for the people of God. Again, we have a foreshadow of Christ, who will stand at the right hand of God, judging all at the last day. The Hebrew word transliterated as Urim means light, while the word Thummim means perfection. Clearly, the high priest was neither light nor perfection for the people of God, but when one considers the fact that God set up the entire outfit as a foreshadowing of the work of Jesus, all is made clear.

THE PRIESTHOOD OF MELCHIZEDEK

Jesus Christ is such a great high priest that being an antitype of the Mosaic high priest was not enough to express everything about his ministry as priest before the throne of God. Jesus is also a priest according to the order of Melchizedek. We are wading into some deep water here.

> *We have this hope as an anchor for the soul, firm and secure. It enters the inner sanctuary behind the curtain, where Jesus, who went before us, has entered on our behalf. He has become a priest forever, in the order of Melchizedek* (Hebrews 6:19,20).

We have already seen the somewhat mysterious Melchizedek as a prefigure of Jesus Christ. Melchizedek was a priest of God, not by birth as were the sons of Aaron, but through direct appointment by God. As the Hebrew writer points out, Abraham the "father" of Levi by Jewish custom, offered tribute to Melchizedek and Melchizedek blessed Abraham in return. *"And without a doubt the lesser is blessed by the greater."* This event near the gates of Salem (Jerusalem) serves as a foreshadow of the fact that the priesthood of Jesus Christ is much greater than the priesthood of the sons of Abraham.

The writer of Hebrews gets to the bottom of why the priesthood—even the high priesthood—of the sons of Aaron was not sufficient foreshadow for the great high priest, Jesus Christ:

> *If perfection could have been attained through the Levitical priesthood...why was there still need for another priest to come— one on the order of Melchizedek, not in the order of Aaron?... And what we have said is even more clear if another priest like Melchizedek appears, one who has become a priest not on the basis of a regulation as to his ancestry but on the basis of the power of an indestructible life. For it is declared: "You are a priest forever in the order of Melchizedek"* (Hebrews 7:11, 15-17).

The priesthood of Aaron was not sufficient as foreshadow of Christ for two reasons. First, the sons of Aaron became priests by virtue of birth, whereas both Melchizedek and Jesus were priests by divine choice. Second, the sons of Aaron died, while Melchizedek never died. Like Enoch before him (Genesis 5:24), and Elijah after him (2 Kings 2:11,12), Melchizedek was taken away by God. He never suffered physical death. Actually, Jesus did suffer physical death, but death could not keep its hold on him. He was raised from the dead on the third day and like Enoch, Melchizedek and Elijah, God took Jesus from the earth to be with him in heaven. Truly Jesus is the son of (the antitype to) the priest Melchizedek. Again, we see foreshadowing in the Old Testament of the teaching on eternal life in the New Testament.

Every single aspect of the rules and regulations, the garments and the ministry of the high priest of Israel points toward the great and spectacular high priest of the New Covenant, Jesus Christ. In a couple of ways the Aaronic high priest could not fully foreshadow the priesthood of Jesus Christ, so God provided Melchizedek to broaden the image. Could God have provided any greater picture of the ministerial role of his Son and our savior, Jesus Christ? When we look at the office of priest and of high priest in Israel, we can surely say they tell us the Messiah is coming.

CHAPTER FIVE

The Mosaic Covenant Prefigures the New Covenant in Christ

The Law is only a shadow of the good things that are coming—not the realities themselves.
Hebrews 10:1

Therefore do not let anyone judge you by what you eat or drink, or with regard to a religious festival, a New Moon celebration or a Sabbath day. These are a shadow of the things that were to come; the reality, however, is found in Christ.
Colossians 2:16,17

Imagine the scene. After freeing his people from slavery in Egypt by great wonders and signs, God brought them to Mount Sinai. Here God established a covenant with his people. God told Moses to set boundaries at the foot of the mountain because anyone who set foot on the holy mountain while God appeared to Moses would be killed. Moses spent two full days consecrating the people. All the people washed their bodies and their clothes and abstained from sexual relations. Tension was building, as the people knew something great was about to happen. God had his people's full attention.

Exactly as Moses had told them earlier, God came upon the mountain with great power on the third day.

On the morning of the third day there was thunder and lightning, with a thick cloud over the mountain. Mount Sinai was covered with smoke, because the LORD descended on it in fire. The

> smoke billowed up from it like smoke from a furnace, the whole mountain trembled violently, and the sound of the trumpet grew louder and louder.... When the people saw the thunder and lightning and heard the trumpet and saw the mountain in smoke, they trembled with fear (Exodus 19:16-19, 20:18).

Given this awe-inspiring sign, it is not hard to see why the people were terrified. And thus was the Law received by Moses and the people of God. God has a way of announcing great changes with demonstrative signs. The reception of the first covenant was certainly no exception to this rule. About four hundred years earlier, God had chosen Abraham as the man through whom to bless the world. Later, as Moses sat at the foot of Mount Sinai, God set up his covenant and gave his Law to Abraham's descendants. On this day, the Jewish religion began.

If the temple was the focus of religion and worship for the Jews, then the Law of Moses was the focus of their daily lives, at least for those who remained faithful to the Old Covenant. What to eat, when to plant crops, health practices, marriage, death, taxes,...it seemed as if even the most minute aspect of the lives of God's people was governed by the Law given at Sinai.

What was the essence—the heart—of the Law of Moses? Many would say that the Ten Commandments are the essence of the Law of Moses. The Ten Commandments certainly meant a lot to the Jewish people, as they were placed in the ark, but the Ten Commandments are definitely not the heart of the Law of Moses. The heart of the Law could be stated as follows:

> "Keep my decrees and laws, for the man who obeys them will live by them. I am the LORD" (Leviticus 18:5).

The essence of the First Covenant was a compact with a promise, sealed in blood. God told his people that if they would keep all the laws he gave them at Mount Sinai, they would be greatly blessed in the land he was going to give them. At first glance, this may have seemed like a great thing, but consider the implications. The problem comes in having to keep all the laws:

> "Cursed is the man who does not uphold the words of this law by carrying them out" (Deuteronomy 27:26).

> "Take to heart all the words I have solemnly declared to you this day, so that you may command your children to obey carefully all the words of this law. They are not just idle words for you—they are your life. By them you will live long in the land you are crossing the Jordan to possess" (Deuteronomy 32:46,47).
>
> "You must distinguish between the holy and the profane, between the unclean and the clean, and you must teach the Israelites all the decrees the LORD has given them through Moses" (Leviticus 10:10,11).
>
> "Be holy because I, the Lord your God, am holy...I am the LORD your God" (Leviticus 19:1).
>
> "If you follow my decrees and are careful to obey my commands, I will send you rain in its season... But if you will not listen to me and carry out **all these commands,** and if you... fail to carry out **all my commands,** and so violate my covenant, then I will do this to you: I will bring upon you sudden terror, wasting diseases..." (Leviticus 26:3,4,14-16).

The problem with the covenant God established through the Law of Moses on Sinai is that the people were unable to keep up their end of the contract. Who could live a life in which they never failed at any point of the law given to Moses? As Paul said in Galatians 2:21, righteousness could not be gained through the law.

But what about all those sacrifices? Surely all that blood of bulls and goats was not being shed for nothing. Were they not intended to make up for the difference between the Jew's performance and God's expectations? The answer is yes...and no... The sacrifices instituted at Sinai were a shadow, as was the covenant they were based on. Shadows do not bring forgiveness, they do not make perfect. Only the real thing can bridge the awesome chasm between our attempts at right living and true righteousness. And thus we had the need for the antitype to the covenant established through Moses: the New Covenant. Consider Hebrews 10:1-4:

> *The law* (at Sinai) *is only a shadow of the good things that are coming—not the realities themselves. For this reason it can never, by the same sacrifices repeated endlessly year after year, make perfect those who draw near to worship. If it could, would*

> they not have stopped being offered? For the worshipers would have been cleansed once for all, and would not have felt guilty for their sins. But these sacrifices are an annual reminder of sins, because it is impossible for the blood of bulls and goats to take away sins.

There you have it. The law, in other words the Law of Moses, was a foreshadow. God had never intended it to be the final answer for the sins of his people. As the life of Moses was a prefigure of the life and ministry of Jesus Christ, so the covenant established through Moses was a prefigure of the covenant established through Jesus Christ. Moses was a prophetic prefigure of the reality revealed in Christ. The same is true of the law given to Moses at Sinai. It is a foreshadow of the fully realized New Covenant in Christ.

Perhaps some might find this hard to accept. How could one thousand four hundred years and literally millions of sacrifices—millions of gallons of blood shed—be meaningless? How could the one true God institute such a thing? Let the dozens of examples already given stand as irrefutable proof of the principle that God uses the people and events in the Old Testament as foreshadows of the reality he was to reveal to us in Jesus Christ. They had great meaning as a foreshadow.

Besides, the sacrifices performed all those years in the desert and in Jerusalem certainly were not meaningless to the Jews themselves. They were pregnant with meaning. Through the sacrifices in the Old Testament, God was teaching both the physical and the spiritual children of Abraham some fundamental principles about our relationship with him, as we will see.

To the Jew who might complain, "Why did you make us go through this whole charade?" God might reply, "This was no charade. In my mind, it was as if my son Jesus had been slain all along. I gave you the Law of Moses as a teacher, a tutor. I needed to prepare a people through whom to bless the world. And besides, it is not as if I did not tell you I would be making a new and greater covenant founded on better promises. What did my prophet Jeremiah tell you?"

> "The time is coming," declares the LORD,
> "When I will make a new covenant with the
>   house of Israel and with the house of Judah.

> It will not be like the covenant I made with their
> forefathers when I took them by the hand out
> of Egypt, because they broke my covenant,
> though I was a husband to them,"
> > declares the LORD.
> "This is the covenant I will make with the house
> of Israel after that time," declares the LORD.
> "I will put my law in their minds and write it on their hearts .
> I will be their God and they will be my people.
> No longer will a man teach his neighbor, or a
> man his brother, saying 'Know the LORD,'
> because they will all know me, from the least
> of them to the greatest," declares the LORD.
> "For I will forgive their wickedness and will
> remember their sins no more" (Jeremiah 31:31-34).

It is not as if the Law of Moses was bad. It is just that the antitype is immeasurably greater. The New Covenant is the fulfillment—the completion, of the covenant established at Sinai. Isn't that what Jesus said in the Sermon on the Mount? *"Do not think that I have come to abolish the Law or the Prophets; I have not come to abolish them but to fulfill them"* (Matthew 5:17). The antitype did not abolish the type. It brought it to completion and fulfilled its requirements. How much greater is the New Covenant, established and sealed by the blood of Jesus!

The covenant established on Mount Sinai was truly an awesome thing. The fire and smoke which covered the entire mountain were an unmistakeable sign of that. However, if we have learned anything from the types and antitypes in the Old and New Testaments, surely it is that the latter is greater than the former. This author will not be able to improve on the writer of Hebrews:

> *You have not come to a mountain that can be touched and is burning with fire; to darkness, gloom and storm; to a trumpet blast or to such a voice speaking words, so that those who heard it begged that no further word be spoken to them...But you have come to Mount Zion, to the heavenly Jerusalem, the city of the living God. You have come to thousands upon thousands of angels in joyful assembly, to the church of the firstborn, whose*

names are written in heaven. You have come to God, the judge of all men, to the spirits of righteous men made perfect, to Jesus the mediator of a new covenant, and to the sprinkled blood that speaks a better word than the blood of Abel* (Hebrews 12:18-24).

When Jewish Christian readers came to this point in the Hebrew letter, they knew exactly what the writer was referring to when he mentioned the mountain, the fire, darkness and trumpet blast—Hebrews twelve is a reminder of the giving of the Law of Moses on Sinai. God's first covenant was great, but the New Covenant was infinitely greater. It brought perfection.

Again, one might be tempted to ask why God introduced something which was not perfect in the first place? *"The former regulation is set aside because it was weak and useless (for the law made nothing perfect)"* (Hebrews 7:18). Why not skip right to perfection: the covenant which was sealed by the blood of Jesus? There were many reasons. One of these is faith. It takes more faith to accept the second covenant because it involves things which are unseen. The Jews could see the temple in Jerusalem. They could not mistake the implications of the pillar of cloud by day and of fire by night. When the Sea of Reeds parted, the people of God did not struggle with interpreting the message: March!

The antitypes of all these things are spiritual. They are invisible. In the words of Jesus to a skeptical Thomas, *"Because you have seen me, you have believed; blessed are those who have not seen and yet have believed."* We are of those who have not seen, and yet whom God expects to believe. As Paul said, *"we live by faith, not by sight"* (2 Corinthians 5:7). When God created the types in the Old Testament and their fulfillment in the New, he provided for us positive proof of the reality of the second and greater covenant. God expects Christians to live by faith, not by sight. However, with the prophetic nature of the types in the Old Testament, it is far from blind faith. The fulfillment of type and antitype in the law is a major part of the evidence to support that faith.

A second reason the Law of Moses is of great value is that the law given on Sinai was a great teacher. So much about the nature of God and the kind of relationship he wants with his people can be gleaned from a careful study of the Law of Moses. The law and the covenant established through Moses prepared the Jews both intellectually and spiritually for the change of covenant God had in mind. If only more had been willing to make the change of mind and heart needed to become followers of the second Moses.

> *What shall we say, then? Is the law sin? Certainly not! Indeed I would not have known what sin was except through the law. For I would not have known what it was to covet if the law had not said, "Do not covet...."*
>
> *Did that which is good, then, become death to me? By no means! But in order that sin might be recognized as sin, it produced death in me through what was good, so that through the commandment sin might become utterly sinful"* (Romans 7:7,13).

For the Jews, and for anyone else willing to look carefully at the Law of Moses, the true nature of sin and its effect on our relationship with God was made very clear. It is hard to fully understand the good news of eternal forgiveness under the New Covenant without first fully understanding the bad news of the depravity of sin and our inability to stop sinning. The Jew's fruitless attempts to follow perfectly the Law of Moses teaches both them and us that lesson. The message is that human effort can not and will not produce a right relationship with God.

Paul expresses the idea that the Law is a great teacher in Galatians as well:

> *What, then, was the purpose of the Law? It was added because of transgressions until the Seed* (that is Jesus Christ) *to whom the promise referred had come....Is the law, therefore, opposed to the promises of God? Absolutely not! For if a law had been given that could impart life, then righteousness would certainly have come by the law....So* **the law was put in charge to lead us to Christ,** *that we might be justified by faith* (Galatians 3:19,21,24).

Until we are ready for the big exam, we need a tutor. Until we are ready for the "pros" we need a coach. Until we are ready to take on full responsibility, we need a mentor. That is what the Law of Moses was. It explained God to us, it led the way; it showed us what was coming. The Law of Moses did not get the Jews to heaven, but it led them to Christ. However when Christ came, it was time to put behind childish things and time to take up the fulfillment of God's plan in the New Covenant.

The New Covenant in Christ as already mentioned, is an antitype to the Mosaic Covenant. Under the former covenant, the agreement between God and his people could be described in its essence as "The man who does these things will live by them." What is this New Covenant which was established so that we could escape the consequences of the law of sin and death?

> *For this reason Christ is the mediator of a new covenant, that those who are called may receive the promised eternal inheritance—now that he has died as a ransom to set them free from the sins committed under the first covenant* (Hebrews 9:15).

In this section of Hebrews, the writer goes on to explain the type/antitype relationship between the first and the second covenants in more detail. Both were essentially like a will. Both were only sealed by the death of the one who made the covenant. The Hebrew writer quotes Moses from Exodus 24:8: *"This is the blood of the covenant that the Lord has made with you,"* going on to explain that this was why Moses sprinkled blood both in the tabernacle and on all the items used in the ceremonies of the first covenant. *"Without the shedding of blood there is no forgiveness"* (Hebrews 9:22).

As with the type, so with the antitype. The New Covenant could only be put into effect and sealed with the death of him who willed it: Jesus Christ. His blood was required to cleanse the items in the heavenly tabernacle. The writer of Hebrews could summarize the antitype—the New Covenant in Christ—as follows:

> *So Christ was sacrificed once to take away the sins of many people; and he will appear a second time, not to bear sin, but to bring salvation to those who are waiting for him* (Hebrews 9:28).

Just like the first covenant, the second covenant was a compact with a promise, sealed in blood.

FORESHADOWS IN THE LAW OF MOSES

There are many parallels between the Old and the New Covenant in which the foreshadow is a physical thing while the New Covenant realization is a spiritual thing. The Law of Moses in the Old Testament becomes the *"the law of the Spirit of life"* (Romans 8:2), through Jesus Christ in the New Testament. The bulls and goats whose blood was used in the sacrifices under the Law of Moses were required for the Jewish worshippers to be unblemished physically. How much greater is the sacrifice in the New Covenant! The antitype sacrifice, Jesus Christ, leads an unblemished life, not physically but spiritually.

As a second example of the physical/spiritual parallels between the covenants, following the former covenant led to largely physical blessings. *"See, I set before you today life and prosperity, death and destruction. For I command you today to love the LORD your God, to walk in his ways, and to keep his commands, decrees and laws; then you will live and increase, and the LORD your God will bless you in the land you are entering to possess"* (Deuteronomy 30:15,16). Many miss this point, so let it be said again. The promise of the Old Covenant was principally that God would give physical blessings. God promised good crops, many children, rain at the proper time, milk and honey and freedom from attacks from their enemies. Physically unblemished sacrifices led to physical blessings. Because the sacrifice in the New Covenant was unblemished spiritually, not physically, the blessing under the second covenant is spiritual. It includes forgiveness of sin and a relationship with God. *"Praise be to the God and Father of Our Lord Jesus Christ, who has blessed us in the heavenly realms with every spiritual blessing in Christ"* (Ephesians 1:3). The first chapter of Ephesians goes on to list these spiritual blessings, including being holy and blameless, being adopted as sons of God, receiving his glorious grace, redemption, forgiveness of sins, being chosen, included in Christ and marked with the seal, the promised Holy Spirit. Every single one of these spiritual gifts is foreshadowed in the physical blessings given to Israel in the Promised Land.

So, what do we learn about God and about the New Covenant through its foreshadow; the first covenant? For one, we learned from the Old Covenant that God wants a relationship with his people through which he can bless them. Even from a cursory glance into Leviticus it is hard to miss the fact that God gave many laws to Israel, through Moses. Let us get the big picture. What was the purpose of these laws? For us who read the New Testament, they are foreshadows of things found in Jesus Christ. But what did these laws mean for Israel? In general, the laws given to Israel provided direct physical benefit or kept them pure so that they could be in a relationship with Yahweh.

HEALTH REGULATIONS

There are many examples of laws which God gave Israel so that they could be blessed with physical health and with happy relationships with one another. For example, God commanded that they abstain from certain meats. It just so happens that each of the meats which God commanded they not eat (pork, meat of carnivores, shellfish etc.) carries a relatively high likelihood of causing deadly disease, while the meats they were allowed to eat (fish, lamb, beef, etc.) tend to be much safer to eat, even if not thoroughly cooked. Other examples could be cited. God gave laws for quarantine in the case of certain diseases. God gave laws about the touching of dead bodies and rules about sexual behavior, all of which brought great health benefit to Israel if obeyed.[1]

God made it clear that he wanted to give them good health. *"If you listen carefully to the voice of the LORD your God and do what is right in his eyes, if you pay attention to his commands and keep all his decrees, I will not bring on you any of the diseases I brought on the Egyptians, for I am the LORD who heals you"* (Exodus 15:26). Despite the complete lack of scientific knowledge of the time, the Mosaic Law is filled with effective and wise health laws. This is one piece of evidence, among many, that the Pentateuch is inspired by God. It is interesting to notice the historical fact that the Jewish people have always been able to survive great tragedy, war and persecutions. One contributing factor is that to the extent that they followed the laws given them by Moses, they lived healthier lives than their neighbors and grew numerically.

The type in the Law of Moses is good physical health. The antitype in the New Testament is good spiritual health. The wasting diseases such as leprosy which were prevented by following God's commands given to Moses, which also made them ceremonially unclean, foreshadow sin and its debilitating effect in our life which is prevented by obeying God and by taking part in the New Covenant in Jesus Christ. The Jews who obeyed the Law of Moses were protected from the devastating effects of the physical diseases of the Egyptians. Those who follow Christ will avoid the devastating effects of the spiritual disease of Egypt: sin. We will not be perfect in this life, but God will give us every spiritual blessing (Ephesians 1:3). Physical blessings are a wonderful thing, but spiritual blessings—peace of mind, forgiveness, freedom from guilt, personal relationship with the God of the universe—these are greater blessings!

CLEAN VERSUS UNCLEAN

As stated previously, many of the Laws handed down through Moses had beneficial health implications. Good physical health for the Jews has as its antitype good spiritual health for the spiritual children of Moses. Although the Mosaic law included many health regulations, an even greater proportion of the laws given to Israel at Sinai were regulations for maintaining ceremonial cleanness. There were laws for maintaining cleanness for all the people of Israel. There were also special laws for ceremonial cleanness for the priests, and still more stringent laws for the high priest. It is easy to get lost reading Numbers, Leviticus and Deuteronomy in all the rules for avoiding uncleanness.

In order for a Christian to understand the relevance of these laws, it is useful to bear in mind the antitype to ceremonial cleanness. Being ceremonially clean to the Jews meant that they were able to present acceptable sacrifices and to worship God. It is not hard to recognize the fulfillment of this foreshadowing in the New Covenant. Ceremonial cleanness is the type, while the antitype in Christ is being cleansed from sin. In order to present our lives as living sacrifices to God, which is our spiritual worship (to paraphrase Romans 12:2), we must avoid being polluted by the world. One thing which is made crystal clear from the Law of Moses is that keeping our life free of sin is very important to God.

Just to give a feeling for some of the rules regarding uncleanness for the Aaronic priests, consider a list taken from Leviticus chapter twenty-one. In order to be ceremonially clean, and able to minister before their God, the high priest was not even allowed in the room with a dead person. The priests were not allowed to shave their heads or the edges of their beards. *"A priest must not make himself ceremonially unclean"* (v. 1). *"They must be holy to their God and must not profane the name of their God"* (v. 6). They were not to marry a woman who had been a prostitute or had been divorced. In the same chapter, the high priest was disqualified for serving before God for any of a number of physical defects. The list goes on. Rules for all the people for maintaining cleanness, not just for the priests, included such prohibitions as mating different kinds of animals, planting fields with two kinds of seeds, eating meat with blood still in it, and so forth. There were laws against cruelty to animals, various sorts of sexual relations, as well as rules for dealing with rebellious children. Many of these laws are physical foreshadowings of spiritual principles for those who are under the New Covenant.

All these regulations are foreshadows of the sort of purity and freedom from sin that God wants for his children under the second and greater covenant. Remember that the forgiven disciple of Jesus is a priest. He or she must make every possible effort to avoid spiritual uncleanness.

> *"Everyone who confesses the name of the Lord must turn away from wickedness."*
>
> *In a large house there are articles not only of gold and silver, but also of wood and clay; some are for noble purposes and some for ignoble. If a man cleanses himself from the latter, he will be an instrument for noble purposes, made holy, useful to the Master and prepared to do any good work.*
>
> *Flee the evil desires of youth, and pursue righteousness, faith, love and peace along with those who call on the Lord out of a pure heart* (2 Timothy 2:19,20-22).

The New Testament warns repeatedly against being polluted by the world. *"For the grace of God has appeared to all men. It teaches us to say 'No' to ungodliness and worldy passions and to live self-controlled, upright and godly lives in this present age"* (Titus 2:11,12). If the multitude of laws for ceremonial uncleanness makes anything clear, it is that God expects us to make every possible effort to be free from sin and impurity.

Although one can list a number of examples of specific laws given at Sinai which are types of spiritual principles laid down in the New Testament, it is most important to get the big picture. What the covenants have in common is that under both dispensations, those who come before God are expected to give very careful attention to remaining holy. Having said that, in both covenants God provided a way to bridge the gap (actually the massive chasm) between the requirement of holiness and the actual performance of those who sincerely tried to stay righteous. Under the former covenant, blood sacrifice was provided to atone for physical uncleanness (many specifics of the sacrificial system will be given in the next chapter). Under Christ, the blood of Jesus is provided to atone for spiritual uncleanness. The overall sense one gets in either case is that there is no excuse for us to sin willfully.

> *My dear children, I write this to you so that you will not sin. But if anyone does sin, we have one who speaks to the Father in our defense—Jesus Christ, the Righteous One. He is the atoning sacrifice for our sins, and not only for ours, but also for the sins of the whole world"* (1 John 2:1,2).

Under the first Covenant, the people of God were required to keep ceremonially clean. God knew that they would never be able to follow his decrees perfectly, so he provided the sacrificial system in part to make up for the difference between sincere effort and perfection. The sacrifices in the tabernacle and later at the temple made atonement with God so that his people could be physically blessed. Similarly, in Christ, his followers are taught to make every effort to remain spiritually clean, but God provides the atoning sacrifice of Jesus Christ to cover the sins that even the most sincere Christian will inevitably commit.

BLOOD, BLOOD AND MORE BLOOD

The type and antitype relationship between the Law of Moses and the law of the spirit of life in Christ has other lessons to teach us. Under the Law of Moses, even what would seem a minor offense required blood sacrifice. In fact, Israel was even required to offer blood sacrifices for unintentional sins of which they were not aware!

> *"If the whole Israelite community sins unintentionally and does what is forbidden in any of the LORD'S commands, even though the community is unaware of the matter, they are guilty. When they become aware of the sin they committed, the assembly*

> must bring a young bull as a sin offering and present it before the Tent of Meeting. The elders of the community are to lay their hands on the bull's head before the LORD. Then the appointed priest is to take some of the bull's blood into the Tent of Meeting. He shall dip his finger into the blood and sprinkle it before the LORD seven times in front of the curtain. He is to put some of the blood on the horns of the altar that is before the LORD in the Tent of Meeting. The rest of the blood he shall pour out at the base of the altar of burnt offering at the entrance to the Tent of Meeting" (Leviticus 4:13-18).

This is a very graphic scene. Try to imagine the effect on those whose bull was sacrificed. Seeing the bull's throat slit and seeing the gallons of blood being spilled out must have made a very strong impression on the people, especially because it was for sins they were not even aware of. Never mind the sins they were very cognizant of.

As mentioned before, on the great sacrifice days in Jerusalem the Brook of Kidron ran red. The message is clear. Sin creates a very big problem between God and his people. The price to bring redemption is dear indeed. The penalty for sin is death. No infraction of God's law is too small to incur a death penalty.

> *"For the life of every creature is in the blood..."* (Leviticus 17:11).

> *For the wages of sin is death...* (Romans 6:23).

> *In fact, the law requires that nearly everything be cleansed with blood, and without the shedding of blood there is no forgiveness* (Hebrews 9:22).

These passages make Paul's statement that the law leads us to Christ take on an awful and an awesome meaning. Sin is a horrible thing in God's eyes. It is very costly. The blood of bulls brought ceremonial cleanness. How much greater the blood of the antitype: Jesus Christ. It is tragically easy for those who are forgiven by the blood of Jesus to forget the incredible price at which they were bought. It is even easier to forget the penalty which stood over our heads. One lie, one furtive glance, one jealous act led to death. Think of the blood spurting out as the bull dropped to its knees and breathed its last. Think of yourself and your sin. Think of the blood of Jesus.

FROM SLAVERY TO FREEDOM

In some ways the Law of Moses teaches about the law of the Spirit of life by things which are similar. In other ways it teaches us about what is to be found through types whose antitypes are analogous, but in some sense actually opposite. The Law of Moses involved principally physical activities which brought principally physical blessings. The Christian Covenant involves principally spiritual activities which bring principally spiritual blessings. As example, the Law of Moses required very carefully defined, regulated activities. The antitype in the New Testament calls for worship based not on ceremony or regulated activity, but on the heart and a loving relationship. To that extent, the antitype is opposite to the type. To put it in very strong terms, the Old Covenant implied slavery, while the New Covenant implies freedom. Many examples of this principle could be given.

For example, under the Old Covenant, worship was highly regulated, involving much ceremony. Priests had well-defined outfits to wear, dates of religious ceremonies were fixed, who had roles in worship were determined at least in part by birth. The Passover Seder involved a definite ritual. *Yom Kippur* involved the priests performing a carefully choreographed series of steps (more on that in chapter seven). The rules for worship on the Old Testament have as their antitype freedom of form in worship. The New Covenant is not completely without prescribed worship as it includes the Lord's Supper. However, beyond that, worship as described in the New Testament is amazingly open-ended. The priest of the New Covenant may pray any time he or she wants. No ceremony is required to come directly before the throne of God. No special garments are required. God provides virtually no specific commands for the public worship, other than that it should be orderly. *"But everything should be done in a fitting and orderly way"* (1 Corinthians 14:40). It would appear that the New Covenant involves more trust on God's part concerning our worship of him. It involves freedom. *"This is the covenant I will make with them...I will put my law in their minds and write it on their hearts"* (Jeremiah 31:33).

The Law of Moses required contribution from the wealth which God gave to his people. The size of the contribution was carefully defined. *"Be sure to set aside a tenth of all that your fields produce each year"* (Deuteronomy 14:22). Despite some who have tried to impose Old Covenant tithing as a rule for those under the New Covenant, the fact is that the standard for those in Christ is to give sacrificially according to what the worshippers decides in their heart to give. *"Each man should give what he has decided in his heart to give, not reluctantly, or under compulsion, for God loves a cheerful giver"* (2 Corinthians 9:7). There is great freedom here. God trusts those under the New Covenant to decide for themselves what to give. Hopefully, they will prove his trust to be well placed!

Under the Old Covenant, times of rest, reflection and meditation upon God were regulated and enforced. All were required to take a weekly time from their busy schedule to observe a Sabbath-rest to God.

> *"Observe the Sabbath, because it is holy to you. Anyone who desecrates it must be put to death; whoever does any work on that day must be cut off from his people"* (Exodus 31:14).

Our human tendency is to not rely on God, but rather on our own ability to work in order to take care of our physical needs. This would help explain why God attached such strong warnings to observation of the Sabbath. Our modern word sabbatical comes from the Hebrew root. Even our own educational institutions recognize the need for time to rest and reflect.

God's people were required to observe Sabbath years as well.

> *"For six years sow your fields, and for six years prune your vineyards and gather their crops. But in the seventh year the land is to have a Sabbath rest, a Sabbath to the Lord...Whatever the land yields during the Sabbath year will be food for you— for yourself, your manservant and maidservant, and the hired worker and temporary resident who live among you, as well as for your livestock and the wild animals in your land"* (Leviticus 25:3,4,6,7).

One can imagine it took a great deal of faith to observe a Sabbath-year. It is not natural for human beings to stop tilling and sowing and to simply rely on the blessings of God for all our sustenance, particularly for an entire year.

Not only this, but every fiftieth year, God required in the Law of Moses that his people take a Jubilee year. The Jubilee was an extra year of rest and reliance on God on top of the Sabbath years. At this time, the people were required to release their slaves and cancel all debts (see Leviticus 25:8-5 for details on the year of jubilee). Two years in a row without sowing and reaping required great faith indeed, especially for those who had built up wealth through owning people and through loaning money.

In all these laws, God was telling Israel something about rest and reliance on him, but he is telling us something as well. Under the second covenant, we have freedom in Christ. God does not prescribe a set Sabbath day or year for those who are in Christ. Yet, God still expects us to live a life of rest and dependence upon him. *"Come to me, all you who are weary and burdened, and I will give you rest. Take my yoke upon you and learn from me, for I am gentle and humble in heart, and you will find rest for your souls"* (Matthew 11:28,29). This is not a suggestion but a commandment of Jesus. Again, we see that the antitype to the Sabbath is less defined and ritualistic. God is trusting our heart and our love for him to cause us to fulfill the requirement of the Old Covenant in freedom from regulation. Those who consider themselves disciples of Jesus would do well to examine their lives in this area. Has God's trust born fruit in a life which fully trusts in him? Do we struggle to carve out quiet, restful times with God in our busy schedule? Do we allow the pursuit of financial security to crowd out simply enjoying life as a saved person? In our modern culture following the pattern of the antitype to the Sabbath and Jubilee—resting in God—may be the most difficult of all of Jesus' commands.

Many other examples could be given of laws, rules and regulations under the first covenant being a type with the antitype in Christ involving the same concept only based on freedom and trust on God's part. We should be thankful that *"He sets aside the first to establish the second"* (Hebrews 10:9). Why did God do this? Because the Law of Moses was not based on faith. True, loving, trusting faith which leads to obedience was God's desire from the beginning.

> *All who rely on observing the law are under a curse, for it is written: "Cursed is everyone who does not continue to do everything written in the Book of the Law"* (quoting Habakkuk 2:4).

> *Clearly no one is justified before God by the law, because "The righteous will live by faith." The law is not based on faith; on the contrary, "The man who does these things will live by them." Christ redeemed us from the curse of the law by becoming a curse for us...* (Galatians 3:10-13).

This is very strong language, but it is the heart of the matter. It is the heart of the gospel. It is the heart of the New Covenant. Since before God set it up, the type was intended to work only as a shadow, a tutor, a school master, to lead us to the antitype: *"The law of the Spirit of life which set me free from the law of sin and death"* (Romans 8:2).

PREFIGURE IN THE MOSAIC COVENANT	EQUIVALENT IN THE NEW COVENANT
Obedience to physically defined rules required.	Obedience to Spiritual principles required.
Physical blessings promised	Spiritual blessings promised
Ceremonial uncleanness.	Sin and separation from God.
Sacrifice bridges the chasm between law and effort.	Sacrifice bridges the chasm between law and effort.
Sealed with the blood of bulls and goats.	Sealed with the blood of Jesus Christ.
Mediated by a High Priest.	Mediated by THE High Priest, Jesus Christ.
Laws, rules and regulations for behavior.	Behavior based on spiritual principle and love.
Tithing.	Sacrifice and giving from the heart.
Sabbath.	Come... I will give you rest. Relying on Jesus.
Death.	Life.

Paul puts this concept in even stronger terms in Colossians 2:13-17, where God says to those who were formerly under the Law of Moses:

> When you were dead in your sins and in the uncircumcision of your sinful nature, God made you alive with Christ. He forgave us all our sins, **having cancelled the written code, with its regulations** that was against us and that stood opposed to us; he took it away, nailing it to the cross. And having disarmed the powers and authorities, he made a public spectacle of them, triumphing over them by the cross. Therefore do not let anyone judge you by what you eat or drink or with regard to a religious festival, a New Moon celebration or a Sabbath day. **These are a shadow of the things that were to come;** the reality, however, is found in Christ."

As great as the Law given at Sinai was, in the final analysis it led to slavery. It stood opposed to us, not because God is opposed to us, but because we needed to be taught that salvation through human effort is worse than vain. It is the height of arrogance. A relationship with God has always been based on the love and grace of the almighty God. Here Paul states in no uncertain terms that God never intended the Law of Moses to be the final word, but only a shadow (foreshadow) of what he intended all along to offer in Christ. Let's be taught by the Law of Moses to put the full weight of our trust in the love, the sacrifice, and the grace of Jesus Christ.

SUMMARY

Thunder, lightning and a thick cloud over the mountain; smoke, shaking of the earth and the sound of a trumpet; all combine to tell us that the law and the covenant given to God's people through Moses was truly a wonderful and awesome thing. As great as the Law of Moses was, God intended it all along to be a mere foreshadow of the far more wonderful New Covenant in Christ.

The former covenant was inadequate in that it was based on human effort and physically unblemished sacrifices, rather than on the blood of the unblemished life of Jesus Christ. Nevertheless, the Law of Moses served a great purpose. It led us to Christ. Physical blessing based on unachievable perfect obedience gave way to spiritual blessing based upon reliance on the only one who ever lived a perfect life: Jesus Christ.

The Old Covenant, as glorious as it was, brought only death, while the New Covenant brings life;

> Now if the ministry that brought death, which was engraved in letters on stone, came with glory, so that the Israelites could not look steadily at the face of Moses because of its glory, fading though it was, will not the ministry of the Spirit be even more glorious? If the ministry that condemns men is glorious, how much more glorious is the ministry that brings righteousness! For what was glorious has no glory now in comparison with the surpassing glory. And if what was fading away came with glory, how much greater is the glory of that which lasts! (2 Corinthians 3:7-11).

The fading away of the glow on Moses' face shows us that the Old Covenant, which is a foreshadowing of the New, is a glorious thing, but one which would fade with time. Hopefully we, in the light of the gospel of Jesus, will be able to see the glory of the gospel clearly, for Paul says of the Jews that, *"their minds were made dull, for to this day the same veil remains when the old covenant is read...But whenever anyone turns to the Lord, the veil is taken away"* (2 Corinthians 3:14,16). Those who truly behold Christ come into the light of the glory of God.

Through the law given at Sinai, God taught us that more than anything else, he wants a relationship with his people. He taught us that sin is a terrible thing, resulting in death and separation. The Law of Moses teaches us that there is absolutely no room for a cavalier attitude toward our own sin. Nevertheless, through the Old Covenant, God told us that the mighty chasm separating our own almost pitiful effort at perfection was to be crossed through the blood sacrifice of Jesus Christ. No longer is our relationship with God based on slavery to a set of rules we could never obey perfectly. It is based on the perfect law of freedom in Christ. The Law of Moses was great, but the law of the spirit of life in Christ is infinitely greater. Let us rejoice with Paul as he declares:

> *Therefore, there is now no condemnation for those who are in Christ Jesus, for through Christ Jesus the law of the Spirit of Life set me free from the law of sin and death* (Romans 8:1,2).

Thanks be to God through Jesus Christ our Lord!

Endnotes

[1] For more on medical implications of the Law of Moses, see John Oakes, *Reasons for Belief—A Handbook of Christian Evidences* (available at www.ipibooks.com), pp. 242-254.

CHAPTER SIX

Old Testament Ritual Sacrifice Points to New Testament Sacrifice

Therefore I urge you, brothers, in view of God's mercy to offer your bodies as living sacrifices, holy and pleasing to God—which is your spiritual worship.

Romans 12:1

For those of us living in a modern, Western culture, it is difficult to imagine the bloody ritual sacrifices which were a part of normal life for the Jews. Most of us would be repulsed by the sight of such activity. This would not be the case in some modern cities such as Tehran, where ritual sacrifice of lambs and goats is commonplace. Ritual sacrifice was not a new concept when Moses brought the Law to God's people at Sinai. Archaeological evidence tells us that the idea of taking an object of value and offering it up in order to appease the gods is an idea nearly as old as humanity. For millennia, people have offered their most prized possessions, even their own children, at altars devoted to beings of their own imagination. When Paul entered Athens, he saw altars devoted to many gods. There were altars to non-Greek gods such as Ishtar and Isis as well as many of the Greek gods, and, of course, Athena. In fact, just to cover themselves, they even had an altar with the inscription, *"TO AN UNKNOWN GOD"* (Acts 17:23).

Sacrifice has always been about giving up something of personal value in order to express the sincerity of the giver and to obtain the favor of the one to whom the sacrifice is offered. However, throughout human history, the problem has always been that the sincerity of the giver did not have the power to appease a god which did not exist. It is a pitiful thing to contemplate the amount of blood and smoke devoted over the centuries to creations of human fantasy resulting from the fear of the unknown.

The existence of sacrificial systems among virtually every human culture since before the dawn of history tells us that it is inherent in human nature to believe that sacrifice is needed to achieve a right relationship with that power which controls our destiny. In the Bible, one only has to wait until Genesis chapter four to find Cain and Abel offering sacrifices to God. It is God who put this instinct into the human heart. In all this, God was preparing our hearts and minds to accept the sacrifices ordained in the Law of Moses. Even more so, God was preparing us to receive and to offer the sacrifices commanded in the New Testament, the greatest of which, of course, is the sacrifice of Jesus Christ. The sacrifice of Jesus Christ on the cross was neither an accident nor an afterthought on the part of God. Jesus is *"the Lamb of God, slain from the creation of the world"* (Revelation 13:8). Of course the skeptic has every right to question this claim, but the evidence of type and antitype found in this chapter will show that the God who inspired the writing of the Bible had these sacrifices in mind since the fall of man.

Sacrifices commanded in the New Testament? This may be a new concept for the reader. In this section we will see that each one of the sacrifices described in detail in the law given at Sinai was intended to anticipate and to teach about an important aspect of sacrifice as fulfilled in their antitypes in the New Testament.

It would be safe to say that most Christians become lost in the details when they read what may seem like a confusing array of sacrifices described in the Old Testament, especially in Leviticus. Surely most Bible readers have asked themselves why God put all that detail in there. Can God expect us to get anything out of all this? In Leviticus, we find trespass offerings, sin offerings, burnt offerings, drink offerings, grain offerings and thank offerings. Were the Jews able to keep all this straight? The answer is absolutely yes. The Mosaic sacrificial system to the Jews was a bit like the game of baseball to the average American. For anyone raised in a culture unfamiliar with the game, baseball is a confusing set of seemingly meaningless rules. However, for many Americans baseball is a part of daily life. The rules are understood and taken for granted. The same would apply to the sacrificial system and the Jews. For us it may seem a confusing array of meaningless rules, but for the Jews during the time before Christ it was a part of daily life, understood and taken for granted by all—a national pass-time.

The sacrificial system given under the first covenant was of great significance to the Jews. They understood that through offering these sacrifices they were able to keep a right relationship with God and to live a blessed life under the protection of Yahweh. The sacrifices at the temple were at the heart of Judaism. However, God intended them to be a foreshadowing of something far greater for those who would come to have a relationship with him under the second covenant in Jesus Christ.

> *The blood of goats and bulls and the ashes of a heifer sprinkled on those who are ceremonially unclean sanctify them so that they are outwardly clean. How much more, then, will the blood of Christ, who through the eternal Spirit offered himself unblemished to God, cleanse our consciences from acts that lead to death, so that we may serve the living God!* (Hebrews 9:13,14).

If the Mosaic sacrifices have a fuller significance to us than to the Jews, surely it is worth the effort to understand what God is trying to teach us, even if it means slogging through a few details to reach that end. Believe it or not, it is easier to understand the sacrificial system in Leviticus and its significance to followers of Jesus than it is to understand the game of baseball!

THE LEVITICAL SACRIFICIAL SYSTEM

It will be helpful to give a general introduction to the sacrifices ordained under the Law of Moses before describing type and antitype in the two testaments. To begin with, the reader may be surprised to know that not all the sacrifices performed by the priests were for forgiveness of sins (or the first covenant equivalent; ceremonial cleanness). One can divide the sacrifices into those which were for worship and those which were intended to deal with sin. Another way to describe the division is between those sacrifices which were for worship of God and those which made it possible to worship God in the first place.

When reading about the sacrifices in Leviticus, there is a straightforward way to know whether one is reading about a sacrifice intended as worship or one which is for dealing with individual or corporate sin. The book of Leviticus is consistent in describing the worship sacrifices as *"an aroma, pleasing to the LORD."* For example, consider Leviticus 1:9, Leviticus 2:2 and Leviticus 3:5. The sacrifices for sin definitely were not a pleasing aroma to God and they are never described in that way. On the contrary, they involve things which God hates. Leviticus chapters four and five do not mention anything about sin sacrifices pleasing God. The distinction between the two types of sacrifice is also recognized in the New Testament. *"Every high priest is selected from among men and is appointed to represent them in matters related to God, to offer gifts and sacrifices for sins"* (Hebrews 5:1). In this case, the "gifts" are the sweet-savor, worship sacrifices, while the "sacrifices for sins" would be the sin offerings.

It is traditional to separate the sacrifices described in Leviticus and elsewhere into five main types, with the other sacrifices as subcategories. The three main sweet savor sacrifices were the burnt offering (*olah* in Hebrew), the grain offering (*minchah*), and the fellowship offering (*shelem*). The two sacrifices which were intended by God to deal with sin are the sin offering (*chatat*) and the trespass offering (*asham*). The details of these sacrifices, their purpose in the Old Covenant and their antitype meaning in the New Testament are the focus of this chapter.

Other offerings could be mentioned as well. One of these is the drink offering (*nesek* in Hebrew). This offering was usually given along with one of the worship offerings. Because the drink offering was always included when Jews gave a grain offering, it is often not mentioned as one of the five principal offerings and is listed under the grain offering. There are sub-categories under the fellowship offering as well. One of these is the thank-offering (often called the peace offering). Another is the vow offering, while the third is the free-will offering. These three sacrifices are very similar, differing mainly in the intention of the worshipper. In fact, the traditional names for these sacrifices indicate their purpose.

Each of these sacrifices was to be made, either at the tabernacle or later, at the Temple in Jerusalem. Also, each of them was performed by priests from the line of Aaron, although the Jewish worshipper was occasionally allowed to take part in at least part of the ceremony, especially in the worship sacrifices. Some of these sacrifices were to be offered on a regular basis, either daily, or weekly or at a New Moon festival or one of the other ordained festivals. Others were to be offered whenever the need or desire arose on the part of the individual.

A secondary goal of this chapter is to separate and describe each of the sacrifices so that the reader can understand the Jewish perspective on the sacrificial system. The principal goal, of course, is to show how all of these sacrifices were intended by God to teach us about aspects of sacrifice to him under the New Covenant. The worship sacrifices will be dealt with first because they appear first in the book of Leviticus. These sacrifices will teach us about personal sacrifice in our daily lives and specifically about those made by our greatest example, Jesus Christ. While the worship sacrifices are prefigures of our personal worship of God, the sin sacrifices prefigure the sacrificial ministry of Jesus Christ.

THE BURNT OFFERING (olah)

The burnt offering is described in Leviticus chapter one. This was a sacrifice of worship—a sweet savor offering. This offering was in general voluntary, although burnt offerings were also given ritually for the whole community twice a day (see Numbers 28). For the Jew, the burnt offering represented a voluntary dedication or commitment of something of value to the Lord. God asked the Jews to take a valued possession and literally burn it up on an altar devoted to him. This sacrifice speaks volumes about total commitment and dedication. Once you burn up your possessions, there is certainly no getting them back. The burnt sacrifice maintains the same antitype meaning in the New Testament as well, as we will see.

The details of the performance of this sacrifice may be summarized as follows. The burnt offering was to be an animal of the herd (a bull) or the flock (a sheep), or for a poor person, a bird could be substituted. The worshipper first laid his hands on the head of the sacrifice to symbolize that the offering represented himself. The animal had to be without defect. It was then sacrificed and the blood was sprinkled on the altar. The head was burned, while the body was very thoroughly washed before also burning it on the altar. *"It is a burnt offering, an offering made by fire, an aroma pleasing to the* LORD" (Leviticus 1:13). When the burnt offering was complete, there was nothing left but ashes.

The burnt offering held deep significance to the Jews. It represented for them a total dedication of life and heart to Yahweh. It is also loaded with meaning and foreshadow for those under the New Covenant. Because it is a sweet savor sacrifice, it bears significance both for the sacrifice of Jesus and for our own personal sacrifice.

It is not mere coincidence that in the burnt offering the head was not cleansed, while the body was thoroughly cleaned. This is because this sacrifice is a foreshadowing of the sacrifice and dedication both of Jesus Christ and of his church to God. Jesus is the head of the church.

> *And God placed all things under his feet and appointed him to be head over everything for the church, which is his body, the fullness of him who fills everything in every way* (Ephesians 1:22,23).

> *Instead, speaking the truth in love, we will in all things grow up into the Head, that is Christ* (Ephesians 4:15).

> *Husbands, love your wives, just as Christ loved the church and gave himself up for her to make her holy, cleansing her by the washing with water through the word, and to present her to himself as a radiant church...After all, no one ever hated his own body, but he feeds and cares for it, just as Christ does the church—for we are members of his body* (Ephesians 5:25-30).

Jesus certainly presented himself to God as a burnt offering. Yet, as the head of the body, he did not need cleansing, as he was without sin. However, the body of the animal, representing the body of Christ, the church, needed cleansing. The Aaronic priests probably were not aware of the powerful imagery and prophecy in the washing of the body but not the head. This had to be a mystery to them. For us, the mystery is revealed in the gospel.

In his lifetime, Jesus presented his own body as a living sacrifice. We are not talking here about his death but his life as an offering.

> *Be imitators of God, therefore, as dearly loved children and live a life of love, just as Christ loved us and gave himself up for us as a fragrant offering and sacrifice to God* (Ephesians 5:1,2).

In this passage, Paul is making reference to the burnt offering. Notice that he is referring to a fragrant offering and a giving up of himself. The point is that Jesus offered his life as as a total dedication to God for our sake and that we ought to offer ourselves to God as a burnt offering sacrifice of love as well.

God is asking for the same burnt offering from us, although we need washing before we are prepared to give it! The burnt offering is not about salvation. It is not "required." It is a voluntary dedication of oneself to God—a thing which is very pleasing to God. Look at Romans 12:1,2. It takes on a whole new and a fuller meaning in this context:

> "Therefore, I urge you, brothers, in view of God's mercy, **to offer your bodies as living sacrifices,** holy and pleasing to God— **this is your spiritual act of worship.**"

The reference to the burnt offering is clear, as is the application to those under the New Covenant. God is calling us to make a burnt offering of our lives, not in order to be cleansed, but because we have been cleansed. Note he says *"in view of God's mercy."* In other words, given that Jesus has already cleansed us and prepared us for the burnt offering, let us come to God and present our lives on the altar of our faith in total dedication and love to him. This is only a reasonable response. Have you presented your life as a living sacrifice? Are you holding back something? It is not a matter of salvation but a matter of love and response to that love. Are you willing to have your life used up for God, leaving only a pile of ashes here on the earth? If you do so, it will be a pleasing aroma to our God.

Our attitude ought to be the same as that of Paul:

> *I eagerly expect and hope that I will in no way be ashamed, but will have sufficient courage so that now, as always, Christ will be exalted in my body, whether by life or by death. For me to live is Christ and to die is gain. If I am to go on living in the body, this will mean fruitful labor for me* (Philippians 1:20-22).

Paul's sincere hope was that his body and his life could be presented as an offering to God—a burnt offering of dedication to the Head, which is Christ. Is that your hope?

One of the great things about the burnt sacrifice—and therefore about the Christian sacrificial life—is that it is truly voluntary. There is a great difference between dedicating something because it is required and dedicating something because your heart is behind it. We learn from the Old Testament, of all places, that this is the essence of the Christian life. God is waiting in eager expectation that we will offer ourselves to him as living sacrifices, not in order to be saved, but out of gratitude because we are saved.

THE GRAIN OFFERING (minchah)

The grain offering is described in detail in Leviticus chapter two. Unlike the burnt offering, the grain offering was not voluntary. The Jews were required to give a grain offering, but it was the size of the offering which was voluntary. For the Jew, the grain offering was giving of the first fruits of their labor to God. It was a gift in response to the physical gifts that God had given them. From the grain offering, Christians can learn about contributing from the first fruits of their labor: money! How does God feel about our contribution?

Actually, there was more to the grain offering than just grain. The worshipper was to bring a mixture of grain, oil, incense (Leviticus 2:1-10), and in some cases salt (Leviticus 2:13). The mixture was sometimes cooked as bread. A portion was burned on the altar, and the rest was given to take care of the needs of Aaron and his sons. The grain offering was at least partially intended to take care of those who ministered before the Lord. It was a worship offering, *"an aroma pleasing to the Lord"* (Leviticus 2:9). Leviticus two specified some things that definitely were not to be combined with the grain offering. It was forbidden to include any kind of leaven or yeast as well as honey (Leviticus 2:11).

For the Jews, the purpose of the grain offering was two-fold. It was intended to remind them that their physical blessings were from God, not simply produced from their own effort. God expected them to return a portion of their blessings as tribute to remind them of where their physical blessings originated. The grain offering was also intended to take care of the physical needs of those who devoted themselves in a special way to the ministry before the Lord—the priests and the Levites.

It is easy see what God intended the grain offering to foreshadow for those who are under the New Covenant. God expects us to bring to him an offering from the first fruits of our labor as well. Through the grain offering, God was telling us that giving from what he has blessed us with is not an option. We are required to give in order to take care of the needs of the church and of those who serve God in a special way. God expects us to give from our first fruits. In other words, our giving should not be an after-thought, or from what is left over after our own "needs" are taken care of. It is a matter of faith to give from our first fruits because when we have only gathered the first fruits, we are not absolutely certain that the last fruits will be enough to sustain us. Trust is involved in this sacrifice.

Let us look at type and antitype in the details of this offering. The grain offering obviously included grain. Grain is the fruit of careful, sustained labor. God expects us to work, to earn something from that work and to give from what we earn. One reason we work, of course, is to take care of our physical needs. A secondary reason to work is so that we can bring an offering to God.

The offering also included oil. One effect of the oil, of course, was to make the bread taste good (remember that the priests and Levites ate part of the offering). In the Bible, oil consistently represents the anointing (choosing) of God. Jesus was anointed with the oil of joy (Hebrews 1:9). We all have an anointing from the Holy One (1 John 2:20). God has chosen each of his children. Their offering of the fruits of their labor reminds them of that fact.

The grain offering also included incense. In the Bible, incense consistently represents our offerings of prayer to God (Revelation 5:8, Revelation 8:3, Luke 1:10). In this, God is telling us that our offerings should be given with prayer.

The grain offering often included salt as well. Salt represents eternity, something permanent, a lasting covenant, an eternal reward (Mark 9:49,50, Colossians 4:6, Matthew 5:13, 2 Chronicles 13:5, Numbers 18:19). Although the food which was offered on the altar was perishable, it produced rewards in heaven which are eternal. Similarly for us: our earthly treasures are a temporary thing, but in giving of our physical treasures to God, we are receiving a heavenly reward which will never spoil or perish.

> *"Do not store up for yourselves treasures on earth, where moth and rust destroy, and where thieves break in and steal. But*

> store up for yourselves treasures in heaven, where moth and rust do not destroy, and where thieves do not break in and steal. For where your treasure is, there you heart will be also" (Matthew 6:19-21).

God is teaching us a lot about our sacrificial giving to take care of the needs of his kingdom through the grain offering.

The things which were not allowed to be included in the grain offering are important foreshadows as well. Leaven was not allowed. Jesus used leaven to represent sin and evil influences. *"Be on your guard against the yeast of the Pharisees which is hypocrisy"* (Luke 12:1). Paul used the same theme:

> *Don't you know that a little yeast works through the whole batch of dough? Get rid of the old yeast that you may be a new batch without yeast—as you really are. For Christ, our Passover lamb, has been sacrificed. Therefore let us keep the Festival, not with the old yeast, the yeast of malice and wickedness, but with the bread without yeast, the bread of sincerity and truth* (1 Corinthians 5:6-8).

In the grain offering, God is telling us to give of our first fruits, but to watch for the influence of every kind of sin in our lives. An offering which is tainted with greed and evil desire is worse than no offering at all.

The grain offering was to exclude yeast and also honey. For the Jews, honey represented that which is decaying. Ours is to be a living sacrifice, coming from new wine skins, made new in *"washing of rebirth and renewal by the Holy Spirit"* (Titus 3:5).

The most obvious New Testament application of the grain offering is found in 2 Corinthians 8 and 9. The Macedonian churches pleaded with Paul for the opportunity to take care of the needs of the saints. They gave first to God, then to Paul's needs, and presumably last to their own personal needs. They had a "good excuse" to be cautious in their giving because they were poor, but they gave generously nevertheless. Paul reminds them that Jesus set an example of giving a grain-offering by giving to the point that he was made poor so that the saints could be made rich. Giving to the needs of the local church is not optional, but the extent of giving is, *"for God loves a cheerful giver"* (2 Corinthians 9:7). Paul associates prayer (incense) with the offering (2 Corinthians

9:12,14) as well as eternal blessings (salt) (2 Corinthians 9:6-11).

Jesus certainly gave a grain offering. In fact, he left all his earthly possessions behind in order to pursue his ministry to the needs of his people. How are you doing in your grain offering? Are you giving your first fruits? Are you holding back—wanting to see how the harvest will finish before you give? Is your offering combined with prayer, or is it just routine? Is your offering mixed with the leaven of bitterness and greed? If so, do not stop giving, but exclude the leaven from your gift. Let us give an acceptable grain offering to God, an aroma pleasing to the Lord.

THE DRINK OFFERING (nesek)

As previously mentioned, the drink offering was related to the grain offering. Drink offerings were almost always given in tandem with grain offerings (Exodus 29:41, Leviticus 23:13 and Numbers 28:31, for example). They were a worship offering: a sweet savor sacrifice. The drink offering was the simplest of the sacrifices ordained in the Mosaic system. It involved simply pouring wine out on the altar.

Although the drink offering was simple, it offered to the Jews a vivid picture of worship. When one empties a container of grain or other produce, it is a simple matter to scoop it back up into the container, although some may be lost. When liquid is spilled from a cup onto the ground, it is irretrievable. There is something final about pouring out a drink offering, which served to remind the Jews of their irretrievable and total dedication to God.

David made a sort of a drink offering in 2 Samuel 23:16. He had expressed his thirst in front of three of his bravest and most loyal soldiers while his pursuer King Saul was camped close by. At extreme risk to their own lives, these soldiers broke through Saul's lines and brought an offering of water to David, stolen right out from under the noses of King Saul's troops. In a vivid scene, David turned their devotion to him into a drink offering of devotion to God as he poured the precious water out on the ground.

The drink offering is a foreshadowing of the kind of total devotion God wants us to have for Jesus Christ, the son of David (by the way, the above incident is another example of how David's life is a prefigure of the Messiah.) As with all the worship offerings, Jesus set the supreme example. His life was poured out for God in every imaginable way. Jesus himself said at the Last Supper that the wine represented his blood *"which is poured out for you"* (Luke 22:20). In Romans 5:5 we are reminded that God irretrievably poured out his love for us in the Holy Spirit.

As Jesus fulfilled the antitype of the drink offering through his life, so should we do our best to do the same. Paul challenged the Philippians with his life:

> *...I did not run or labor for nothing. But even if I am poured out like a drink offering on the sacrifice and service coming from your faith, I am glad and rejoice with all of you. So you too should be glad and rejoice with me* (Philippians 2:16,17).

For Paul, being a drink offering was not a burden but a joy. He was able to claim that his entire Christian life was a drink offering. He held nothing back in his cup at the end of his life.

> *For I am already being poured out like a drink offering, and the time has come for my departure. I have fought the good fight, I have finished the race, I have kept the faith* (2 Timothy 4:6,7).

What a great honor to pour our lives out at the foot of the altar in sacrifice and service to God! What am I holding back? What little side reservoir of life am I keeping in reserve? What am I saving it for? Let yourself be poured out for God.

One further comment about the grain and the drink offerings should be made. Perhaps the reader thought of the possibility that there is a type and antitype relationship between the combined grain and drink offerings and the Lord's Supper. It is tempting to see the "obvious" analogy here, but obvious analogies can sometimes not be valid. In this case, the Lord's supper may include unleavened bread and wine together, but it is nevertheless not a fulfillment of the grain and drink offerings. The Lord's Supper is an act of worship but it is not at offering, it is a remembrance of the death of Jesus Christ. In fact, we will see in chapter seven that the Lord's Supper is actually the New Testament antitype of the Passover. The Passover, like the Lord's Supper is a remembrance of a blood sacrifice and the resultant salvation. More will be said on that later.

THE FELLOWSHIP OFFERING (shelem)

The fellowship offering is the third major category of worship sacrifices. This offering has been traditionally known as the peace offering because it was translated that way in the King James Version. There are three slightly different versions of the fellowship offering, depending on the intent of the giver. These are the thank-offering (Leviticus 7:11-15), the vow-offering (Leviticus 11:16 and 22:23), and the free-will offering (Leviticus 22:23). All of these were *"an aroma, pleasing to the LORD"* (Leviticus 3:5). As with the other fragrant aroma offerings, the fellowship offering was not intended to bring forgiveness of sin. The general intent of the fellowship offering was to offer a gift of thanks to God for some special blessing—whether it was for a blessing received or one which was being expectantly prayed for. The bottom line is that the fellowship offering was a party!

The details of the fellowship offering are described in Leviticus chapter three. The worshiper was to provide an animal from his own herd. It was to be an animal without defect. As with the burnt offering, the worshiper laid his hands on the animal before the sacrifice so that the animal could represent himself to God. Following this, the priest sacrificed the animal, sprinkling some of the blood on the sides of the altar. The kidneys and the fat and other parts of the entrails were burned on the altar. The rest of the animal was to be cooked and eaten. It was not eaten by the priests but by the one giving the offering along with his family and friends in a feast celebrated before the Lord. The meat was to be eaten the same day.

For the Jew, the fellowship offering was all about celebrating his or her relationship with God. Remember that a principal aspect of the first covenant was for God to give physical blessings to his people, whether it be children, blessed marriages, successful harvests or so forth. God wanted his people to celebrate their personal victories together and to use the event as an opportunity for them to remember that all blessings come from God.

Let us consider the separate meaning of the three types of fellowship offering. The thank-offering was intended as a feast to celebrate and to offer thanks for a specific blessing already received. The vow offering was a feast anticipating a future blessing of God. For example, if a woman was pregnant, and the worshipper wanted to celebrate, but to also ask God to bless the birth, she might give a vow offering. The free-will offering was exactly what is implied by the name. In this case, the worshiper is simply excited about being in a covenant relationship with God and wants to celebrate, but not necessarily for any specific blessing.

Of course, the fellowship offering has much to teach Christian as well as the Jew. God intended all along for it to be a foreshadowing of Christian worship. One of the important aspects of the free will offering was that the feast was to be celebrated and the meat eaten on a single day. God wanted the Jews and Christians as well to celebrate the daily blessings he gives us. Christianity is definitely not only about giving up things; about sacrifice and self-denial. These are absolutely part of the life of the disciple, but a large part of God's desire for us under the New Covenant is to experience spiritual blessings. God wants us to live a life of daily celebration of the blessings we have in Christ.

> *"I have come that they may have life, and have it to the full"* (John 10:10).

> *"I tell you the truth," Jesus replied, "no one who has left home or brothers or sisters or mother or father or children or fields for me and the gospel will fail to receive a hundred times as much in this present age...and in the age to come, eternal life"* (Mark 10:29,30).

> *Praise be to God the Father of our Lord Jesus Christ, who has blessed us in the heavenly realms with every spiritual blessing in Christ* (Ephesians 1:3).

Christian worship involves sacrifice. It involves absolute dedication to God, as the other worship sacrifices remind us. Let us not forget, though, that God promises to fill the devoted, dedicated, sacrificial life with spiritual blessings beyond measure. We tend to focus on the negative. Problems tend to overwhelm us, but the follower of Jesus must celebrate the many blessings given by God.

The Mark 10 passage promises the follower of Jesus one hundred fold blessing in relationships; if not in quantity, certainly in quality. Let us enjoy and celebrate these relationships. These are blessings given by God. We should have regular parties to celebrate both spiritual rebirths (baptisms) and physical births. There should be small parties and big parties, and sometimes even one-on-one parties alone with God. *"Be joyful always; pray continually; give thanks in all circumstances, for this is God's will for you in Christ Jesus"* (1 Thessalonians 5:16). In this passage, one can see an aspect of the free-will offering (rejoice always), of the vow offering (pray continually) and of the thank offering (in all circumstances). This is more than coincidence. Paul, a Pharisee, has the fellowship offering in mind. If the reader is a Christian, are you excited about your life in Christ? Do you focus on the problems, or do you spend more time celebrating the blessings? If you are not yet a Christian, you need to make a decision and join the party.

One interesting fact about the fellowship/*shelem* offering is that it was often placed on top of the burnt offering/*olah* sacrifice. This indicates that the blessings of God are based on and produced through our dedication to him. The greater the devotion offered, the greater the blessing given by God. It is not that our good deeds and sacrifices to God earn the blessings. The New Testament makes it clear what we deserve based on our sin. Our devotion does not earn the blessings, but that is just how God works. The blessings are the natural response of God to our sacrifice to him.

Another aspect of the fellowship offering is that it had to be a clean animal. Leviticus 22:17-29 describes in some detail the types of deformities which made an animal defiled and therefore unacceptable. God does not accept defiled offerings. Of course, uncleanness in the first covenant is the type of sin in the second covenant. Praise God that once a person is forgiven of sins through the blood of Jesus, he or she is automatically clean and able to offer burnt offerings, free-will offerings and thank-offerings at any time. Those who are not washed in the blood of Jesus are not fit to offer worship to God. This may be frustrating. In may even seem unfair, but that is how God works. In the words of Romans 8:7, "*the sinful mind is hostile to God.*" We must take care of first things first. If a person is not saved, he or she should put their religious offerings aside and get into a right relationship with God. Only then can that person make sweet smelling offerings before the spiritual tabernacle in the presence of God.

THE BLOOD SACRIFICES

The sacrifices already discussed have been about our worship of God under the New Covenant. The last two sacrifices are definitely not foreshadows of our worship of God. These are the sacrifices required for forgiveness of sins in order to put us into a relationship with God. Although the worship offerings were covered first in this chapter (following the order in Leviticus), the fact is that without the sin offering and the guilt offering, the burnt, grain and fellowship offerings would be of no value. Our relationship with God is predicated on the forgiveness of sins. Unless we are made clean from our sin, our commitment, our gifts and all our other attempts at worship are in vain.

> *"Surely the arm of the LORD is not too short to save,*
> *nor his ear too dull to hear.*
> *But your iniquities have separated you from your God;*
> *Your sins have hidden his face from you,*
> *so that he will not hear.*
> *For your hands are stained with blood,*
> *your fingers with guilt.*
> *Your lips have spoken lies,*
> *and your tongue mutters wicked things"* (Isaiah 59:1-3).

> *"There is no one righteous, not even one;*
> *there is no one who understands,*
> *no one who seeks God.*
> *All have turned away,*
> *they have together become worthless;*
> *there is no one who does good,*
> *not even one"* (Romans 3:10-12).

The sin problem had to be resolved before worship was acceptable. This brings us to the sin and the guilt offering.

The two redemption offerings are quite similar in form. To the uninitiated, there is relatively little difference between the actual ceremonies of the two sacrifices. At first glance, the two sacrifices seem to be for a similar purpose as well. However, a careful study will reveal that the two sacrifices were for significantly different categories of transgressions.

In general, the sin offering was for trespasses against God's authority. In other words, the sin offering was to deal with sins directly against the authority of God. It has been said that in essence, the sin offering is for violations of the first four of the Ten Commandments. The sin offering and the offenses it was meant to deal with are described in the next section.

In general, the guilt offering was for sins of one Jew against a fellow Jew or against the Jewish people as a whole. These were offenses of personal property (as opposed to God's property). It has been said that the last six of the Ten Commandments are a summary of the laws which, when violated, required a guilt offering. This may be an oversimplification, but it can be helpful in distinguishing the two types of sacrifices for forgiveness of sins.

Before moving on to the specifics of the two sacrifices, it would bear mentioning one very important point which applies to both. The fact is that under the Law of Moses, there was no provision made for deliberate sin against God or against a fellow Jew.

> "The LORD said to Moses, "Say to the Israelites: 'When anyone sins **unintentionally** and does what is forbidden in any of the LORD'S commands..." (Leviticus 4:1).

> "If the whole Israelite community sins **unintentionally** and does what is forbidden in any of the LORD'S commands,..." (Leviticus 4:13).

> "When a person commits a violation and sins **unintentionally** in regard to any of the LORD'S holy things..." (Leviticus 5:14).

Specifically, there was no provision for forgiveness of intentional murder, blasphemy against God, adultary, idolatry and other sins which could not be committed accidentally. There are hints in the Old Testament that upon a deep repentance and extreme abhorrence of the evil committed, God held out the possibility of forgiveness. The case of David's sin in commiting adultery with Bathsheba, and ordering the death of her husband in battle (1 Samuel 11 and 12), followed by David's abject repentance, as seen in Psalm 51 is one example of this principle. However, in general, the Mosaic system did not make provision for those who blatantly broke the commandments of the Law.

How are we to view this fact, and what does it foreshadow in the New Covenant? A hint at the answer can be found in Hebrews 10:26-31:

> *If we **deliberately keep on sinning** after we have received the knowledge of the truth, no sacrifice for sins is left, but only a fearful expectation of judgment and of raging fire that will consume the enemies of God. Anyone who rejected the law of Moses died without mercy on the testimony of two or three witnesses. How much more severely do you think a man deserves to be punished who has trampled the Son of God under foot, who has treated as an unholy thing the blood of the covenant that sanctified him, and who has insulted the Spirit of grace? For we know him who said, "It is mine to avenge; I will repay," and again, "The Lord will judge his people." It is a dreadful thing to fall into the hands of the living God.*

The plan of redemption in the Old Covenant is a wonderful thing. Its antitype in the New Covenant is even far greater. However, God's grace does not extend to those who stubbornly refuse his loving kindness and turn back to willfully continuing in sin. This is a sobering teaching! God is consistent about willful sin in both covenants. This has implications for those who would teach the doctrine known as "once saved, always saved."

It is not that God wants those whose hearts are given to him to live in constant fear of hell and damnation every time they sin. On the contrary, it is God's intent for those who are in Christ to come into his presence with confidence, in full expectation of God's blessings.

> *Therefore, brothers, since we have confidence to enter the Most Holy Place by the blood of Jesus, by a new and living way opened for us through the curtain, that is his body, and since we have a great priest over the house of God, let us draw near to God with a sincere heart in full assurance of faith, having our hearts sprinkled to cleanse us from a guilty conscience and having our bodies washed with pure water* (Hebrews 10:19-22).

God wants and even expects those who are forgiven by the blood of the New Covenant to come to him with confidence and full assurance of faith. Nevertheless, let our confidence be seasoned with the sober knowledge, both from the Old and the New Covenant, that God will not tolerate continued, stubborn, willful violations of his law.

THE SIN OFFERING (chatat)

As already mentioned, the sin offering was intended to provide forgiveness for offenses against the authority of God. It is not a foreshadowing of anything we might do. Rather, it is a foreshadowing of the redemptive work of Jesus Christ himself. The details of the sin offering are described in Leviticus 4:1-5:13, as well as in Leviticus 6:24-30.

In the sin offering, the offending person, or a representative if the sin was corporate, was to bring an unblemished animal[1] to the priest. He was to lay his hands on the animal as a symbol of imparting the sin onto the animal. Significantly, the sinner himself actually sacrificed the animal, unlike the worship sacrifices. Hopefully, this brought home the seriousness of his offenses to the sinner. Then the priest sprinkled the blood seven times before the curtain leading to the Most Holy Place as well as on the horns of the altar of incense in front of the curtain. This is quite different from the worship sacrifices, where the blood was never brought into the Holy Place. After this, the rest of the blood was spilled out at the foot of the altar of burnt offering, as in the worship sacrifices. Next, the kidneys and associated fat on the kidneys and the liver (as with the burnt and the fellowship offering) were burned on the altar. The rest of the animal, including the hide, the organs, the head, the bones and the meat, were carried outside the camp to be burned.

Every single aspect of this sacrifice is a foreshadowing of the redemptive work of Jesus Christ. First, the sacrifice had to be unblemished. Jesus was also an unblemished sacrifice for our sins. In fact, based on this qualification, he is the only person who has ever lived on this earth who would have been qualified to be made a sin sacrifice. *"For you know that it was not with perishable things...that you were redeemed from the empty way of life handed down to you from your forefathers, but with the precious blood of Christ, a lamb without blemish or defect"* (1 Peter 1:18,19).

Second, the sinner laid his hands on the sacrifice. This is reminiscent of Isaiah 53:6, *"and the LORD has laid on him the iniquity of us all."* This was the source of the greatest pain for Jesus when he anticipated going to the cross. *"My soul is overwhelmed with sorrow to the point of death"* (Matthew 26:38), and even while he was on the cross; *"My God, my God, why have you forsaken me"* (Matthew 27:46). Based on his own knowledge of the sin offering, we can assume that Jesus was aware of what was to happen to him on the cross. In the sacrificial death of Jesus, God laid on him the sins of every person who has ever lived. *"God made him who knew no sin to be sin for us, so that in him we might become the righteousness of God"* (2 Corinthians 5:21). Can one even begin to imagine how devastating that was to Jesus? A man without sin—God in the flesh, took full responsibility for every sin ever committed by humanity. In accepting this responsibility, he accepted death.

Next, the sinner himself actually killed the animal. Please consider the implications of this action. You or I may not have actually driven the nails into the hands and feet of Jesus, but God considers us responsible for having killed his son. The words of the people in the crowd when Jesus was condemned speak volumes for us. *"Let his blood be on us and on our children"* (Matthew 27:25). God fulfilled their request, for better or for worse. Peter said to a group of thousands of Jews assembled in Jerusalem on the day of Pentecost, *"God has made this Jesus, whom you crucified, both Lord and Christ"* (Acts 2:36). It is worth noting that only a small fraction of this crowd was even in Jerusalem at the time of his execution. It is not a stretch to apply *"whom you crucified"* to all sinners, especially in view of the foreshadow in the sin offering. In fact, in the sin offering, when a corporate sin was committed, a single representative killed the animal as a representative of all the offenders. The analogy here is clear.

The blood of the sin sacrifice was sprinkled on the curtain and on the altar of incense, inside the Holy Place. Jesus did not enter the earthly Holy Place with his blood, but as the Hebrew writer tells us:

> *When Christ came as high priest of the good things that are already here, he went through the greater and more perfect tabernacle that is not man-made, that is to say, not a part of this creation. He did not enter by means of the blood of goats and calves; but he entered the Most Holy Place once for all by his own blood, having obtained eternal redemption. The blood of goats and bulls and the ashes of a heifer, sprinkled on those who are ceremonially unclean sanctify them so that they are outwardly clean.*

> *How much more, then, will the blood of Christ, who through the eternal Spirit offered himself unblemished to God, cleanse our consciences from acts that lead to death so that we may serve the living God* (Hebrews 9:11-14).

The blood of Jesus was brought right into the presence of the living God in the heavenly tabernacle, of which the tabernacle or temple in Jerusalem was only a copy. Similarly, some of the blood from the sin offering had to be brought into the Holy Place. The sin offering is an awesome prefigure of things to come. Remember that at the moment Jesus breathed his last, the curtain in the temple was ripped asunder from top to bottom. From that moment, God was no longer dwelling in the temple in Jerusalem. Rather, God was present in the heavenly tabernacle where the blood of Jesus does its work.

Next, the offering was burned. Other than the kidneys and certain fat portions which were burned on the altar of sacrifice, the body was burned outside the camp. God commanded that the body from the sin sacrifice be burned outside the camp as a symbol of removing the sin from among his people. There are many examples in the Law of Moses in which unclean things had to be taken outside the camp to keep the community ceremonially clean. This, too, is a foreshadow of the sacrificial death of Jesus. For symbolic reasons, Jesus was killed outside the city of Jerusalem at Golgotha. As we have already seen, the sin of the whole world was laid on Jesus when he was killed as a sin sacrifice, which required him to be crucified outside the city of Jerusalem. The way the Hebrew writer put it:

> *The high priest carries the blood of animals into the Most Holy Place as a sin offering, but the bodies are burned outside the camp. And so Jesus also suffered outside the city gate to make the people holy through his own blood. Let us, then, go to him outside the camp, bearing the disgrace he bore* (Hebrews 13:11-13).

Here we have another example of the enemies of Jesus unwittingly helping fulfill a prophecy of the Messiah. This provides still more evidence, not only that the Bible is the inspired word of God, but that God was in control of every event which surrounded the death of Jesus Christ.

We can see that every detail of the Mosaic sin sacrifice was a foreshadowing of the sacrifice of Jesus Christ for the sins of the whole world. As is usual, the thing which is prefigured is far greater than the original. As Hebrews makes plain:

> *This is an illustration for the present time, indicating that the gifts and sacrifices being offered were not able to clear the conscience of the worshiper. They are only a matter of food and drink and various ceremonial washings—external regulations applying until the time of the new order* (Hebrews 9:9,10).

If the blood of the sin sacrifice had any power to forgive the sins of the Jews, it was only given that power by future reference to the only sacrifice which has ever been able to make a sinner truly clean—the blood of Jesus Christ. When he saw Jesus, John the Baptist declared, *"Look, the Lamb of God, who takes away the sin of the world!"* (John 1:29). Remember that from God's perspective, Jesus is a lamb slain from the creation of the world, or as Peter put it, *"He was chosen* (as an unblemished sacrifice) *before the creation of the world"* (1 Peter 1:20). Remember, too, that in the sin sacrifice, the lamb was the correct sacrifice for the common people. Praise God for Jesus, our sin sacrifice.

THE GUILT OFFERING (asham)

The second sacrifice for the sin of the people under the Mosaic system was the guilt offering. This sacrifice is sometimes known as the trespass offering, which can help to clarify its distinction from the sin offering. The guilt offering was intended to deal with "trespasses" against ones' neighbor (and sometimes against God). The details of this sacrifice are described in Leviticus 5:14-6:7 and Leviticus 7:1-10. The main point of the guilt offering to the Jew was that the person who sins against his or her fellow man, will be put out of fellowship with God unless they reconcile with those they sinned against. Sins against people are sins against God.

There were two very significant differences between the sin offering and the guilt offering other than the type of sin they were intended to remove. The guilt offering was only to be offered by an individual. There was no such thing as a corporate sin against an individual. Each person was to take personal responsibility for his or her own actions. The second major difference between the sin and the guilt offering is that the guilt offering always included restitution for the offense. It was required that the restitution be made before the sacrifice was offered. The offender was required to make his relationship right with his neighbor before he could repair his relationship with God through a sacrifice. Here we can see that God is concerned with our relationship with him and with one another. This is certainly a major theme in the New Testament as well.

The details of this sacrifice were as follows. If the violation was against God, such as failing to bring in a tithe, the worshiper was required to make up the full amount, plus 20% and to bring a ram for the sacrifice. If the offense was against a fellow Jew, such as stealing, failing to return a lost animal and so forth, the same full restitution plus twenty percent was required, plus a ram for the sacrifice of atonement. After confessing and making restitution, he killed the ram, the blood was spilled out at the foot of the altar and the animal was burned up on the altar.

The guilt offerings were always intended by God to be a foreshadow of the ministry of Jesus Christ. The New Testament antitype of this offering is unique in that it involves both our own action to make our relationship with our brother or sister right and the sacrifice of Jesus to make us right with the Father. One finds in the messianic prophecy Isaiah 53:10, that, *"it was the LORD's will to crush him and cause him to suffer, and though the LORD makes his life a guilt offering, he will see his offspring and prolong his days."* When God made Jesus a guilt offering, he had in mind *"his offspring,"* which is the disciples of Jesus whose relationships with one another will be made right through the ministry of Jesus.

Romans 3:25 talks about God presenting Jesus as a sacrifice of atonement. Through Jesus, as in the guilt offering, we are made *"at one"* with both our fellow man and with God. Jesus even provided specific instructions for how his followers were to fulfill the New Testament equivalent of the guilt offering in Matthew 5:23,24:

> *"Therefore, if you are offering your gift at the altar and there remember that your brother has something against you, leave your gift there in front of the altar. First go and be reconciled to your brother; then come and offer your gift."*

The parallel here with the guilt offering is unmistakeable. Christians do not bring offerings to the temple, but the point of

	Old Testament Sacrifice	New Testament Sacrifice	Scripture Reference
Sweet Savor Sacrifices	The Burnt Offering	Jesus' and our devotion to God	Ephesians 5: 1,2 Romans 12: 1, 2
	The Grain Offering	Giving back a contribution to God	Matthew 6: 19-21 Romans 8, 9
	The Drink Offering	Pouring out our life for God	Luke 22: 20 Philippians 2: 16
	The Fellowship Offering	Celebrating our blessings from God	John 10: 10 1 Thess 5: 16
Blood Sacrifices	The Sin Offering	Jesus' sacrifice for our sins	1 Peter 1: 18, 19 2 Cor 5: 21
	The Guilt Offering	Maintaining a relationship with one another	Matthew 5: 23, 24

Jesus is that if we are worshiping God, yet sinned against our brother, then as in the guilt offering, we must give first priority to confessing and getting it right with our brother. Notice that, as is usual in the New Covenant, a legal requirement (full restitution plus twenty percent) is not defined. Instead Jesus leaves us free to work out the details in love with our brother or sister. The point in either case is that if we are out of fellowship with our brother or sister, it will inevitably affect our relationship with God, and God expects us to make resolving conflict quickly a very high priority.

In summary, all the sacrifices invoked by God under the Aaronic priesthood were intended to prefigure the work and ministry of Jesus Christ. These sacrifices were the heart of Judaism and they therefore had great significance to the Jews. However, their true meaning finds its ultimate fulfillment in Jesus Christ. In studying out these sacrifices as types and their New Testament antitypes, we learn a great deal about the kinds of sacrifices God wants from those under the New Covenant. God wants us to give generously from the physical blessings he has given us. God expects us to devote our lives without reservation—to pour ourselves out for him. God wants us to be devoted, but he also wants us to be exuberant about having a relationship with him.

Parties are the order of the day. We are reminded of our absolute, abject dependence for salvation and a relationship with God on the sacrifice of Jesus Christ on the cross. The blood of Jesus is the only way to a right relationship with God and with one another. Praise God for the lamb, chosen before the creation of the world.

Endnotes

1 The higher the position of leadership of the offender, the more valuable the animal required to make atonement. Priests and elders of the community were to bring a bull, lesser leaders were to bring a male goat, while the common people were to bring a female goat or a lamb.

The Old Covenant Feasts Prefigure Specific Aspects of the Christian Life

Get rid of the old yeast that you may be a new batch without yeast—as you really are. For Christ, our Passover lamb, has been sacrificed. Therefore let us keep the Festival, not with the old yeast, the yeast of malice and wickedness, but with bread made without yeast, the bread of sincerity and truth.

1 Corinthians 5:7,8

"When you enter the land that the Lord will give you as he promised, observe this ceremony. And when your children ask you, 'What does this ceremony mean to you?' then tell them, 'It is the Passover sacrifice to our LORD who passed over the houses of the Israelites in Egypt and spared our homes when he struck down the Egyptians'" (Exodus 12:25-27). With these and other words, God commanded his people, through Moses, to celebrate the Passover. The Passover is a reminder of the night that the destroying angel passed through Egypt to kill the firstborn in every household. The firstborn of Israel were saved from death through the blood of a lamb, sprinkled on the wooden beam over their doors. The angel "passed over" these houses.

"For I received from the Lord what I also passed on to you: The Lord Jesus on the night he was betrayed, took bread, and when he had given thanks, he broke it and said, 'This is my body, which is for you; do this in remembrance of me.' In the same way, after supper he took the cup, saying 'This cup is the new

covenant in my blood; do this, whenever you drink it, in remembrance of me.' For whenever you eat this bread and drink this cup, you proclaim the Lord's death until he comes" (1 Corinthians 11:23-26).

With these and other words, God commanded spiritual Israel, through Paul, to celebrate the Lord's Supper. The Lord's Supper is a reminder of the death of the Lamb of God, Jesus Christ, whose blood was poured out over a wooden beam in order to save those under the New Covenant. The Passover was given by God to Abraham's physical descendants as a remembrance of their salvation from physical death, while the Lord's Supper was given by God to Abraham's spiritual descendants as a remembrance of their salvation from spiritual death.

Is the parallel an accident? Consider the fact that when Jesus instituted the Lord's Supper, he and his apostles were celebrating the Passover meal. Both the Passover meal and the Lord's Supper include unleavened bread and wine. The death of Jesus on the cross occurred on the same day that the Jews celebrated the Passover. As with the type, so with the antitype. On the night Jesus was betrayed, he was well aware of the signifigance of the timing of this last meal with his apostles. He had already said to his followers that he had come, not to abolish the law, but to fulfill it (Matthew 5:17). On the night of his last Passover on the earth, he was about to demonstrate this claim by fulfilling what was foreshadow in the Passover. Once again, we see God using an event in the history of his chosen people as a prefigure of a key aspect of the New Covenant. God had planned all along to make the death of Jesus be an antitype to the death of the Passover lamb which had occurred over fourteen centuries earlier. He also planned from the very beginning to make the Passover feast and the Lord's Supper a type/antitype pair.

When one reads the Old Testament, especially the book of Leviticus, it is hard to miss the fact that God instituted a great number of ceremonies, festivals and feasts. These feasts were given by God to his people with two general purposes in mind. Some of the feasts were intended to help Israel to remember specific events in their past (or in one case, in their future) which could help them to reflect on how much they needed to rely on him. The others were intended, not to remember any one specific event, but to cause them to contemplate the blessings they had in a relationship with him. We will see that the antitypes to these feasts in the New Testament have the same purpose.

There are seven major feasts instituted in the book of Leviticus. All seven are described in some detail in Leviticus chapter twenty-three. In addition, more information and commandments related to these feasts are scattered throughout Leviticus, as well as Exodus, Numbers, Deuteronomy and elsewhere. The seven feasts can be separated into two categories. There were five one-day feasts. These were the Passover, the Feast of Firstfruits, the Feast of Weeks (also known as the Feast of Pentecost), the Feast of trumpets (the Jewish New Year feast) and the Day of Atonement. Each of the feasts was intended to remind Israel of a specific event in the nation of Israel and its relationship with God. It will be shown in this chapter that each of the five one-day feasts are types of specific days/events in the life of a Christian which God wants us to be reminded of as well.

The other two feasts could better be described as festivals, as they occurred over a seven day period. These were the Feast of Unleavened bread, a seven day period of communal worship which was preceded by the Passover. The Feast of First Fruits was celebrated on the second day of Unleavened Bread as well. The second week-long festival was the Feast of Tabernacles (also known as the Feast of Booths). The Day of Atonement fell on a date five days before the Feast of Tabernacles. Both of the week-long festivals were intended by God to be reminders of the nature of their relationship with him. Of course, their antitypes in the New Covenant will serve the same purpose as well.

Other prescribed festivals of the Jews bear mentioning in this context as well. There was the weekly day of rest, the Sabbath, which was described in an earlier chapter as a type. There were also the monthly New Moon festivals. In the earliest times, these were celebrated on the day following the first appearance of a new moon in the sky. Later, the Jews prepared a calendar years in advance, including designated New Moon days based on astronomical calculations. This allowed the Jews to prepare ahead of time for these festivals. The dates of all seven Jewish festivals were set based on the timing of the New Moons. In addition, the Jews had their Sabbath years and Jubilee years, as mentioned previously.

Lastly, there are two additional feasts celebrated by most Jews which were instituted after Sinai, and which therefore are not mentioned in the Pentateuch. These are the Feast of Purim and the Feast of Hannukah. The Feast of Purim is a three day festival established to remember the salvation of the Jews from their persecutors during the time of Esther (Esther 9:26-32). Hanukkah (or Chanukkah) is an eight day festival which was created by the Jews in the second century B.C. to commemorate the reconsecration of the Temple after the horrible persecutions and desecration of the temple under Antiochus Epiphanes in 167-164 B.C.

There is one obvious teaching which one can glean from all these feasts and festivals. If one can assume that they were all given by God to his people, then it becomes clear that from God's perspective, it is very important for those who are in a relationship with him to spend time remembering the many blessings he has given them. The importance of remembering the blessings of God is stressed repeatedly in the Old Testament. For example, consider Deuteronomy 8:10-19. This is an extended quote, but it has a powerful message:

> When you have eaten and are satisfied, praise the LORD your God for the good land he has given you. Be careful that you **do not forget the LORD your God,** failing to observe his commands, his laws and his decrees that I am giving you this day. Otherwise, when you eat and are satisfied, when you build fine houses and settle down, and when your herds and flocks grow large and your silver and gold increase and all you have is multiplied, then your heart will become proud and **you will forget the LORD your God** who brought you out of Egypt, out of the land of slavery. He led you through the vast and dreadful desert, that thirsty and waterless land, with its venomous snakes and scorpions. He brought you water out of hard rock. He gave you manna to eat in the desert, something your fathers had never known, to humble and to test you so that in the end it might go well with you. You might say to yourself, "My power and the strength of my hands have produced this wealth for me." But **remember the LORD your God,** for it is he who gives you the ability to produce wealth, and so confirms his covenant, which he swore to your forefathers, at is is today.
>
> **If you ever forget the LORD your God** and follow other gods and worship and bow down to them, I testify against you today that you will surely be destroyed.

It may not be obvious at first glance but there is a great danger lurking behind any blessings which one receives from God. When we are blessed by God, the tendency to forget where the blessings come from and to begin to give ourselves the credit for our "accomplishments" is always present. The festivals and feasts in the Old Covenant were given specifically so that the Jews would not ever forget from where their blessings came.

Are those under the New Covenant immune from the temptation to forget where their blessings came from? Clearly not. *"What do you have that you did not receive? And if you did receive it, why do you boast as though you did not?"* (1 Corinthians 4:7). Apparently the Corinthian disciples struggled with this sin. Remember that the Old Testament laws were a shadow of things to come. If the Old Covenant feasts were intended to help the Jews to remember God's blessings, then they were intended to do the same for those who are Christians. This is a very good reason to study the type/antitype relationship implied by the Old Testament festivals. God expects and even demands that we take the time to remember our blessings and to be thankful for them.

THE PASSOVER (pesach)[1]

The Passover (*pesach* in Hebrew) was a one-day feast instituted by God in order that the Jews would remember the "passing over" of the destroying angel, when the firstborn of every household in Egypt was killed. This was the last of the plagues which God brought on Egypt so that Pharaoh would let God's people go out into the desert to worship him. Remember from chapter one that the entire event of leaving Egypt, passing through the Sea of Reeds and entering the wilderness is a foreshadow of those under the New Covenant leaving their life of sin and entering into a saved relationship with God. God established the Passover because he wanted the Jews to never forget that it was only by his miraculous power that they were saved, both from slavery and from the destroying angel.

To this very day, Jews hold the Passover to be their second most significant feast, after *Yom Kippur,* the Day of Atonement. Every Jewish family, even some of the least religiously observant, celebrates a Passover meal in their homes very similar to the one instituted by God in Exodus chapter twelve. Very precise directions were given by God in Exodus for how the Passover meal was to be celebrated. Every single detail of this meal has deep significance for those who are saved by the blood of Jesus. We will see that God intended the Passover meal all along to be a reminder, not just for the Jews, but for Christians.

The historical record of the Passover is found in Exodus chapters eleven through thirteen. God had already brought nine unnatural disasters, commonly known as "plagues" on Egypt in order to convince Pharaoh to let his people go out into the desert to worship him. After some of the plagues, Pharaoh had repented and agreed to let the Jews go out to worship, only to change his mind and harden his heart when he thought about the implications of letting them free, even for a short time. God told Moses *"I will bring one more plague on Pharaoh and on Egypt. After that, he will let you go from here, and when he does, he will drive you out completely"* (Exodus 11:1). So Moses shared with the people what God had told him; *"About midnight I will go throughout Egypt. Every firstborn son in Egypt will die, from the firstborn son of Pharaoh, who sits on the throne, to the firstborn son of the slave girl, who is at her hand mill, and all the firstborn of the cattle as well"* (Exodus 11:4,5). Since the Jews themselves were slaves, this terrifying plague would presumably include the firstborn sons of every Jewish family. With few exceptions, the previous nine plagues had affected both Jew and Egyptian.

God provided his people with a way to avoid this disastrous plague. Each family was to take a year old male lamb *"without defect,"* slaughter it at twilight and put some of the blood of that sacrifice on the sides and tops of the wooden doorframes on their homes. God promised that if they would perform this sacrifice, he would "pass over" their houses when he came to destroy the first born in Egypt. The families were to eat the slaughtered lamb that night. Prophetically, God told them not to break any of the bones of the lamb they slaughtered (Exodus 12:46). They were also instructed to eat unleavened bread and bitter herbs with their Passover meal. God told them to eat the meal in haste, *"...with your cloak tucked into your belt, your sandals on your feet and your staff in your hand"* (Exodus 12:11).

What God had told Moses is exactly what happened. On that same night, the LORD struck down the firstborn sons throughout Egypt, right up to Pharaoh's house, except for those whose houses were marked with the blood of the Passover lamb. Pharaoh called Moses and Aaron into his palace and ordered them to leave into the desert to worship Yahweh. Unlike in his previous similar orders, he told them to go with their herds and belongings. The Jews went on their way laden with many valuable gifts from their Egyptian neighbors—eager to see them go. The Jews left in such haste that they were unable to add leaven to their bread dough. The rest of the story of the Exodus has already been described in chapter one. The people escaped from slavery in Egypt, symbolic of those under the New Covenant escaping from slavery to sin. They were only able to escape by passing through the waters of the Red Sea, as they were baptized into Moses.

At the same time that God performed the Passover miracle, he also instructed his people to perform a ritual Passover meal every year from that day forward as a reminder of how he had freed them from their captivity:[2]

> *"This is a day you are to commemorate; for the generations to come, you shall celebrate it as a festival to the LORD—a lasting ordinance"* (Exodus 12:14).

> *"When you enter the land that the LORD will give you as he promised, observe this ceremony. And when your children ask you, 'What does this ceremony mean to you?' tell them, 'It is the Passover sacrifice to the LORD, who passed over the houses of the Israelites in Egypt and spared our homes when he struck down the Egyptians'"* (Exodus 12:25-27).

If there ever was a command God gave to the Jews which they have followed religiously, it is the command to celebrate the Passover meal annually.

Every year, Jewish families perform a ritual cleansing of all yeast from their house before celebrating the Passover. On the night of the Passover meal, known as the "Seder," the extended family gathers together to share the meal of lamb, unleavened bread and bitter herbs. The lamb is eaten to remember the sacrifice and the escape from destruction. The unleavened bread is to remember the haste of their escape from slavery. The bitter herbs are eaten to remind them of the bitterness of enslavement under Pharaoh. Traditionally, the patriarch of the family reads from set passages in Exodus. Before the readings it is traditional to choose a young boy from the family to ask four questions. One of these is "What does this mean?" (Exodus 13:4), after which the whole group is taught about the meaning of the Passover. The other three questions are, "Why is this night different from all other nights?" "Why on this night do we only eat unleavened bread?" and "Why eat bitter herbs?" Traditionally, three pieces of unleavened bread are used. The third piece of bread is broken, hidden away, only to be recovered and distributed to all later. Additionally, four cups of wine are shared. For the Jews, the third cup, shared just at the end of the supper, is known as the cup of redemption.

Every single detail of this feast serves as a wonderful foreshadowing of salvation in Jesus Christ. To quote from Phillip Lester[3], "The essence of the Passover is that of the Lord's Supper. It is all about remembering where we have come from, the bitterness of our enslavement (to sin), and the price of our deliverance by the blood of the Lamb." The Passover of the Jews is a type, while the Lord's Supper is the antitype. In fact, it would probably be more accurate to call the meal on the night Jesus was betrayed the Last Seder, rather than the Last Supper. This truly was the last Passover meal before the Passover found its fulfillment in the New Testament antitype—The Lord's Supper (Not that there is anything wrong with a Christian celebrating a Seder meal). This is exactly what Jesus meant as he shared the Last Supper with his closest friends:

> Then came the day of Unleavened Bread on which the Passover lamb had to be sacrificed. Jesus sent Peter and John, saying "Go and make preparations for us to eat the Passover...."
> When the hour had come, Jesus and his apostles reclined at the table. And he said unto them, "I have eagerly desired to eat this Passover with you before I suffer. For I tell you, I will not eat it again until it finds fulfillment in the kingdom of God" (Luke 22:7,8,14-16).

It this passage, Jesus is telling the disciples that the next Passover celebration would be in the form of its New Covenant antitype—the Lord's Supper. We are reminded one more time of Jesus' claim that he did not come to bring the law to an end but to bring it to fulfillment in the New Covenant.

Consider some of the type/antitype relationships between the Passover and the Lord's Supper. As mentioned in the introduction to this chapter, when God made the Passover to be a type of the Lord's Supper he was not being subtle, given that Jesus celebrated the Last Supper on the night of the Passover meal. In the

Passover meal, an innocent lamb is sacrificed. The Lord's Supper commemorates the death of Jesus who, *"was led like a lamb to the slaughter, and as a sheep before his shearers is silent, so he did not open his mouth."* The Passover lamb had to be without physical defect. The antitype to the lamb, Jesus Christ was without spiritual defect. He never sinned.

The original Passover lambs were killed to save people who were under a death sentence, as the death angel was to pass through Egypt that night. The Lord's Supper commemorates Jesus' death for a people who were under a spiritual death sentence. *"But because of his great love for us, God, who is rich in mercy, made us alive with Christ even when we were dead in transgressions—it is by grace you have been saved"* (Ephesians 2:4,5). The Passover lamb's sacrificial blood was sprinkled on the wooden cross-beam over the Israelite's doors. When they did this, the Jews had no idea whatever that they were prefiguratively acting out what happened to the blood of Jesus, *"the lamb of God who takes away the sins of the world"* (John 1:29), which was to be shed on a cross-beam fourteen centuries later. Because of the blood of the Passover lamb, God "passed over" the houses of the Jews. Because of the blood of the Lamb of God, *"slain from the creation of the world,"* God will pass over the sin in our own personal house—our lives.

The five type/antitype parallels already mentioned are only the beginning. God commanded the Jews not to break any of the bones of the Passover lamb, *"Do not break any of the bones"* (Exodus 12:46). How did the Jews interpret this seemingly obscure command? What did God have in mind? It was a mystery to them. The mystery is revealed in the gospel. The command to not break any of the bones of the Passover lamb is a prophecy of the antitype to the Passover lamb, Jesus Christ. It is reminiscent of the messianic prophecy in Psalms 22:17, *"I can count all my bones."*

Jesus was crucified along with two thieves. Jesus died first of the three, most likely because of the extremely rough treatment he received even before being crucified. Because the crucifixion happened on the same day as the Passover meal, the Jews wanted the bodies taken down from the cross before sunset. When they made this request, the Roman soldiers broke the bones of the two thieves crucified along with Jesus. They did this because it was common knowledge that once the condemned person's legs were broken, he could no longer push himself up to breathe. The two thieves therefore died within a few minutes. When the soldiers came to Jesus, they did not break his legs because he had already died (John 19:31-33). Thus was fulfilled the prophecy, dutifully acted out every year, when the Jews carefully avoided breaking any of the bones of the Passover lamb.

The Jews had to flee Egypt so quickly that they were not even able to add leaven their bread. We have already seen in chapter six that leaven in the Old Testament is a type of sin in the New Testament. Jesus expects those who follow him to flee from their life of spiritual slavery in sin without looking back (Luke 9:62). Of course, both the Passover meal and the Lord's Supper include the eating of unleavened bread. In the Lord's Supper the unleavened bread is meant to symbolize the body of Jesus whose life was without leaven (sin). Before the Passover meal, Jews go through a traditional searching of the house to remove any possible leaven from their homes. Similarly, God expects us before we even take the Lord's Supper to look at our own personal spiritual house in order to discard the unspiritual leaven we will inevitably find there:

> *A man ought to examine himself before he eats of the bread and drinks of the cup* (1 Corinthians 11:28).
>
> *Your boasting is not good. Don't you know that a little yeast works through the whole batch of dough? Get rid of the old yeast that you may be a new batch without yeast—* ***as you really are.*** *For Christ, our Passover lamb, has been sacrificed. Therefore let us keep the Festival...* (1 Corinthians 5:6,7,8).

Here, the imagery of the Passover meal and the Lord's Supper is closely intertwined. Note that the Lord's Supper is both a reminder of the already accomplished fact of being without sin and a call to walk away from current sin in our lives.

As part of the Passover meal, God commanded the eating of bitter herbs. This was to remind the Jews of the bitterness of slavery in Egypt. One would think that the Jews would never forget how terrible it was to be in bondage. One would be wrong. While wandering in the wilderness, the Jews soon forgot the horrors of slavery and longed to return to Egypt (Numbers 20:5,6). This is why God gave them the Passover as a remembrance, not only of the amazing miracle of their release from bondage, but also as a reminder of the bitterness of slavery. What a great foreshadow for those under the New Covenant who celebrate the Lord's Supper. One would think that it would be easy for a disciple of Jesus to remember how bitter the life of sin was and how amazingly better their life is under the Good Shepherd Jesus Christ who gives life to the full (paraphrasing John 10:10,11). Again, one would be very wrong. Christians need to be reminded how truly bitter life under slavery to sin was. Here the imagery of the Passover meal and that of the Lord's Supper are closely intertwined.

Although it is not commanded in the Pentateuch, the Jews have an ancient tradition of sharing three loaves of bread and four cups of wine. The third piece of unleavened bread is broken into pieces and the pieces are hidden around the house. After the meal, the family searches the house, recovering the pieces and sharing them together. Little do most of them know that they are acting out a foreshadow of the bodily resurrection of Jesus in this interesting part of the Passover meal. The traditional third cup of wine is drunk immediately after the meal. The Jews recognize this as the cup of redemption. This third cup is the one Jesus took on the night he was sacrificed as a Passover lamb. *"After supper he took the cup, saying, 'This is the new covenant in my blood...'"* If only the Jews who shared this third cup had any idea how prophetic the cup of redemption was to become when Jesus shared it with his apostles the night before he gave a sacrifice for redemption of the whole world.

There are three themes in this chapter. One of these is that the entire Old Testament points to Jesus Christ. The second is that the abundant and intricate foreshadowings in the Old Testament prove beyond a doubt that the Bible is inspired by God. The additional theme in this chapter is that God wants and even expects those who come to him to take time to make a regular habit of remembering what he has done in their lives. In both the Passover and the Lord's Supper, God is calling Christians to remember the death of the sacrificial lamb Jesus Christ and the miracle of salvation which it works in the lives of those who put their faith in the blood of the Paschal lamb.

Perhaps Christian parents would do well to institute their own ceremony similar to the four questions asked by Jewish children. Ritual remembering is valuable to all disciples of Jesus. This truth applies even more so to their children. In order to bring home the parallel message of the Lord's Supper and the Passover, one helpful idea would be for a Christian family or a group of disciples of Jesus to celebrate a Passover Seder together. What might make this even more encouraging would be to invite a Jewish Christian to take part. The point is that in these two ceremonies God is telling us that we need to be reminded of the bitterness of sin and the wonderful salvation wrought by the blood of the Passover lamb.

THE FEAST OF FIRSTFRUITS

Most believers in Jesus are at least casually aware of the Passover and the fact that it occurs somewhere near the time of the death of Jesus in the Jewish calendar. By contrast, Christians in general know absolutely nothing about the Feast of Firstfruits: when it is celebrated, its purpose in the Law of Moses, and especially its role as a foreshadow of the Christian dispensation.

The Feast of Firstfruits was instituted as part of the Law of Moses at Sinai. The purpose, timing and ceremony of the feast are found in Leviticus 23:9-14. Basically, this feast was created by God in order for the people to celebrate the promise inherent in the very first fruit of the harvest of their crops. It was not so much a harvest festival, but an anticipation-of-the-harvest festival. Firstfruits was celebrated several weeks before any crop was harvested. The Jews took a portion of the grain when it just began to produce a head of seeds—well before it became mature. Many ancient people had harvest festivals, but the Jews must have been unique among their neighbors to have a festival for a harvest which still lay in the future. To create an analogy, if one were to plant a large garden with many different crops, the Feast of Firstfruits would be celebrated when that very first crop was on the plants, but definitely not yet mature enough to eat. If one lived in the central United States, this would happen in May at the earliest, but in Palestine this fell in March or April. This first fruit of one's garden would be brought before God and dedicated to him both in recognition that all good fruit comes from him and in anticipation of and request for a good harvest the rest of the year.

> "When you enter the land I am going to give you and you reap its harvest, bring to the priest a sheaf of the first grain of the harvest. He is to wave the sheaf before the Lord so it will be accepted on your behalf; the priest is to wave it on the day after the Sabbath" (Leviticus 23:10,11).

For our purposes, the timing of the Feast of Firstfruits is vitally important. As one can see from the passage above, this festival was celebrated on the day after the Sabbath. Which Sabbath? Actually, in the Jewish calendar, the Feast of Firstfruits came to be celebrated on the day after the Sabbath which fell during the Feast of Unleavened Bread. It is possible to get confused here, so let us examine this carefully. For Jewish people, the term "Passover" has evolved to cover the Passover meal, or Seder, the seven-day Feast of Unleavened Bread which directly followed the Passover and the Feast of Firstfruits which falls on the second day of the Feast of Unleavened Bread. In other words, for the Jews, the Passover covers eight days and three festivals, beginning with the preparatory Passover meal, including the entire Feast of Unleavened Bread and the one-day Feast of Firstfruits.

If one considers the timing of the Feast of Firstfruits carefully, a riveting conclusion jumps out. Jesus was resurrected from the dead on the Feast of Firstfruits! Jesus was crucified on Friday[4], the day of the Passover Feast, which was the 14th of *Nisan*. The following day, the 15th of *Nisan* was a Sabbath and was also the first day of the Feast of Unleavened Bread. The third day, the 16th of *Nisan*, a Sunday, was the Feast of Firstfruits. It was also the day Jesus rose from the dead. God gave the Feast of Firstfruits to the Jews so that they would remember that they were entirely dependent on him for their physical blessings. As is by now a very familiar pattern, God also had a deeper spiritual meaning in the Feast of Firstfruits for those who would be saved under the New Covenant. The Feast of Firstfruits is a reminder of our total dependence on God to inherit eternal life. It is also a foreshadow of the resurrection of Jesus.

In the Old Covenant type, the Feast of Firstfruits, the firstfruit if the harvest was brought and presented to Yahweh. The presentation of the firstfruits of their fields represented an expectation on the part of the Jews of an abundant future harvest. In the antitype, the resurrection, Jesus arose as the first fruits from the dead. The resurrection of Jesus is the firstfruits, the harbinger and the promise of the final resurrection of all mankind. *"Multitudes who sleep in the dust of the earth will awake: some to everlasting life, others to shame and everlasting contempt"* (Daniel 12:2). To support this claim, consider 1 Corinthians 15:20,21 where Paul is discussing the resurrection of the dead:

> But Christ has indeed been raised from the dead, the firstfruits of those who have fallen asleep. For since death came through a man, the resurrection of the dead comes also through a man.

In other words, the resurrection of Jesus is the firstfruits of all those who have died. It is a promise of a future harvest of souls—the resurrection from the dead. Based on this passage we can assume that Paul was well aware that the resurrection of Jesus was the antitype to the Feast of Firstfruits.

It is worth noting that Jesus was not the first person in the Bible resurrected from the dead. One could mention Lazarus (John 11) or the Shunnamite woman's son (2 Kings 4:8-37) and others. However, in each of these cases, we are led to assume that the person miraculously raised to life later died in the usual way. Jesus is the firstfruits from the dead in that he rose to everlasting life with God.

Consider also Colossians 1:18:

> And he is the head of the body, the church; he is the beginning and the firstborn from among the dead, so that in everything he might have the supremacy.

Jesus is the firstborn—the firstfruits from among those who have died and been raised to eternal life with God. As Paul told his hearers in Athens, the resurrection of Jesus proves that God has set aside a day in which all men will be judged with justice (Acts 17:31). This is true because Jesus is the first fruit of a vastly larger harvest which will be resurrected from among the dead to face judgment. From the giving of the Law of Moses on, the Jews celebrated the gathering of the physical firstfruits, never realizing that they were prophetically acting out the resurrection of Jesus and its promise of a harvest of souls at the end of time.

If the resurrection of Jesus is prophesied in the Feast of Firstfruits, a natural question arises. Should those under the New Covenant remember the event in some sort of annual Christian firstfruits ceremony as God told the Jews to do? The answer is that God does not command such a celebration, which leaves it up to individual Christians. The exact historical roots of the religious holiday now known as Easter are somewhat obscure. One can assume that it was started by early church leaders trying to encourage the disciples out of concern that they not forget the resurrection of Jesus. Unfortunately, despite good intentions, over time the church's celebration of the resurrection acquired strong pagan overtones. Easter took on aspects of a fertility rite, even borrowing its name from the pagan god Ishtar.

Christians should probably put aside such pagan aspects in their commemoration of the resurrection of Jesus! However, some have overreacted to the Roman Catholic holiday by declaring it a sin to celebrate Easter. If there is any message to be gleaned from this chapter it is that people tend to forget. Regular reminders of such blessed events as the resurrection of Jesus are a very good thing.

For the Jews, the Feast of Firstfruits was about faith. From the first sign of the development of seed on the grain the Jews celebrated a harvest which did not yet exist, on faith that God would take care of their needs. It is the same for the follower of Jesus. The antitype is all about faith as well. We take the resurrection of Jesus from the dead as a promise of a great future harvest. We understand that we will be part of this harvest of souls for eternity. Why not begin celebrating now? Let the party begin.

THE FEAST OF UNLEAVENED BREAD

As previously noted, the Feast of Unleavened Bread is part of the three celebrations which comprise what became collectively known as the Passover. The Feast of Unleavened Bread was a seven-day festival which was celebrated immediately after the day of the Passover meal, making the entire Passover an eight day event. The Feast of Unleavened Bread was instituted at the same time as the Passover meal, as described in Exodus 12:[5]

The Old Covenant Feasts Prefigure Specific Aspects of the Christian Life   181

> "Celebrate the Feast of Unleavened Bread, because it was on this very day that I brought your divisions out of Egypt. Celebrate this day as a lasting ordinance for the generations to come. In the first month you are to eat bread made without yeast, from the evening of the fourteenth day until the evening of the twenty-first day. For seven days no yeast is to be found in your houses. And whoever eats anything with yeast in it must be cut off from the community of Israel, whether he is an alien or native-born" (Exodus 12:17-19).

One can see from this description that the Feast of Unleavened Bread was designed to celebrate and to remember the Exodus—the release of God's people from captivity and slavery in Egypt. It is important to distinguish the Passover meal from the Feast of Unleavened Bread. The Passover meal was given as a remembrance of Israel's salvation from the destroying angel. It is a foreshadow of salvation through the blood of Jesus as well as a foreshadow of the Lord's Supper. The Feast of Unleavened Bread, on the other hand, was intended as a remembrance of the freedom from slavery which resulted from the Passover event.

Why unleavened bread? For two reasons. One reason was that it was a reminder of the actual events of the Exodus. *"With the dough they had brought from Egypt, they baked cakes of unleavened bread. The dough was without yeast because they had been driven out of Egypt and did not have time to prepare food for themselves"* (Exodus 12:39). The unleavened bread is a reminder of the suddenness and the totality of their release from captivity. As we contemplate this Jewish feast, it can serve the same purpose for us. The second reason God had them use unleavened bread for the seven day feast is that it served as a foreshadow for us of our freedom which is gained when we escape from our own captivity to sin. As we have already seen, yeast is often used in the New Testament as a symbol of the insidious effect of sin, *"A little leaven leavens the whole lump."* This is another example of an Old Covenant feast which is a remembrance of a physical event for the Jews and of a spiritual reality for Christians.

It has already been stated that, the one-day feasts of the Jews were given by God as foreshadows to remind those who are in Christ of a specific event of importance to their spiritual lives, while the week-long festivals were given as foreshadows and reminders of an aspect of Christian living. This will apply to the

Feast of Unleavened Bread. For the Jews it was a remembrance of their freedom from slavery. For the Christian it is a reminder of freedom from sin. Thanks to the Passover event—the sacrificial death of Jesus on the cross—the person who is in Christ is free from the destructive influence of sin in his or her life. Romans 6:5-7 gives us a great reminder of the meaning of all three of the Passover Week festivals.

> *If we have been united with him in his death, we will certainly also be united with him in his resurrection. For we know that our old self was crucified with him so that the body of sin might be rendered powerless, that we should no longer be slaves to sin—because anyone who has died has been freed from sin.*

In this one amazing passage, Paul reminds his readers of the passing over of their sins which resulted from the death of the Passover lamb, Jesus Christ. He also reminds them that without the resurrection of Jesus, which is celebrated in the Feast of Firstfruits, they would not have been raised to live a new life. Most important to the discussion at hand, Paul also reminds his readers that as a result of the Passover and the Firstfruits, they can celebrate a life without leaven—no longer being enslaved to sin. The death of Jesus creates for us a life which is no longer captive to the enslaving aspects of sin.

From the Feast of Unleavened Bread we learn that the Bible is inspired by God! It is amazing how God created these three festivals and was able to interweave their prophetic implications throughout the gospel message. From a practical perspective, we learn that those who are in Christ need to appreciate being forgiven. The Jews took seven days every year out of their busy lives to celebrate freedom from slavery. Freedom from sin is something to be even more excited about. We need to be reminded on a regular basis that no matter what is happening in our lives, be it struggles, challenges or temptations, the simple fact of being free from the destructive, enslaving power of sin is a cause for celebration.

In fact, those who do not celebrate their freedom from sin are in spiritual peril. God gave the Feast of Unleavened Bread to Israel as a regular reminder both of what they had left behind and what they had gained when they left slavery in Egypt. Let us celebrate with our wonderful life of freedom. Let us never act as they did when only a short time after the Exodus the people of Israel became focused on the trials of needing food and water in the desert and actually longed to return to their life of slavery. Yes, this can happen to us. As Paul admonished the Thessalonian disciples, let us *"Be joyful always; pray continually; and give thanks in all circumstances, for this is God's will for you in Christ Jesus"* (1 Thessalonians 5:16).

THE FEAST OF WEEKS/PENTECOST (shavoat)

The fourth feast prescribed in the Old Testament calendar was the Feast of Weeks: *shavoat* in Hebrew. This was the main harvest feast of the Jewish year. The timing of the feast was tied to the Feast of Firstfruits.

> *"From the day after the Sabbath, the day you brought the sheaf of the wave offering, count off seven full weeks. Count off fifty days up to the day after the seventh Sabbath, and then present an offering of new grain to the LORD. From wherever you live, bring two loaves made of two-tenths of an ephah of fine flour, baked with yeast, as a wave offering of firstfruits to the LORD"* (Leviticus 23:15-17).

The Sabbath referred to in this passage from Leviticus is the Passover Sabbath. The day after this Sabbath was the Feast of Firstfruits. The Feast of Weeks got its name from the fact that it fell exactly seven weeks after the Feast of Firstfruits. This feast later came to be known as the Pentecost because it also happens to fall exactly fifty days after the Passover Sabbath.

Notice the phrase *"from wherever you live"* in the passage above. Once Israel entered the Promised Land, they were expected to bring the fruit of their harvest to celebrate the Feast of Weeks in Jerusalem every year, unless it became impossible because they had been scattered too far from the holy city to make the trip. Even then, the Jews were expected to make the journey from such great distances at least at some point in their lives. This fact will be significant when we discuss the New Testament antitype to the Feast of Weeks. In fact, the Jews were expected to travel to the location of the Tabernacle or the Temple three times per year: at Passover, at Pentecost and on the Day of Atonement, which is why these came to be thought of as the three major feasts of Judaism.

The use of the word firstfruits in the above passage can lead to confusion between the Feast of Firstfruits and the Feast of Pentecost. By the time of the Feast of Weeks, which fell in mid May to early June, virtually all the Spring harvest of grain was already in. The Jews were commanded by God to dedicate the firstfruits of all their harvests to him, including the firstfruits of the wombs of their flocks and herds (Exodus 34:19,20), and even their first children. With the Feast of Weeks being the main harvest festival (in fact it is called the Feast of Harvest in Exodus 23:16), it is naturally referred to as a time for dedicating firstfruits. To put it simply, the Feast of Weeks was a firstfruits festival, while the day Jesus was resurrected was the Feast of Firstfruits.

The Feast of Weeks, then, was intended by God as a time for his people to celebrate the harvest of their crops. The people may have done the hard work, but God expected them to remember that in the end it was only through his blessing that they could bring in a crop. The Jews would be perpetually tempted to forget this fact, so God gave them a feast for which they were required to travel to Jerusalem to celebrate. Every year this reminded them that God is responsible for the harvest.

If the Feast of Pentecost is a type, what is the antitype? As with Passover and Firstfruits, God has made it easy for us to determine this one. Seven weeks after Jesus was raised from the dead, tens of thousands of Jews were gathered in Jerusalem from all the nations to which the Jews had been scattered due to their persecutions. They came to Jerusalem to celebrate the Pentecost. Jesus had already ascended into heaven, having told his followers to wait in Jerusalem.

Early that morning, the apostles and other followers gathered together in one place. *"Suddenly a sound like the blowing of a violent wind came from heaven and filled the whole house where they were sitting"* (Acts 2:2). With this attention-grabbing miracle and many others which followed that day, God announced the beginning of his great spiritual harvest. On what Christians now know as "the Day of Pentecost," God poured out the Holy Spirit on the apostles as toungues of fire came to rest on each of them and they were miraculously enabled to speak in the different languages of the Jews from all the nations to which they had been scattered. At this time Peter preached the first public gospel sermon, announcing the New Covenant to the Jews who had come to Jerusalem to celebrate the Feast of Weeks. *"With many other words he warned them; and he pleaded with them, 'Save yourselves from this corrupt generation.' Those who accepted his message were baptized, and about three thousand were added to their number that day"* (Acts 2:40,41). At the Feast of Pentecost, the physical harvest feast of the Jews, the beginning of the spiritual harvest of souls for eternal life was begun. And what a beginning it was! There were about three thousand baptisms on that one day alone.

God used the Feast of Pentecost as a foreshadow of the Day of Pentecost. The physical harvest was a foreshadow of the spiritual harvest. It was also a foreshadow of the outpouring of the Holy Spirit. When God poured out the Holy Spirit on the apostles that Pentecost day, he was announcing that from this day forward, the Holy Spirit would be made available to dwell in anyone who would repent and be baptized.

> Peter replied, "Repent and be baptized, every one of you, in the name of Jesus Christ so that your sins may be forgiven. And you will receive the gift of the Holy Spirit. This promise is for you and your children and for all who are far off—for all whom the Lord our God will call" (Acts 2:38,39).

The Feast of Weeks served as a foreshadow of the spiritual harvest in the Kingdom of God. On the Day of Pentecost, the Christian church had its birthday. Some have argued that after the day Jesus died (Passover) and the day Jesus was resurrected (Firstfruits), the Day of Pentecost is the third most significant day in the entire spiritual history of humanity. No wonder God gave the Jews a feast day to serve as a type of this great day.

What is the message of the Feast of Weeks/Pentecost for those under the New Covenant? God wants us to work very hard to yield a spiritual crop of souls for eternity. Although God brings about the harvest, it does not happen without some human effort. God celebrates over even one soul being saved—enough to set up the Feast of Weeks as a foreshadow of this great harvest. Having said that, let those who bring the harvest of souls into the kingdom of God never forget who gives them the ability to bring in the crop. As Paul told the Corinthian disciples:

> *I planted the seed, Apollos watered it, but God made it grow. So neither he who plants nor he who waters is anything, but only God, who makes things grow. The man who plants and the man who waters have one purpose, and each will be rewarded according to his own labor. For we are God's fellow workers; you are God's field, God's building* (1 Corinthians 3:6-9).

Through the Feast of Pentecost, God teaches us that we should labor like a hard working farmer to bring the spiritual crop of souls into his kingdom, but we should never forget that all the glory goes to the one without whom there would be no harvest at all. And when we see the harvest come, let us celebrate!

THE FEAST OF TRUMPETS (Rosh Hashannah)

In modern Jewish culture, *Rosh Hashannah,* the feast of trumpets, has become one of the most significant religious holidays along with *Yom Kippur,* Hannukuh and the Passover. It is celebrated as the Jewish New Year. In fact, the Hebrew words *Rosh Hashannah* means "head of the year." One should bear in mind that for the Jews there are two major New Years every calendar year. The religious New Year falls on the Passover, which is the fourteenth of *Nisan* in March or April. The civil New Year comes almost six months later, on the first of Tishri, the date of *Rosh Hashannah.* For the Jews, the change of year number occurs on the Feast of Trumpets. For example, October 4, 2005 is the beginning of the year 5766 in the Jewish calendar. On the other hand, when the Jews in the kingdom period kept track of how many years their kings had ruled, they counted their regnal year from the fourteenth of *Nisan,* not the first of *Tishri.* Making matters even harder to keep track of for non-Jews is the fact that both New Year celebrations move around on the modern Gregorian calendar. This is true because the Jews use a lunar calendar. Their months begin with a new moon. Depending on where the new moon falls, the Feast of Trumpets can be anywhere from early September to early October.

At first, it may seem strange to non-Jews to have two New Years, but if one thinks about it, it really is not so different from other cultures. Many of us trace our year from the beginning of the school year in September. For myself as a college professor, when people ask me how my year is going, I usually think back to the previous September, not to the previous January 1st to answer the question.

The Feast of Trumpets has not always been called *Rosh Hashannah* by the Jews. When the holiday was originally instituted, as described in Leviticus 23:24,25, it was called *Yom Teruah,* which translates as the day of sounding the shofar. The shofar was a trumpet made from a ram's horn (see picture below). This explains the name "the Feast of Trumpets."

The original Feast of Trumpets was not necessarily created as a New Year celebration. One can read in Leviticus 23:24,25:

> *"Say to the Israelites: On the first day of the seventh month will be a day of rest for you, a sacred assembly proclaimed with a trumpet call. You must not do any work and you must offer a burnt offering to the LORD."*

There is little said here which could serve as a clue to the purpose of the Feast of Trumpets. The passage in Numbers 29:1-6 doesn't add much to this description. It has already been mentioned that in ancient Israel, the timing of the New Moon was based on actual visual sighting of the slight crescent of a new moon. Out of concern that they might miss the correct day of the New Moon on which *Rosh Hashannah* falls, Jewish teachers actually added a second day to the Feast of Trumpets just in case the crescent moon could not be seen due to clouds in the night sky. The feast took on an aspect of being on guard or being alert—waiting for God's timing. Many rabbis actually suggested that the Jews not sleep at all on the night of *Rosh Hashannah*. The Feast of Trumpets became symbolic of a Day of Judgment for the Jews. Jewish teachers called the Feast of Trumpets to be a day of self-reflection and repentance for Israel in order to be prepared for God's judgment.

There was good reason for the Jews to associate the blowing of the trumpets on *Yom Teruah* with judgment. When they heard the trumpet blast at Sinai they trembled:

> *When the people...they trembled with fear. They stayed at a distance and said to Moses, "Speak to us yourself and we will listen. But do not have God speak to us or we will die."*
> *Moses said to the people, "Do not be afraid. God has come to test you, so that the fear of God will be with you to keep you from sinning"* (Exodus 20:18-20).[6]

When Israel heard the trumpet blast at Sinai it further caused them to associate judgment and repentance with the Feast of Trumpets. As an example, when the Israelite armies surrounded Jericho, it was shofars which were blown, bringing down the walls of the city. All this will help us to understand what God intended the Feast of Trumpets to foreshadow.

The point has already been made that the single-day feasts are all types of a specific event of relevance for the believer in Jesus Christ. The Feast of Trumpets is no exception to this rule. Although the feast has significance to the Jews as well, God intended all along for the Jewish Feast of Trumpets to be a type of the day Jesus will return to the earth to bring an end to this present world and to usher in the final Day of Judgment.

When Jesus described his own return at the end of days, he used very familiar imagery (familiar to the Jews, that is) from the Feast of Trumpets.

> *"At that time the sign of the Son of Man will appear in the sky, and all the nations of the earth will mourn. They will see the Son of Man coming on the clouds of the sky, with power and great glory. And he will send his angels with a loud trumpet call, and they will gather his elect from the four winds, from one end of the heavens to the other"* (Matthew 24:30,31).

Immediately after making this statement, Jesus began a lengthy discourse on being watchful and ready for the day of his coming: *"No one knows the hour..."* (v. 36), *"Therefore keep watch..."* (v. 42), *"So you also must be ready..."* (v. 44), *"Therefore keep watch, because you do not know the day or the hour"* (25:13). This sermon would have fit perfectly with the theme of every Feast of Trumpets celebration for the prior fourteen centuries.

The antitype to the Feast of Trumpets is mentioned in other passages in the New Testament as well. The return of Christ and the resurrection of all humanity at the end of this present age are also described in 1 Corinthians 15:51-53:

> Listen,...we will all be changed—in a flash, in the twinkling of an eye, at the last trumpet. For the trumpet will sound, the dead will be raised imperishable, and we will be changed. For the perishable must clothe itself with the imperishable, and the mortal with immortality.

This final trumpet blast will be the realization of all those annual shofar blasts in Israel. Repentance and watchfulness will bear fruit in eternal life.

Paul returns one more time to this theme in 1 Thessalonians 4:15,16:

> According to the Lord's own word, we tell you that we who are still alive, who are left till the coming of the Lord, will certainly not precede those who have fallen asleep. For the Lord himself will come down from heaven, with a loud command, with the voice of the archangel and with the trumpet call of God, and the dead in Christ will rise first.

After this impressive description of the return of Christ, Paul continues with a call to continual repentance and readiness which may very well have reflected some of the lessons he heard on the Feast of Trumpets as a young Pharisee-in-training.

If one assumes that God designed the entire Old Testament as prophetic preparation for the coming of Jesus and his ministry to the world, then it becomes only reasonable to imagine the festivals he gave to the Jews to be foreshadows of the great moments in the new dispensation brought in by Christ. When one reads the New Testament, it is very clear that the day Jesus comes again, with a loud command, the voice of the archangel and with the trumpet call of God, that will be a very great day indeed. It should not surprise us at all that God provided a foreshadow of this great day in the festivals celebrated by the Jews. The Feast of Trumpets is the Old Testament type. The return of Jesus and the Day of Judgment of all humanity is the antitype. As the Jewish leaders taught, and as Jesus and Paul preached, we would do well to stay watchful and ready for that day. Let us not be like the foolish virgins in Matthew chapter twenty-five who let their lamps go out. Let us live a life of daily repentance and devotion, because as surely as the sun will rise tomorrow, some day that final trumpet blast will sound. Will you be ready?

JEWISH FESTIVAL	ANTITYPE IN THE NEW COVENANT
Passover *(pesach)*	The sacrificial death of Jesus Christ
Feast of firstfruits	The resurrection of Jesus Christ
Feast of unleavened bread	Celebrating being free of sin in our lives
Feast of weeks/ Pentecost *(shavoat)*	The giving of the Holy Spirit and the initiation of the church
Feast of trumpets *(rosh hashanah)*	Judgment day, Jesus coming back
Day of atonement *(yom kippur)*	The day we were saved – spiritual birthday
Feast of Booths *(tabernacles)*	Celebrating life in fellowship with God

THE DAY OF ATONEMENT (Yom Kippur)

The Day of Atonement, *Yom Kippur,* was the most significant festival of the Jewish year. It was the one day of the year when the high preast would enter into the Holy of Holies to make intercession for the sin of all the people for the entire year. Whereas the sin offering and the guilt offering focused on **accepting personal responsibility** for one's sins, the Day of Atonement was about **forgiveness of sins**. Arguably, *Yom Kippur* is the central foreshadow of the entire Old Testament.

Yom Kippur was part of the Fall cycle of festivals of the Jewish religious year, falling somewhere between mid-September and mid-October, depending on the timing of the new moon. The Fall feasts included the one-day Feast of Trumpets and the Day of

The Old Covenant Feasts Prefigure Specific Aspects of the Christian Life

Atonement, as well as the seven-day Feast of Tabernacles. The Day of Atonement fell on the tenth of Tishri in the Jewish calendar, and therefore came nine days after *Rosh Hashannah*. It was one of the three ceremonies which all Jews living within a reasonable distance were required to come to Jerusalem to celebrate. *Yom Kippur* is still observed today by Jews worldwide as one of their high holidays. However, the celebration today is a shell of the original because without the actual sacrifice of the goat in the tabernacle, the central signifigance of the event is lost.

Yom Kippur was instituted with the giving of the Law of Moses on Sinai. The details of the festival are found in Leviticus 16, Leviticus 23:26-32 and Numbers 29:7-11. The focal point of the Day of Atonement was the entrance of the High Priest into the Holy of Holies to scatter the blood of the sacrificial goat on the mercy seat for the sin of all the people. However, to emphasize the holiness of God, an elaborate ceremony, with many other offerings, was required as a prelude to this one awesome sacrifice. *"This is how Aaron* [and all High Priests after him] *is to enter the sanctuary area: with a young bull for a sin offering and a ram for a burnt offering"* (Leviticus 16:3). To help keep the information from becoming overwhelming, the most important events surrounding the *Yom Kippur* ceremony are listed below:

1. The High Priest washes his entire body with water from the laver (more washing than is normally required).

2. The High Priest then puts on an all-white "sacred" linen tunic (as opposed to his normal colorful garments).

3. A young bull is sacrificed for the sins of the High Priest and his family (as well as a ram for a burnt offering).

4. Two goats are selected. One is sacrificed as a sin offering for the whole people. The other will be the scape-goat.

5. The High Priest enters the Holy Place alone. He takes a large censer full of incense and a coal from the altar and carefully places it behind the curtain in front of the Holy of Holies.

6. Once the smoke of the incense has filled the Most Holy Place sufficiently for the High Priest not to be killed by seeing the presence

of God, he passes through the curtain and quickly sprinkles the blood of the bull followed by the blood of the goat on the mercy seat to *"make atonement for the Most Holy Place because of the uncleanness and the rebellion of the Israelites, whatever their sins have been"* (Leviticus 16:16).

7. The High Priest then sprinkles the blood of both sacrifices on the items in the Holy Place and on the altar of burnt offering.

8. He then takes the second goat, the scape-goat, and lays his hands on its head, symbolically imparting the sins of all the people onto the goat. The goat is then chased off into the desert to carry the sins of the people away from the camp.

9. After making the burnt offering on the altar and burning the fat of the sin offering, the bodies of the goat and the bull are carried out of the camp (or out of the city of Jerusalem during the Temple period) to be completely burned.

The Day of Atonement was about forgiveness of sins. The Hebrew word *kapar* (from which we get Kippur) means literally to cover over.[9] *"This is an everlasting covenant for you: Atonement is to be made once a year for all the sins of the Israelites"* (Leviticus 16:34). It served as a foreshadow of the central event in the New Covenant: the entrance of the Great High Priest Jesus Christ by virtue of his own blood into the heavenly Tabernacle to take away the sins of the whole world.

While *Yom Kippur* serves as a foreshadow of the atoning work of Jesus Christ, it tells us at least as much about what the Old Covenant did **not** do as it tells us about what the blood of Jesus **does** do. The High Priest had to wash himself thoroughly at the laver. He had to put on brand new white linen garments. He had to make a separate sacrifice of a bull for his own sins. The antitype to the High Priest, Jesus Christ, was able to enter the heavenly tabernacle for us without any of these steps because he was without sin. The High Priest had to light a censer full of incense behind the Holy of Holies to create such a cloud that he would not be killed by seeing the unobscured presence of God.[7] Jesus was able to come boldly into the presence of the Father in heaven, unobscured by the cloud of incense.

> It was necessary, then, for the copies of the heavenly things to be purified with these sacrifices, but the heavenly things themselves with better sacrifices than these. For Christ did not enter a man-made sanctuary that was only a copy of the true one; he entered heaven itself, now to appear for us in God's presence (Hebrews 9:23,24).

Most significantly of all, the High Priest had to perform this ceremony year after year. This was a painful reminder that the sins of the people were not forgiven once and for all on *Yom Kippur*. The antitype—the sacrifice of Jesus is quite different. *"But now he has appeared once for all at the end of the ages to do away with sin by the sacrifice of himself"* (Hebrews 9:26). The fact is that if the sacrifice of the goat on *Yom Kippur* did bring about forgiveness of sins for Israel at all. It was only in anticipation of the only sacrifice that ever truly removed the sin of humanity: the blood of Jesus Christ. If the antitype sacrifice were never offered, the type would not have had any effect in atoning for sin. All this is summarized and made clear in Hebrews 9:11-14:

> When Christ came as a high priest of the good things that are already here, he went through the greater and more perfect tabernacle that is not man-made, that is to say, not a part of this creation. He did not enter by means of the blood of goats and calves; but he entered the Most Holy Place once for all by his own blood, having obtained eternal redemption. The blood of goats and bulls and the ashes of a heifer sprinkled on those who are ceremonially unclean sanctify them so that they are outwardly clean. How much more, then, will the blood of Christ, who through the eternal Spirit offered himself unblemished to God, cleanse our consciences from acts that lead to death, so that we may serve a living God.

Jesus made those who are saved through his blood to be priests to serve in the heavenly Tabernacle! For those who are saved by the blood of Christ, it is no longer the Day of Atonement; it is a life of atonement! The Day of Atonement is a foreshadow of the day one is personally saved from the consequences of sins.

But there is more to the foreshadow. After the Tabernacle was purified, the High Priest laid his hands on the scape goat. As the sins of the people were symbolically laid onto the scape goat, so the sins of the whole world were laid on Jesus Christ. *"He himself bore our sins in his body on the tree, so that we might die to sins and live for righteousness; by his wounds you have been healed"* (1 Peter 2:24). As the scape goat symbolically carried away the sins of the Jews out of the camp, so Jesus literally carries away the sins of his people away from the "camp" which is their life. *"As far as the east is from the west, so far has he removed our transgressions from us"* (Psalms 103:12). The Jews called the scape goat *azazel*, meaning removal. It is not enough for our sins to be atoned for; they need to be removed from our life.

Not only was the scape goat chased off into the wilderness, never to return, the bodies of the sin sacrifices were also carried outside the camp to be burned. This, too, is a foreshadow of the sacrifice of Jesus. The sin sacrifices had to be burned outside the camp because God will not dwell where there is sin. Similarly, the sacrifice of the antitype, Jesus Christ, had to occur outside the city of Jerusalem:

> *The high priest carries the blood of the animals into the Most Holy Place as a sin offering, but the bodies are burned outside the camp. And so Jesus also suffered outside the city gate* [at Golgotha where he was crucified] *to make the people holy through his own blood. Let us, then, go to him outside the camp, bearing the disgrace he bore. For here we do not have an enduring city, but we are looking forward for the city that is to come* (Hebrews 13:11-14).

Here the Hebrew writer identifies the physical city of Jerusalem as a type of the spiritual Jerusalem where Jesus is ministering even now in the presence of the Father. As the sin sacrifices had to be carried outside of Jerusalem to be burned on the Day of Atonement, so Jesus, who carried the sins of the whole world, had to be taken out of the city gate to be sacrificed.

Yom Kippur, the Day of Atonement, was used by God as a foreshadow of the atoning sacrifice of Jesus Christ. It was God's prophetic statement about how those under the New Covenant were to come directly into the presence of the Most High God through the blood of Jesus. The other six feasts of the Jews were celebrated either as a reminder of something God had done for his people in the past (for example, the Passover) or in anticipation of something God would do in the future (Firstfruits, the Feast of Trumpets). The Day of Atonement was neither of these. It was a celebration of something which happened that very day—atonement for the sins of the people. Every time a disciple of Jesus is baptized into Christ, it is a modern-day fulfillment of the promise foreshadowed in the Day of Atonement. Those who are baptized into Christ are buried with him, they are united with him in his death, they are crucified with him, and they are raised to live with him (Romans 6:2-7). Now, that is something to celebrate.

THE FEAST OF TABERNACLES

The Feast of Tabernacles was a seven-day festival that marked the end of the Fall cycle of religious holidays for the Jews.[8] The Jewish name for this feast is *Sukkot,* which means booths or shacks. This is a very appropriate name because the Jews were required to live in simple booths during the festival. That is why the festival is also known as the Feast of Booths. To make matters even more confusing for the uninitiated, the feast is also known as the Feast of Ingathering (Exodus 23:16) because it occurred at the time of the final bringing in of the Fall harvest of crops. In fact, the Feast of Tabernacles was such an important part of the Jewish life, that it simply came to be known as *"the Feast"* (John 7:37).

Sukkot was ordained by God as the final of three harvest festivals (the others being Firstfruits and Pentecost). It was to be celebrated beginning five days after *Yom Kippur;* from the fifteenth to the twenty-first of *Tishri.* Unlike the somber Day of Atonement, it was intended as a joyous celebration of the blessings of God. Some have appropriately described it as the Jewish Thanksgiving. The specific commandments concerning this festival are found in Leviticus 23:33-43, Exodus 23:16 and Deuteronomy 16:16. In modern Judaism the Feast of Tabernacles has diminished somewhat in importance, but in biblical times it was very significant—at least as significant as Thankgiving is to Americans today. Indeed Josephus, the Jewish historian of the first century A.D. described it as the greatest feast of the Jews.[10] Philo, the first century Jewish philosopher made a similar comment about *Sukkot.*

The celebration of the Feast of Tabernacles involved the Jews building a "booth", a simple, temporary structure, designed to remind them of the booths they had lived in when wandering in the wilderness. These booths were to be small, but of sufficient size for the families to actually spend the night. *"Live in booths for seven days: All native-born Israelites are to live in booths so your descendants will know that I had the Israelites live in booths when I brought them out of Egypt. I am the* LORD *your God"* (Leviticus 23:42,43). All Jews were required to go to Jerusalem to celebrate "The Feast." This may be part of the reason it was during Tabernacles that Ezra made his famous call to revival and repentance (Ezra 10:1-17). As with the other two harvest festivals, the intent was for the Jews to be reminded that all blessings come from God. Firstfruits was about an anticipated blessing, Pentecost about a blessing which was just beginning, and Tabernacles was about thanking God for the completed harvest which had already come in.

Although it is not specifically stated in the Old Testament, the connection between the Day of Atonement and the Feast of Tabernacles is fairly obvious. Through the forgiveness of sins, received on the Day of Atonement, the Jews had a relationship with God, and through that relationship, they were given abundant physical blessings, which they celebrated in the Feast of Booths.

The Feast of Tabernacles, of course, is a foreshadow of something to be celebrated in the New Covenant. The Feast of Tabernacles is an Old Testament foreshadow of our living in a blessed relationship with God through Jesus Christ. A hint of this fact can be found in Ezekiel 37:24,26,27:

> *"My servant David will be king over them, and they will all have one shepherd. They will follow my laws and be careful to keep my decrees....I will make a covenant of peace with them; it will be an everlasting covenant. I will establish them and increase their numbers, and **I will put my sanctuary among them** forever. **My dwelling place will be with them**; I will be their God and they will be my people. Then the nations will know that I the* LORD *make Israel holy, when my sanctuary is among them forever."*

This is a messianic prophecy. *"My servant David"* is a reference to Jesus, the Messiah. In this prophecy, God is telling his people that through the Messiah, his sanctuary, his dwelling place, in other words his tabernacle will be among his people. In Ezekiel, God is saying, I will come and dwell with my people.

Zechariah 14:16-21 is another prophecy about the Feast of Tabernacles with messianic implications. In this passage, Zechariah prophesies that a remnant from the nations that formerly persecuted Israel will be called to the New Jerusalem to celebrate the Feast of Tabernacles.

God has fulfilled the prophecy implied in the Feast of Tabernacles in more than one way. When Jesus lived here among men, God was literally tabernacling with his people. *"The Word became flesh and made his dwelling among us"* (John 1:14). The Greek word translated "lived" in the NIV could be translated a bit more awkwardly, but also more accurately as *"tabernacled."* It is ironic that as the Jews lived in booths at the Feast of Tabernacles during Jesus' ministry, God was literally living and walking—he was tabernacling—among his people. The Feast of Tabernacles was a foreshadow of Jesus—God in the flesh—coming and dwelling with men.

God also completed the antitype to the Feast of Tabernacles when he sent the Holy Spirit to dwell in his people. *"In him the whole building is joined together and rises to become a holy temple on the Lord. And in him you too are being built together to become a dwelling in which God lives by his Spirit"* (Ephesians 2:21,22). Disciples of Jesus are tabernacles, booths, in which God dwells by his Spirit. Jesus made it clear that this would happen:

> *"If you love me, you will obey what I command. And I will ask the Father, and he will give you another Counselor to be with you forever—the Spirit of truth. The world cannot accept him, because it neither sees him nor knows him. But you know him, for he lives with you and will be in you"* (John 14:15-17).

In the Holy Spirit, God dwells in his people, making them a holy temple.

Another relevant passage is 2 Corinthians 5:1-5:

> *Now we know that if the earthly tent* (tabernacle) *we live in is destroyed, we have a building from God, an eternal house in heaven, not built by human hands. Meanwhile, we groan, longing to be clothed with our heavenly dwelling, because when we are clothed, we will not be found naked. For while we are in this tent, we groan and are burdened, because we do not wish to be unclothed but to be clothed with our heavenly dwelling so that what is mortal may be swallowed up in life. Now it is God who has made us for this very purpose and has given us the Spirit as a deposit guaranteeing what is to come.*

Heaven will be one long Feast of Tabernacles. For those who are in Christ, the Holy Spirit is a deposit guaranteeing their seat at that blessed feast.

An interesting aspect of the Jewish celebration of Tabernacles is that each day of the feast, there was a joyous procession of the Jews to the Pool of Siloam, headed by a priest carrying a pitcher. Upon reaching the Pool, the priest filled the pitcher with water. He carried the pitcher through the Water Gate (the source of the name for that gate), back into the temple precincts where, after a threefold blast of trumpets, he poured the water into a silver receptacle on the altar. For the Jews, this reminded them of the water coming out of the rock in the wilderness. This brings added meaning to the events in John chapter seven.

> *"On the last and greatest day of the Feast* (of Tabernacles), *Jesus stood and said in a loud voice, "If a man is thirsty, let him come to me and drink. Whoever believes in me, as the Scripture has said, streams of living water will flow from within him." By this he meant the Spirit, whom those who believed in him were later to receive"* (John 7:37-39).

For the Jews in attendance, the reference to the pouring of water in the Tabernacle ceremony was impossible to miss. For Jesus, Tabernacles was a foreshadow of God dwelling with mankind forever: first with him coming and physically tabernacling with us (John 1:14), second, with God dwelling in us in the form of the Holy Spirit (John 7:38; also John 4:14 and Isaiah 12:8), and finally culminating with us dwelling with God the Father forever in the great and final Tabernacle, which will be heaven.

What do we learn from the Feast of Tabernacles? We learn that God intended all along to dwell with and in his people through Jesus Christ. We learn that this is something which needs to be remembered, to be appreciated and to be celebrated with all of our might. God felt that the Jews needed a week-long annual reminder that he had chosen them, from among all the peoples of the earth, to dwell among them and to bless them. The Jews needed to take an entire week out of their busy lives, to break their routine by living in tents, to be reminded of the great blessing of living in a relationship with God. This being true it is fair to say that followers of Jesus will need continuing reminders to celebrate the blessing of being a living tabernacle in whom God dwells as well. We need to break the routine of daily life. We need to get out of our comfort zone. We need to do something out of the ordinary to celebrate living in a relationship with God. Perhaps having one's own personal Feast of Tabernacles might be helpful. Spending a weekend camping out in the wilderness in a tent, devoting the time to being in and celebrating a relationship with God would be a good idea. The outing could be a one-on-one affair with God, or it could be a group celebration, as it was with the Jews. It would be fair to say that in our super-busy modern culture, we need to celebrate regular Feasts of Tabernacles even more than the Jews did.

Remember that every aspect of the Old Covenant was created for the Jews, but it has an even deeper meaning for those under the New Covenant. Followers of Jesus need to consider how to implement the Feast of Tabernacles in their own lives.

CONCLUSION

In considering the feasts ordained in the Old Testament it becomes clear that God called the Jews to a celebratory life! Being a Jew was not principally about being somber and glum; it was about celebrating the blessings of a life in a covenant relationship with God Almighty. In their festivals, the Jews celebrated past, present and future blessings from God.

In the light of the ministry of Jesus Christ, the festivals of the Jews take on a fuller and deeper meaning. The shadow is found in the Mosaic celebrations. The reality is found in their fulfillment in Christ. For thousands of years the Jews have been telling us about the sacrificial death of Jesus on the cross (Passover), the resurrection of Jesus from the dead (Firstfruits), the birth of the church, and the sending of the Holy Spirit (Pentecost), the return of Jesus Christ at the end of the ages (Trumpets), and, ultimately, about our own personal salvation from our sin (*Yom Kippur*). In light of these amazing truths we, as anticipated by the Law of Moses, should live in daily celebration of being forgiven of our sins (Unleavened Bread) and living in continual fellowship with our Creator (Tabernacles). In the words of 1 Corinthians 5:7-8: *"For Christ, our Passover lamb has been sacrificed. Therefore, let us keep the Festival, not with the old yeast,...but with bread without yeast, the bread of sincerity and truth!"*

Endnotes

1 The author acknowledges help in this section from Phillip Lester and an unpublished article of his *"Passover Reflections."*

2 God instituted the week-long feast of unleavened bread at this time as well, as will be discussed below.

3 Phillip Lester, from his (unpublished) essay, *"Appreciating the Significance of the Passover."*

4 The Jewish day has always begun and ended at sundown. Therefore, the 14th of *Nisan*—the day of the Passover Feast—began on Thursday evening, when Jesus celebrated what came to be known as the Last Supper. It stretched through Thursday night when Jesus was arrested and underwent a mock trial before the Jews. It also included the trial before Pilate and the crucifixion which occurred during the day on Friday.

5 Also see Leviticus 23:4-8.

6 Also, see Isaiah 27:12,13 and Zechariah 9:13-15.

7 Leviticus 16:2.

8 The Jews traditionally celebrate two additional and separate holidays which are tacked on to the end of the Tabernacle week—on the twenty-second and twenty-third of *Tishri*. These are known as *Shemini Atzeret* and *Simkhat Torah*. They are commonly thought of as part of the Feast of Tabernacles, but will not be covered in this chapter.

9 It is interesting to note that the Latin word for goat, *caper,* comes from the Hebrew word *kapar,* meaning atonement.

10 Josephus, *Antiquities of the Jews,* VIII, iv, 1.

Prophecies in the Old Testament Predict Events in the Life of Jesus Christ of Nazareth

"This is what I told you while I was still with you: Everything must be fulfilled that is written about me in the Law of Moses, the Prophets and the Psalms."

Luke 24:44

When Jesus spoke the words recorded in Luke 24:44 to his apostles after his resurrection, he told them not only that the Old Testament was written about him, but that he was in the final phase of fulfilling the specific historical prophecies about the Messiah. In this chapter we will see the truth of this claim proved convincingly. We will see historical messianic prophecies describing in detail everything from the location and details of Jesus' birth, to the location, means and timing of his death. Messianic prophecies in the Old Testament describe and predict the life of Jesus on every level—from the broadest description of his life and ministry down to some of the most minute details of events in his life—all recorded hundreds of years before Jesus was born. As one writer has said, "We will find historic prophecies of Jesus in the Old Testament from Genesis to Zechariah. Prophecies of the Messiah describe him as both a servant and a king, a shepherd and a sheep, the son of David and David's Lord, the priest and the sacrifice, the offerer and the offering.[1] At the end of all this, the reader is left with convincing proof that the Bible is inspired by God and that Jesus Christ is the One, the Messiah, the Lamb of God, slain from the creation of the world.

It would be reasonable to assume that for most who have read the Bible extensively, if they were asked how the Old Testament tells us about Jesus, most would answer that it is through historical prophecies of the Messiah. It was tempting to begin this study with the messianic prophecies for this reason. The predictive prophecies about the Savior of Israel in the Old Testament are so striking as apologetic proof of the inspiration of the Bible, that it could distract from the main point, which is that the entire Old Testament is about Jesus Christ. By now the reader probably gets the point, so it is time to dive into the amazing predictions about the Messiah which saturate the Old Testament scripture.

QUESTIONS TO BEAR IN MIND

The apologetic nature of messianic prophecies has been covered fairly extensively in an earlier book of mine.[2] In that book, the possible objections to the messianic prophecies are dealt with in detail. They will be discussed only very briefly here. Let us imagine taking the extreme skeptical view toward the evidence that the Bible is a product of divine inspiration. A person who takes a skeptical approach to the claim that messianic prophecies prove the inspiration of the Bible might ask the following questions:

1. How do we know that the supposed prophetic passages in the Old Testament are really predictions of the Messiah? Is it not possible that these passages are taken out of their context by apologists and misapplied to Jesus simply to prop up belief in the Bible?

2. Can we be absolutely sure that these writings in the Old Testament really predated the life of Jesus? Could the early church have inserted them into the Old Testament in order to be able to claim that Jesus is the Messiah?

3. How can we be sure that Jesus really did these things—that the witnesses are reliable?

4. Is it not possible that Jesus read the Old Testament and, wanting to claim to be the Messiah, purposefully did some of the things the Messiah is supposed to do so that he could support his claim?

In answer to the first question, we will see as we go through the individual passages that many of them are unmistakeable references to the Messiah. For example, in Isaiah 9:1,2 which, as we will see, predicts that the Messiah will be from Galilee, the passage continues by calling the person from Galilee, *"Wonderful Counselor, Mighty God, Everlasting Father, Prince of Peace"* (Isaiah 9:6). It is hard to deny that this is a prophecy of the Messiah.

As additional evidence that many of the prophecies we will discuss are indeed about the Messiah, there is the fact that most of the Jews of the first century had messianic expectations. They considered passages such as Micah 5:2 (which predicts that a savior will be born in Bethlehem) to be about the expected Messiah. It seems reasonable to assume that any scripture in the Old Testament which was considered by consensus of the Jews in the first century as being about the Messiah is a legitimate messianic prophecy, and therefore that the early Christians did not take their messianic implications out of context. Not all the passages we consider will be "obviously" about the Messiah if taken by themselves in their Old Testament context. However, in general the discussion will be limited to passages which are clearly about the Messiah. A more detailed discussion of the approach used to decide which passages have legitimate messianic reference is included in the appendix. The reader should bear in mind the question of how sure we can be that a passage is in fact messianic when analyzing the prophecies below.

Let us consider question number two. Can we be sure that these really are prophecies of the future? In other words, how do we know that they were written hundreds of years before the events—that they were not later insertions into the Old Testament by zealous Christians, intent on proving that Jesus is the promised Messiah? The answer is that we can know for sure that this criticism of Messianic prophecies does not hold water for two reasons.

First is the manuscript evidence. With the discovery of the Dead Sea Scrolls in the 1940s, we now have manuscripts of all or part of almost every Old Testament book. These scrolls predate the ministry of Jesus by between one hundred and two hundred and fifty years. It would be difficult for proposed deceitful apologists to insert changes into the Old Testament before they were born! Besides this, there is the Septuagint translation of the entire Hebrew Bible into the Greek vernacular which was completed by about 150 B.C. This parallel witness to the Old Testament manuscript makes the claim that the Old Testament was changed to support belief in Christianity untenable. The proposed deceitful apologists would have had to change both the Hebrew and the Greek versions at the same time! Given the requirement of time in order for the Jewish scribes to come to consensus about the inspiriation of individual books, one can conservatively conclude that the entire Old Testament canon was completed by 400 B.C.

There is a second reason we can dismiss the idea that the Old Testament was changed to make it appear that Jesus fulfilled prophecies. The reason is that all along, the Jews have had ultimate custodianship over the Hebrew text of the Old Testament. The Jews put together the most authoritative Hebrew version of the Old Testament known as the Masoretic Text in the 7th and 8th centuries A.D. It's simply unbelievable that the same Jews who rejected Jesus as the Messiah would have changed the Old Testament to support Christian beliefs. Although we may not be able to prove absolutely that the words recorded in Isaiah were written in about 730 B.C. (i.e. during the career of Isaiah) we can state with certainty that every single prophecy we will look at was written hundreds of years before the ministry of Jesus of Nazareth.

What about the third question? Can we be absolutely sure that Jesus did the things recorded by the gospel writers? Is it possible that the New Testament writers stretched the truth or even fabricated stories about Jesus after his ministry in order to manipulate the evidence to support his claims to be the Messiah? In the end, it will be impossible to absolutely prove that every event in the life of Jesus recorded in the gospels, which also fulfilled a messianic prophecy, actually happened. We are forced to trust the word of the original witnesses. However, there are more than a few reasons that it is logical to accept that their eyewitness testimony can be trusted.

First, there is the fact that several of the prophecy fulfillment events are a matter of historical record from pagan and even Jewish authors. Specific prophecies of the Messiah whose fulfillment is a matter of external historical record in Jesus' life include the place of his birth, the fact that Jesus worked many public miracles, and that he was persecuted, arrested and crucified. In addition, we know from historical record that he was executed in Jerusalem, as well as the approximate date of his death, all of which are specifically prophesied in the Old Testament. These facts are testified to by such Roman historians as Tacitus and Pliny the younger, as well as the Jewish historian Josephus and even the Jewish writers of the Talmud.[3]

Then there is the character of the writers themselves. Call Paul, Peter, Luke and Matthew fanatics if you will, but the bottom line is that they absolutely believed in the truth of the message which they taught. One evidence of the reliability of the New Testament as history is the fact that it presents the apostles as real people—with sins and character flaws. However, there is not a single piece of evidence that any of them were anything less than absolutely honest witnesses to the events they recorded. If the apostles and other New Testament writers were out to deceive people about Jesus being the Messiah, how does one explain the fact that most of them were martyred for their faith? There is no evidence that any of the eyewitnesses to the ministry of Jesus later recanted, even on pain of death.[4] If the gospel accounts are fabrications, created to make it appear that Jesus is the Messiah, then it is hard to explain the facts. It is conceivable, perhaps, that one of the conspirators would die for a lie, but it defies what we know of human nature to accept that dozens were martyred for a faith which they knew to be a lie. Jesus really did these things.

What about the fourth question above? Is it conceivable that Jesus might have decided at some point in his life that he wanted to be the Messiah and that he began to willfully manipulate his followers by doing the things the Old Testament said the Messiah would do? The fact is that Jesus was well aware of the Old Testament and he was fully congnizant of the fact that he was living out the events foreshadowed in the scriptures. Nevertheless the scenario whereby Jesus might deceive the people by faking his Messiahship is completely unsupportable. We will see that Jesus fulfilled Old Testament prophecies about the Messiah which include where and when he would be born as well as how he would die and the specifics of his betrayal. As a human being, Jesus obviously would have no ability to manipulate such things (unless, of course, he was God, which would make the issue moot). It is true that a messianic pretender could arrange entering Jerusalem on a donkey (Zechariah 9:9) to deceive the people, but it is hard to imagine him planning that the soldiers at his execution would gamble over his clothing (Psalms 22:18).

Having laid out some apologetic issues, we will now proceed to considering a number of the historical prophecies of the Messiah. For the sake of space, it will obviously be impossible to cover all the messianic prophecies. The passages chosen, however, are a representative list. A discussion of methodology used to decide whether an Old Testament passage is truly a messianic prophecy is found in the appendix.

THE PENTATEUCH

Although they are jam-packed with prefigures and foreshadows, the first five books of the Bible, the Law of Moses, have relatively few direct historical prophecies of the Messiah. Perhaps this makes the few examples of note even more significant. Prophecies with reference to the Messiah not discussed here include Genesis 12:1-3, Genesis 22:17,18 and Numbers 24:17-19.

Genesis 3:15

"And I will put enmity between you and the woman, and between your offspring and hers; he will crush your head and you will strike his heel."

This passage is widely considered the first messianic prophecy. Satan did indeed strike at Jesus' heel, most notably in the temptation in the desert (Matthew 4:1-11, Luke 4:1-13). The blow, however, was not fatal. *"When the devil had finished all this tempting, he left him until an opportune time"* (Luke 4:13). Jesus, the "offspring" of Eve by direct descent, despite being struck in his heel, ultimately crushed the head of Satan as he hung on the cross. Paul certainly saw Genesis 3:15 as prophetic (Romans 16:20). Significantly, this passage is identified as messianic in the Jewish Targum.[5] Satan's final condemnation awaits the end time (Revelation 20:10), when he will be thrown into the lake of fire and burning sulfur. The offspring of Satan, in the form of the great persecutors of God's people, such as Antiochus Epiphanes,[6] Domitian and Diocletian, clearly expressed enmity toward Jesus when they attacked the people of God. The prefigure of the snake and Eve is carried forward to Revelation chapter twelve which describes the war between the Dragon (Satan) and the Woman (in this case, symbolic of the Church of Jesus Christ).

Genesis 49:10,11

> "The scepter will not depart from Judah, nor the ruler's staff from between his feet, until he comes to whom it belongs and the obedience of the nations is his. He will tether his donkey to a vine, his colt to the choicest branch; he will wash his garments in wine, his robes in the blood of grapes."

The scepter in this passage is the royal staff which represents the authority of a king. David, who was from the tribe of Judah, partially fulfilled this prophecy as a foreshadow when he came to rule in Jerusalem. However, the prophecy refers to *"he who comes to whom it belongs and the obedience of the nations is his."* This is clearly a reference to the King of Kings—Jesus Christ (John 18:37). By the way, Jesus, the "Son of David," was also a member of the tribe of Judah on his mother's side, as required by this prophecy.

This passage has several other allusions to Jesus' life and ministry. The donkey and colt anticipate Jesus' royal ride into Jerusalem on a donkey and its colt (Matthew 21:1-5). We see that Jesus is the true vine (John 15:1). It is not hard to see what the wine, which is interestingly called the "blood of grapes," is looking toward. The statement that the blood of grapes would be used to wash his garments seems like a very obscure reference in its Old Testament context, unless one applies it to the sacrifice of Jesus and the imagery in the Lord's Supper. *"These are they who have come out of the great tribulation; they have washed their robes and made them white in the blood of the lamb"* (Revelation 7:14). This prophecy in Genesis, coming as it does earlier in the Bible, makes somewhat less direct statements about the Messiah than we will find in the later prophets.

Deuteronomy 18:15,17-19

> *The LORD your God will raise up for you a prophet like me from among your own brothers. You must listen to him...The LORD said to me: "What they say is good. I will raise up for them a prophet like you from among their brothers; I will put my words in his mouth, and he will tell them everything I command him. If anyone does not listen to my words that the prophet speaks in my name, I myself will call him to account."*

In these words God told Moses, in essence, that he was a prefigure of the great prophet to come. That prophet is the Messiah—Jesus Christ. Jesus was more than a prophet, but prophet he definitely was. In fulfillment of this prophecy, Jesus boldly declared, *"So whatever I say is just what the Father has told me to say"* (John 12:50). The scribes in the crowd that day surely knew he was referring back to the prophecy given to Moses.

MESSIANIC PROPHECIES IN THE PSALMS

There are more messianic prophecies in the Psalms than in any other single Old Testament book, (Isaiah and Zechariah run a close second and third.) Many of the emotional cries by David to his God can be seen as having a double reference, both to himself and to the "Son of David," Jesus Christ. In some cases, one could claim that it is debatable whether the passage is absolutely messianic. (Psalms 2:1-6, Psalms 35:19, Psalm 41:9, Psalms 69:25, Psalms 78:2, Psalms 91:11,12 and others could be mentioned in this context.) In this section, we will look at those prophecies which have the most obvious application to the Christ.

Psalm 16:10,11

> *Therefore my heart is glad...because you will not abandon me to the grave, nor will you let your Holy One see decay. You have made known to me the path of life; you will fill me with joy in your presence, with eternal pleasures at your right hand.*

Psalm 16 is attributed to King David. As Peter pointed out in Acts 2:29, David did indeed die and his body decayed: *"his tomb is here to this day."* In this key passage David was prophesying the resurrection of his direct descendant—the Messiah. How do we know this is a reference to the Messiah? Who else in the Bible could even conceivably be referred to as sitting down at the right hand of God? Certainly David did not have the arrogance to claim the right hand position to God. This is the most direct prophecy in the Old Testament that the Messiah—he who will sit at the Father's right hand—was to be resurrected from the dead. Perhaps this is one of the passages Paul had in mind when he said that Jesus was raised from the dead "according to the Scriptures" (1 Corinthians 15:3).

Psalm 22:1,7,8,15-18

"My God, my God, why have you forsaken me?
  Why are you so far from saving me,
  so far from the words of my groaning?
All who see me mock me;
  they hurl insults, shaking their heads:
"He trusts in the LORD
  let the LORD rescue him.
Let him deliver him,
  since he delights in him."

My strength is dried up like a potsherd,
  and my tongue sticks to the roof of my mouth;
  you lay me in the dust of death.
Dogs have surrounded me;
  a band of evil men has encircled me,
they have pierced my hands and my feet.
  I can count all my bones;
  People stare and gloat over me.
They divide my garments among them
  and cast lots for my clothing."

At first glance, Psalm twenty-two would appear to simply be an emotional cry from David, *"a man after God's own heart,"* to his God, both complaining about his suffering and crying out for deliverance. In fact, it would have been perfectly reasonable for David to feel as if he were forsaken by God when he was being chased by King Saul through the wilderness or when he felt forced to play the part of a crazy man when exiled to Philistia. His enemies probably did mock and insult him at times. However, when one looks at other details in this psalm, there is no way David can simply be writing about himself. Were David's hands and feet ever pierced? Did those who stared at him ever divide his garments among themselves? This is a Messianic prophecy! Try to imagine what David must have thought after he wrote down these words under the influence of the Holy Spirit. Why did I write that? What am I talking about here? I can count all my bones? What is that about, God?

To the Jews reading this psalm before the advent of Jesus Christ, it probably would not have been clear that it was about the Messiah, although they, too, might have wondered what David was talking about. However, historical hindsight makes the conclusion that the psalm is a messianic prophecy unmistakeable. In Psalm twenty-two we are looking at a tableau of the crucifixion scene, written well over one thousand years before it happened!

David may have felt forsaken by God, yet God never forsook him. However, Jesus was literally forsaken by God when the sins of the entire human race were imputed to him. This would explain why he quoted this psalm when at the point of death (Mark 15:34).

Little did Jesus' enemies, the chief priests and teachers of the law, know that God would use them to fulfill prophecies of the Messiah. If they had known, they might have held their tongues, rather than mock him and hurl insults at him. *"In the same way the chief priests and teachers of the law mocked him among themselves. 'He saved others,' they said, 'but he can't save himself! Let this Christ, this King of Israel, come down now from the cross, that we may see and believe.' Those crucified with him also heaped insults on him"* (Mark 15:31,32).

David described the Messiah's tongue sticking to the roof of his mouth. Jesus simply said *"I am thirsty"* (John 19:28). Had Jesus read Psalm 22, and was he just trying to continue to create the false impression that he was the Messiah? We can assume he had read the psalm. We can also assume that he was very thirsty.

Next, David describes the crucifixion scene (*"a band of evil men has encircled me"*) and then makes an amazing statement. *"They have pierced my hands and my feet."* This is an undeniable reference to the crucifixion of Jesus. What makes the idea that David foresaw this even more amazing is the fact that crucifixion was not even invented until six hundred years after David died. Crucifixion, as far as we know from historical documents, was invented by the Persians in the fourth century B.C. Even then, it involved tying a person to a stake. Crucifixion by nailing hands (actually wrists) and feet to a cross was invented by the Romans, over eight hundred years after David wrote. Did the gospel writers make up this story of the crucifixion? The Jewish historian Josephus, as well as the writers of the Talmud mention Jesus being crucified.[7] Might Jesus have arranged this to support his messianic claim? That would be an awfully tough price to pay to sustain a lie. Imagine how Jesus felt as a young man reading Psalm twenty-two, knowing that it was about him! Jesus knew all along what fate awaited him.

But David is not done. *"I can count all my bones"* (v. 17). What was David referring to? It would be reasonably safe to assume that he did not know. Reading John 19:31-37 will supply the answer. Because Jesus and the two thieves were crucified on the day before the Passover Sabbath and because death by crucifixion could take more than twenty-four hours, the Jews asked that the three prisoners be killed so their bodies could be taken down from the crosses before sunset. This was accomplished by breaking the legs of the crucified person, which would prevent their being able to push up on their feet, causing suffocation within minutes. When the soldiers came to Jesus, he was already dead. He had died in considerably less than the usual time, probably because he had already been extensively tortured before being crucified. According to the eye-witness report of the apostle John, Jesus, unlike the two criminals, had none of his bones broken. As mentioned in the last chapter, this event was foreshadowed by the Passover ceremony. God had commanded (Exodus 12:46) that none of the bones of the Passover lamb were to be broken when preparing the Seder meal. We learn two things from this. First, God intended all along for his Son to die for our sins. Second, Psalm twenty-two is inspired by that same God!

We are not done with Psalm twenty-two. *"They divide my garments among them and cast lots for my clothing"* (v. 18). Now, which was it, David, did they divide your garments (one for me, one for you, one for you...) or did they cast lots, i.e. gamble, for your clothes? It would seem impossible for both to be the case. God's word being what it is, will anyone be surprised at this point that they actually did both?

> When the soldiers crucified Jesus, they took his clothes, dividing them into four shares, one for each of them, with the undergarment remaining. This garment was seamless, woven in one piece from top to bottom.
> "Let's not tear it," they said to one another. "Let's decide by lot who will get it" (John 19:23, 24).

This comes from an eyewitness to the events. Was John a liar? Consider his life and decide for yourself. This prophecy fulfillment has an attention-grabbing property to it, but the thing to focus in on is that Jesus, knowingly, willingly, gave up his life for you and me. Remember the previous statement by David prophesying Jesus' words on the cross, *"My God, my God, why have you forsaken me?"*

Psalm 31:5

> *Into your hands I commit my spirit;*
> *Redeem me, O LORD, the God of truth.*

Seen in isolation, the skeptic could claim that this passage is taken out of context if applied to Jesus Christ. However, given the totality of the poignant scene at the cross, it seems beyond possibility that Jesus just happened to pull out this somewhat obscure passage in Psalms while on the cross and near death. As Luke records, these are the last words of Jesus. *"It was now about the sixth hour...Jesus called out in a loud voice, 'Father, into your hands I commit my spirit.' When he had said this, he breathed his last"* (Luke 23:44,46). It is interesting to note that the other messianic prophecies in the Bible record a number of facts about Jesus, but the Psalms, being emotion-laden poetry, generally predict the most emotional aspects of the life and death of the Messiah.

Psalm 69:8,9,21

> *I am a stranger to my brothers,*
> *An alien to my own mother's sons;*
> *for zeal for your house consumes me,*
> *and the insults of those who insult you fall on me.*

> They put gall in my food
> and gave me vinegar for my thirst."

The prophecy in Psalm 69 is an example of the rule just stated. David was a zealous man. Jesus, the *"son of David"* was more so, as evidenced by the scene in John 2:13-17. When Jesus came into the temple, he saw greedy people making a profit from the sincere efforts of God's people to offer sacrifice to Him. Providing possible sacrifices for the people was not the problem. Making a killing off of the killing was. This got Jesus quite upset. He made a whip, driving the animals out, overturning the tables of the profitable money changers (only the Jewish shekel was accepted at the temple, providing another way to make a nice profit), saying, *"Get these out of here! How dare you turn my Father's house into a market"* (v.16). The disciples were not noted for recognizing messianic prophecies as they were being fulfilled. This was one exception. Even the seemingly somewhat slow disciples remembered at that time the statement in Psalm 69:9, *"Zeal for your house will consume me."*

Verse twenty-one takes us out of David's life and back to the crucifixion scene. The Hebrew word translated as gall here is a general term meaning poison or bitter weeds or herbs. It is doubtful that David ever suffered this particular treatment. This is a messianic prophecy. In Matthew 27:34 the apostle remembers that *"They offered him wine to drink, mixed with gall."* Mark is more specific, mentioning wine and the herb myrrh, which was used as a drug to deaden pain (Mark 15:23). Luke and John complete the picture, mentioning wine vinegar (Luke 23:36, John 19:29).

Psalm 110:1,4

> The LORD says to my Lord: "Sit at my right hand
> until I make your enemies a footstool for your feet."
>
> The LORD has sworn and will not change his mind:
> "You are a priest forever in the order of Melchizedek."

Psalm 110 is notably different from those we have already studied. It is called a royal psalm by virtue of its subject. Here we do not find the suffering savior, but the Messiah reigning as priest and king. Of course, Jesus was all these things. When David said, *"The* LORD *said to my Lord,"* who was he referring to? Did David have two different Lords? Not that he was aware of. That is how we know this scripture is about the Messiah. In the text, the first LORD (note all capitals) is the word *YHWH,* sometimes translated Yahweh, whereas the second Lord (note smaller case letters) used the Hebrew word *adon,* meaning lord or master. The former LORD refers to God the Father, while the second Lord is God the Son, Jesus Christ. That certainly is how Peter interpreted this passage in his sermon in Acts chapter two (Acts 2:33-35), where he accurately points out both that Jesus is now exalted to the right hand of the Father, and that David most certainly did not ascend to heaven. David, by the power of the Holy Spirit, got it exactly right.

Verse four is a prophecy that the Messiah will be a priest, but not a priest from the order of Aaron or of Levi. Rather, the Lord's anointed will be a priest of a very different kind. The Messiah will be a priest in the order of Melchizedek (by special appointment, rather than physical descent). This was discussed in the chapter on the Old Testament priesthood as a foreshadow of the ministry of Christ. God gave his people plenty of warning that a new kind of priesthood was in the offing.

Psalm 118:22,23 (also Isaiah 28:16)

The stone the builders rejected
  has become the capstone;
the LORD *has done this,*
  and it is marvelous in his eyes.

This, the last of the messianic prophecies from the Psalms to be covered here, is a psalm of praise. It is not specifically attributed to David. Hints that this is a messianic statement are found in the immediate context of these verses. For example, there is the phrase, *"I will not die but live"* (v. 17). Another statement which points to this passage being about the Messiah is; *"This is the gate of the* LORD *through which the righteous may enter,"* (v. 20) which certainly puts into mind the statement of Jesus, *"I am the gate; whoever enters through me will be saved"* (John 10:9). We learn from this psalm that the Messiah will be a stone whom the builders reject. Presumably, those who reject the stone are the Jews generally, or more specifically the Jewish teachers, scribes and Pharisees. This prophecy calls to mind the tearful scene as Jesus looked over Jerusalem. *"O Jerusalem, Jerusalem, you who kill the prophets and stone those sent to you, how often I have longed to gather your children together, as a hen gathers her chicks under her wings, but you were not willing"* (Matthew 23:37).

The marvelous thing is that God has raised up the stone, rejected and killed by the Jews. The Father resurrected the Son, making him into the capstone. Peter quotes from Psalms 118:22,23, saying *"It is by the name of Jesus Christ of Nazareth, whom you crucified, but whom God raised from the dead, that this man stands before you completely healed"* (Acts 4:10). The word translated capstone in Psalms 118:22 is actually two Hebrew words *pinna*, meaning cornerstone, and *rosh,* meaning head or highest in authority. According to the Psalmist, the Messiah will move from rejection to being both the cornerstone, the defining foundation (Ephesians 2:20) and the peak, the pinnacle of God's authority, for as Jesus said, *"All authority in heaven and on earth has been give to me"* (Matthew 28:18). And it most certainly has!

Messianic Prophecies in Isaiah

By sheer numbers, the Psalms may have more prophecies of the Messiah than any other book, but Isaiah contains the most well-known messianic predictions. Significantly, it contains the greatest number of prophecies which were generally acknowledged to be messianic by the Jews during the lifetime of Jesus Christ, as we will see. Given that the Jews saw these Isaiah prophecies as applying to the Messiah, there is no legitimate way to claim that over-zealous Christians somehow read details of Jesus' ministry out of context from what is written in the book of Isaiah. It is noteworthy that after the time of Jesus, the Rabbis removed many of the messianic prophecies from their customary daily readings of the Old Testament, for obvious reasons, when one considers the implications of these passages.[8] As with the

Psalms, not all the messianic prophecies in Isaiah will be covered, but rather those which are most convincingly messianic. Prophecies not discussed here include Isaiah 4:2-4, Isaiah 16:5, Isaiah 22:20-22, Isaiah 40:9-11, Isaiah 49:5,6, Isaiah 55:4,5 and others.

Isaiah 7:14

> *Therefore the Lord himself will give you a sign: The virgin will be with child and will give birth to a son, and will call him Immanuel.*

From the point of view of the apologist, this is probably the most controversial prophecy of the Messiah because of the fact that the Hebrew text can be interpreted in two different ways: the difference having a radical effect on one's view of what it says about the incarnation of Jesus. The Hebrew word translated here as virgin is *alma,* which has as its normal meaning, girl, maiden or young woman. In certain contexts it can also be translated as virgin. In the Old Testament this word is translated as maiden or maidens four times, as girl once and as virgin or virgins twice. Making the interpretation even more dicey is the fact that Hebrew at that time had another word whose normal meaning was virgin:*betula*. This word unambiguously meant a woman who has not had sexual relations. It is used fifty-one times in the Old Testament.

So did God, through Isaiah, prophesy that the Messiah would be born of a virgin? First of all, the word Immanuel is a transliteration of the Hebrew for God among us. This prophecy unambiguously mentions both a sign from God and a woman with a child who would be given the name God-with-us. Why do most translators use virgin here? Is it because they are biased and like the fact that the passage then becomes a prediction of the virgin birth? The answer is that most scholars use the word virgin in this case for two reasons. First, the Jews themselves, when they translated this passage into Greek in the Septuagint version, translated the Hebrew word *alma* into a Greek word which definitely means virgin. Apparently, the Jews at that time, who knew their own language and culture better than us, saw this as being a prophecy of their Messiah being born of a virgin. The second reason most scholars would prefer virgin here is the same reason, presumably, that the Jews who made the Greek translation in the second century B.C. did so. The context of the passage seems to demand this translation. Otherwise, how would it be a sign from God if a married woman or even an unmarried woman who had sex were to have a child? It is very clear that Isaiah 7:14 is a statement that the Messiah would be from a miraculous birth. Why, then, did God, through Isaiah, use the word *alma,* rather than *betula?* Perhaps to stress that Mary, the mother of the Messiah, was so young.

For myself, when I speak publicly on messianic prophecies, I do not include Isaiah 7:14 in my very short list of prophecies to cover, not because I do not believe it is a prophecy of the virgin birth, but simply because the interpretation is debatable. In addition, the skeptics can and do make the charge that Mary was not really a virgin, and who can really prove it one way or another at this point? Let us leave it at this: Mary certainly claimed that her son's birth was miraculous, in complete agreement with Isaiah 7:14.

Isaiah 9:1,6,7

> *Nevertheless, there will be no more gloom for those who were in distress. In the past he humbled the land of Zebulun and the land of Naphtali, but in the future he will honor Galilee of the Gentiles, by the way of the sea, along the Jordan...*
> *For to us a child is born, to us a son is given,*
>   *and the government will be on his shoulders.*
> *And he will be called Wonderful Counselor,*
>   *Mighty God, Everlasting Father, Prince of Peace.*
> *Of the increase of his government and peace*
>   *there will be no end.*
> *He will reign on David's throne and over his kingdom,*
>   *Establishing and upholding it with justice and righteousness*
>   *from that time on and forever.*
> *The zeal of the* LORD *Almighty will accomplish this.*

This is about as unambiguously a messianic prophecy as any. Isaiah describes a figure who is born of woman, but who is Wonderful Counselor, Mighty God, Prince of Peace. The Jews of Jesus' day would recognize this as messianic because of the reference to David's throne. What is Isaiah referring to when he mentions Zebulun and Napthali? If one looks at a map of the approximate borders of the Israelite tribes, one will see that Zebulun and Naphtali are at the heart of the area of Jewish settlement which came to be known as "Galilee" in Roman times (see map below). In fact, if one compares a map of Roman-era Palestine to the map of the tribal territories, one thing which sticks out is that Nazareth is right on the border between the two territories. Isaiah is prophesying that the Messiah will bring honor to Galilee, and more specifically to the lands of Zebulun and Naphtali. It just so happens that Jesus was raised in Galilee—specifically in the small town of Nazareth. It is not as if Jesus could have arranged to fulfill this messianic prophecy (unless, again, he were God). It is also worth noting that extra-biblical sources confirm that Jesus was from Nazareth. In fact, his enemies sarcastically called him *"The Nazarene."* (Mark 14:67, Acts 24:5). Ironically, one of the charges his enemies made against Jesus was that he could not be a prophet, since he was from Galilee. *"Are you from Galilee, too? Look into it, and you will find that a prophet does not come out of Galilee"* (John 7:52). These critics forgot that Jonah was from Galilee. They also forgot the prophecy in Isaiah that God would honor Galilee through his Messiah. When we look at Micah 5:2, this prophecy will seem even more remarkable.

Isaiah 11:1,2

> *A shoot will come up from the stump of Jesse;*
> *From his roots a Branch will bear fruit.*
> *The Spirit of the Lord will rest on him—*
> *the Spirit of wisdom and of understanding,*
> *the Spirit of counsel and power*
> *the Spirit of knowledge and of the fear of the LORD.*

According to Isaiah, one with wisdom, knowledge and power, who is full of the Spirit of God, will come. He will be like a root—a branch from Jesse. Any Jew would know that this is Jesse, the father of King David. God had already promised to David that:

> *"I will raise up your offspring to succeed you, who will come from your own body, and I will establish his kingdom. He is the one who will build a house for my Name, and I will establish the throne of his kingdom forever. I will be his father and he will be my son...Your house and your kingdom will endure forever before me; your throne will be established forever"* (2 Samuel 7:12-16).

The promise of God to David was fulfilled, in part, through his physical son Solomon, who built the temple. However, the physical throne of Israel/Judah was destroyed forever in 586 B.C. when Nebuchadnezzar burned Jerusalem and leveled the temple. The passage in 2 Samuel, which predicts an eternal throne, is a clear reference to the expected Messiah, who will be a descendant of David (2 Samuel 7:12-16), from the "root" of Jesse (Isaiah 11:1). The Jews expected the Messiah, as prophesied in Isaiah 11, to be a direct descendant of King David.

That is exactly what Jesus was. Even if we did not have the geneaologies in Matthew 1:1-16 and Luke 3:23-38, confirming Jesus' descent from the line of David, we could still know that Jesus was from King David's line. We know this from the fact that the census called for by Augustus required all to return to their ancestral towns.[9] Mary and Joseph had to return to Bethlehem, which was the tribal territory of Jesse and of David (1 Samuel 16:4-13). Again we have a messianic prophecy fulfilled by Jesus which is a matter of undeniable historical record over which Jesus (as a human being) had no control. If Jesus was simply trying to fulfill messianic prophecies to prop up a bogus messianic claim, it would have been hard for him to arrange to be descended from David.

But there is a bit more to be gleaned here before we move on. In Matthew 2:23 one finds an interesting statement. After establishing the fact that Jesus' family settled in Nazareth, Matthew declares that this fulfilled a statement of the prophets: *"He will be called a Nazarene."* One will not find the statement *"He will be called a Nazarene"* anywhere in the Old Testament. Is Matthew mistaken? The question is cleared up when one looks a bit closer at the word Nazarene. The word Nazareth in Greek is *nazaret* which means sprout or branch. It comes from the Hebrew word *netser,* which also means branch, and is the word used in Isaiah 11:1. Other prophecies calling the Messiah *"the Branch"* include Jeremiah 23:5, Zechariah 3:8 and Zechariah 6:12.

This is an amazing set of circumstances! God arranged, first, to tell us that his Messiah would be descended from Jesse and David. Second, he arranged to have Jesus be born by direct descent from, or as a branch of David. Third, he told us in the Old Testament that his son would be called *"the Branch".* Fourth, he managed to arrange that Jesus was raised in a town named *"branch"* so that he could be called a Nazarene (branch). To add to the stunning set

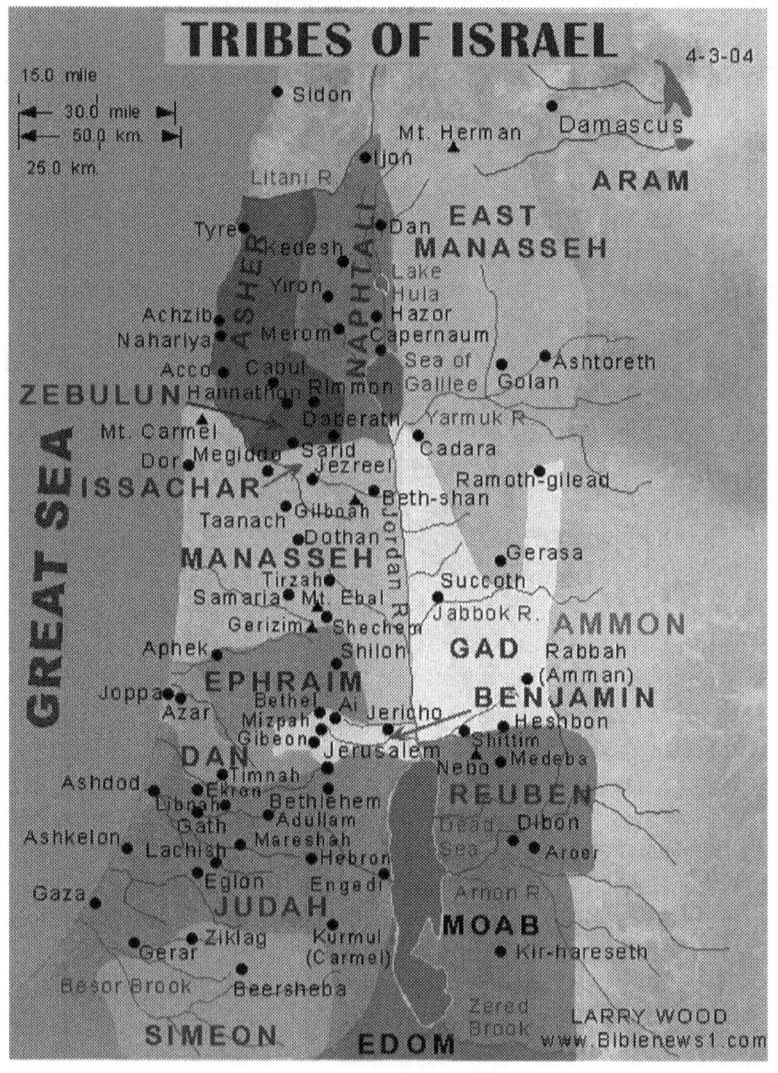

Prophecies in the Old Testament Predict Events in the Life of Jesus Christ of Nazareth

of circumstances, God managed to have this town called branch (Nazareth) be right on the border between Zebulun and Naphtali. If that is a bit confusing for you, imagine God setting it all up!

This is all fascinating information to ponder, but it is very important to remember the main theme. God is sending the Messiah, bringing salvation.

Isaiah 35:5,6

> *Then will the eyes of the blind be opened*
> *and the ears of the deaf unstopped.*
> *Then will the lame leap like a deer,*
> *and the tongue of the dumb shout for joy.*
> *Water will gush forth in the wilderness*
> *and streams in the desert."*

That this is a messianic prophecy is shown by the context in Isaiah 35. *"Water will gush forth in the wilderness," "And a highway will be there; it will be called the Way of Holiness"* (v. 8), *"But only the redeemed will walk there, and the ransomed of the Lord will return"* (v. 9). According to Isaiah, the advent of the Messiah will be accompanied by healings of the blind (Matthew 9:27-31, Mark 8:22-26, John 9:1-7 and others), the deaf (Mark 7:32-35, Mark 9:17-27) and the lame (Mark 2:3-12, John 5:1-8 and many more). As a little touch of prophetic detail, the man healed in Acts 3:1-10 (admittedly healed by Peter in the name of Jesus of Nazareth, rather than by Jesus himself) was *"walking and jumping and praising God."* Jesus fulfilled this prophecy, to say the least. Crowds of thousands came to him from great distances for the opportunity to be healed. Many of these miracles were performed in the public arena. At the first gospel sermon, Peter reminded the people that Jesus was a worker of miracles, wonders and signs, *"as you yourselves know"* (Acts 2:22). Even the Jews who vehemently opposed Jesus could not deny that he worked wonders like no one before him. In fact, the Jewish writers of the Talmud admitted in a backhanded way that he worked miracles, accusing Jesus of practicing sorcery.[10]

Isaiah 42:1-3

> *"Here is my servant whom I uphold,*
> *my chosen one in whom I delight;*

> *I will put my Spirit on him*
> *and he will bring justice to the nations.*
> *He will not shout or cry out,*
> *or raise his voice in the streets.*
> *A bruised reed he will not break,*
> *and a smoldering wick he will not snuff out."*

Here is a servant who will bring justice to the nations. The Messiah will have an amazing impact on the world. Spiritually, he will have a thundering voice, yet he will be supernaturally humble at the same time. He establishes justice for humanity without shouting—without even raising his voice. What an amazing metaphor: *"A bruised reed he will not break."* Is there another figure in world history who fits this description better than Jesus of Nazareth? Jesus could disband an angry, murderous crowd by a look of conviction, by an appeal to conscience or by a moment of pregnant silence (John 8:1-11).

Isaiah 53:1-12

The material in Isaiah chapter fifty-three is without a doubt the most well-known of messianic prophecy. Some, but not all Jews saw this as messianic material.[11] To many Jews it was hard to justify their concept of the Messiah as a political savior, a Davidic Messiah, who would restore the fortunes of Israel with the suffering servant of Isaiah fifty-three. Some Jews even envisioned separate persons in the suffering servant of Isaiah 53 and the restorer of Israel. Much of the prophetic material concerning the spiritual restoration of Israel will be covered in the chapter on prophecies of the kingdom.

The inspiring aspect of the prophecies of both a suffering servant and of a conquering king is that Jesus fulfilled them all. The reason the Jews failed to make the connection is that they misinterpreted the nature of the revived kingdom of Israel. As Jesus said, *"My kingdom is not of this world"* (John 18:36). Much more will be said on this later.

There is so much material in Isaiah chapter fifty-three, that it will be broken into sections in our treatment.

> *Who has believed our message*
> *and to whom has the arm of the LORD been revealed?*

> *He grew up before him like a tender shoot,*
> *and like a root out of dry ground.*
> *He had no beauty or majesty to attract us to him,*
> *nothing in his appearance that we should desire him.*
> *He was despised and rejected by men,*
> *a man of sorrows, and familiar with suffering.*
> *Like one from whom men hide their faces*
> *he was despised, and we esteemed him not*
> (Isaiah 53:1-3).

None of his contemporaries in either biblical or other sources described the physical appearance of Jesus. Apparently, there was nothing either strikingly attractive or repulsive in Jesus' physical appearance. One thing which is not disputed: he was despised and rejected by men. When given a choice between Jesus and the violent criminal Barabbas, the crowd of Jews chose the latter. Although Jesus lived a joyous life, he was a man of great sorrows and suffering. At one point, even his own family doubted his sanity. The people in his home town tried to kill him (Luke 4:16-30). His closest friends abandoned him at his darkest hour. Finally, the people whom he had come to save had him tortured and killed. Truly the Hebrew writer could say of Jesus that *"he learned obedience from what he suffered"* (Hebrews 5:8).

> *Surely he took up our infirmities*
> *and carried our sorrows,*
> *yet we considered him stricken by God,*
> *smitten by him, and afflicted.*
> *But he was pierced for our transgressions,*
> *he was crushed for our iniquities;*
> *the punishment that brought us peace was upon him,*
> *and by his wounds we are healed.*
> *We all, like sheep, have gone astray,*
> *each of us has turned to his own way;*
> *And the LORD laid on him the iniquity of us all*
> (Isaiah 53:4-6).

Jesus was indeed pierced for our transgressions. John reports this detail of the crucifixion in John 19:31-37. As already mentioned in the context of Psalms twenty-two, the Roman soldiers did not break Jesus' legs when they were asked to end the lives of Jesus and the two criminals at his side because he was already dead. In order to make absolutely sure of his death, a soldier drove a spear deep into his side, bringing forth a flow of blood and water.[12] John was an eye-witness of this event. Little did the soldier who jabbed the spear into Jesus' side know that he was fulfilling the prophecy uttered by Isaiah over seven hundred years before. The wonderful statement, *"by his wounds we are healed,"* brings us back to the whole point of this prophecy. The Messiah is coming, bringing salvation. The phrase, *"the LORD has laid on him the iniquity of us all,"* is a reference to the laying of hands on the scape-goat during the *Yom Kippur* ceremony to remove the sins of the people. It is also a prophecy that the suffering Messiah would be our scape-goat, taking upon himself the sins of all people on the cross.

> *He was oppressed and afflicted,*
>   *yet he did not open his mouth;*
> *he was led like a lamb to the slaughter,*
>   *and as a sheep before her shearers is silent,*
>   *so he did not open his mouth.*
> *By oppression and judgment, he was taken away.*
>   *And who can speak of his descendants?*
> *For he was cut off from the land of the living;*
>   *for the transgression of my people he was stricken.*
> *He was assigned a grave with the wicked,*
>   *and with the rich in his death,*
> *though he had done no violence,*
>   *nor was any deceit in his mouth*
> (Isaiah 53:7-9).

One of the most amazing aspects of the events which led up to the crucifixion of Jesus is that when he was accused, he refused to defend himself. *"When he was accused by the chief priests and the elders, he gave no answer"* (Matthew 27:12). Truly, Jesus was led like a sheep before his shearers. The difference is that a sheep is not smart enough to know what is coming, while Jesus most certainly did. *"Who can speak of his descendants?"* This is an ironic question. Jesus was cut off in the prime of his life and had no physical descendants. Yet those who take on the faith of Abraham become spiritual descendants of Abraham, sons or daughters of God and brothers or sisters of Jesus.

Although Jesus was very poor himself, he did have a small number of wealthy supporters. *"As evening approached, there* came a rich man from Arimathea, named Joseph, who had himself become a disciple of Jesus. Going to Pilate, he asked for Jesus' body, and Pilate ordered that it be given to him" (Matthew 27:57,58). Despite his poverty, Jesus was buried in a new tomb which had been carved out for the family members of Joseph, a wealthy Jew. And thus Jesus fulfilled the prophecy of Isaiah. He was *"assigned a grave with the wicked, and with the rich in his death."*

> *Yet it was the LORD'S will to crush him*
>   *and cause him to suffer,*
> *And though the LORD makes his life a guilt offering,*
>   *he will see his offspring and prolong his days,*
>   *and the will of the LORD will prosper in his hand.*
> *After the suffering of his soul,*
>   *he will see the light of life and be satisfied;*
> *by his knowledge my righteous servant will justify many,*
>   *and he will bear their iniquities.*
> *Therefore I will give him a portion among the great,*
>   *and he will divide the spoils with the strong,*
> *because he poured out his life unto death,*
>   *and was numbered with the transgressors.*
> *For he bore the sin of many,*
>   *and made intercession for the transgressors* (Isaiah 53:10-12).

As already stated, although the Messiah was cut off and had no physical descendants, through his giving of himself as a guilt offering, Jesus was able to see his spiritual offspring—the church. Isaiah also prophesied the resurrection of the suffering servant. *"After the suffering of his soul, he will see the light of life."* As Paul said in 1 Corinthians 15:5, Christ was raised, *"according to the Scriptures."* The fulfillment of this prophecy is one of the central facts of Christianity. In a reference to the drink offering, Isaiah states that the Messiah will pour out his life unto death. Jesus willingly gave himself as a drink offering for us. This beautiful passage is a mixture of historical prophecy of the Messiah and a clear statement of the gospel of Jesus Christ. Praise God that we have passed from shadow to reality—that the Mystery has been revealed. On the cross, Jesus willingly bore the sin of many and interceded with his Father for us.

Prophecies in the Old Testament Predict Events in the Life of Jesus Christ of Nazareth

Old Testament Prophecy	Content	New Testament Fulfillment
Genesis 3:15	Satan will attack the Messiah, but the Messiah will destroy the work of Satan.	Matthew 4:11, Luke 4:1-13
Genesis 49:10,11	The Messiah will be from Judah (also hints about a vine, colt, branch and blood/grapes)	Matthew 1:2,3
Deuteronomy 18:15-18	God will raise up a prophet like, but greater than Moses.	Matthew 21:11, Mark 6:15
Psalm 16:10,11	The Messiah will not be abandoned to the grave (will be resurrected).	John 2:19, Luke 24:1-7
Psalm 22:15-18	The Messiah will be crucified, his bones will not be broken, his clothing will be divided and gambled over.	John 19:6,7; 19:31-34; John 19:23,24
Psalm 31:5	The Messiah will commit his spirit into the hands of God.	Luke 23:46
Psalm 69:9,21	The Messiah will show zeal for God's house. He will be given gall and vinegar to drink.	John 2:12-17, Matthew 27:34, Luke 23:36
Psalm 110:1,4	The Messiah will be a priest in the order of Melchizedek.	Hebrews 7:11-18
Psalm 118:22,23	The Messiah will be rejected, but will become the foundation of the Kingdom of God.	Matthew 23:37 Acts 4:10
Isaiah 7:14	The Messiah will be born of a virgin.	Luke 1:26-38
Isaiah 9:1,2,6,7	The Messiah will be from Galilee; in the region of Zebulun and Naphtali.	Hebrews 7:11-18
Isaiah 11:1,2	The Messiah will be descended from Jesse and will be a Branch (Nazarene).	Matthew 1:5,6; John 1:45,46; Matthew 2:23
Isaiah 35:5,6	The Messiah will heal the deaf, the blind and the physically disabled.	Mark 7:22-25, 8:22-26, 2:3-12
Isaiah 42:1-4	The Messiah will be miraculously humble.	John 8:1-11
Isaiah 53	The Messiah will be despised and rejected by men, he will suffer and be pierced, he will take on himself the sin of mankind, he will be silent before his accusers, and will be buried with the rich.	Matthew 27:15-18 John 19:33-35, Mark 14:60,61, 15:3-5; Mark 15:42-46
Daniel 9:24-27	The Messiah will come to Jerusalem to bring salvation somewhere between AD 26-33.	Luke 3:1,2
Micah 5:2	The Messiah will be born in Bethlehem Ephrathah.	Luke 2:1-7
Zechariah 6:9-15	The Messiah will be a king and a priest, and will bring harmony between the two.	John 18:37 Hebrews 7:11-17
Zechariah 9:9-11	The Messiah will ride as king into Jerusalem riding on a donkey and the colt of that donkey.	Matthew 21:1-7
Zechariah 11:10-14	The Messiah will be betrayed for 30 pieces of silver. Money will be thrown to "the potter."	Matthew 26:14-16 Matthew 27:6,7
Zechariah 13:7	When the Messiah is attacked, his "sheep" will be scattered.	Mark 14:50,51

Messianic Prophecies in the other prophets

There are a number of messianic prophecies scattered throughout the other books of the prophets, especially in Zechariah. There is almost as much specific messianic prophecy in Zechariah as in Isaiah or Psalms. For the sake of space, we will only cover those which are most obviously messianic and which include new information about the Messiah we have not already seen. Messianic prophecies in these books which are not covered here include Jeremiah 23:5, Jeremiah 33:14-22, Ezekiel 21:27, Haggai 2:23, Zechariah 3:1-8, and Zechariah 4:12-14.

Daniel 9:24-27

The book of Daniel has more historical prophecy than any other in the Bible. In the sixth century B.C., Daniel wrote a history book of the Near East for the next two thousand years. Daniel tells the history of the Babylonian, Persian, Greek and Roman Empires both with a broad brush and in striking detail, hundreds of years before these events. All these prophecies are covered thoroughly in my book *Daniel, Prophet to the Nations*.[13] There are prophecies of the Kingdom of God in Daniel as well (see chapter nine). The messianic prophecy in Daniel is found in chapter nine.

> *"Seventy 'sevens' are decreed for your people and your holy city to finish transgression, to put an end to sin, to atone for wickedness, to bring in everlasting righteousness, to seal up vision and prophecy and to anoint the most holy.*
>
> *Know and understand this: From the issuing of the decree to restore and rebuild Jerusalem until the Anointed One, the ruler, comes, there will be seven 'sevens.' It will be rebuilt with streets and a trench, but in times of trouble. After sixty-two 'sevens,' the Anointed One will be cut off and will have nothing. The people of the ruler who will come will destroy the city and the sanctuary. The end will come like a flood: War will continue until the end, and desolations have been decreed. He will confirm a covenant with many for one 'seven,' but in the middle of that 'seven' he will put an end to sacrifice and offerring. And one who causes desolation will place abominations on a wing of the temple until the end that is decreed is poured out on him"* (Daniel 9:24-27).

The Jews in the first century were well aware that this was a prophecy of the Messiah. The word Messiah comes from the Greek for anointed one. Could it be any clearer? The phrases, *"to atone for wickedness, to bring in everlasting righteousness, to seal up vision and prophecy and to anoint the most holy"* have the unmistakeable imprint of messianic prophecy.

What is the meaning of the seventy "sevens?" It seems that it refers to a period of time, but if one were reading this prophecy before its fulfillment, the exact meaning of this phrase would be debatable. In hindsight, there can be little doubt what it refers to. Seventy times seven is four hundred and ninety. Is it four hundred and ninety days? Months? Years? Or is it some indeterminate amount of time? History and the appearance of the Messiah in Jerusalem will answer this question for us. It is definitely four hundred and ninety years.

The key to interpreting the timing of this prophecy is found in verse twenty-five. *"From the issuing of the decree to restore and rebuild Jerusalem, until the Anointed One* (i.e. the Messiah) *comes..."* When Cyrus destroyed the Babylonian Empire in 539 B.C., he set in motion the process which led to the return of God's people from exile in Mesopotamia to reoccupy the Promised Land. All this had been prophesied by God. In about 730 B.C., Isaiah wrote, *"This is what the LORD says... 'I will raise up Cyrus in my righteousness: I will make all his ways straight. He will rebuild my city and set my exiles free'"* (Isaiah 44:28-45:1,13). God had reemphasized this prophecy in Jeremiah 25:11,12, *"these nations will serve the king of Babylon seventy years. But when the seventy years are fulfilled, I will punish the king of Babylon and his nation."*

After the Persian Emperor Cyrus had destroyed the Babylonian power, there was more than one decree to free the Jews which could conceivably be what Daniel's prophecy refers to. There was the decree of Cyrus in 539 B.C., found in Ezra 1:2-4, which led to the first return of captives to Jerusalem. This decree authorized the rebuilding of the Temple, not necessarily the city of Jerusalem. There were two other decrees in support of an Israelite return issued by Persian emperors that we know of. The first of these is found in Ezra 7:13-26. It was issued *"in the fifth month of the seventh year of the king."* The king referred to in Ezra seven is Artaxerxes. This decree was issued in 458 B.C. It provided for large funds to rebuild the city of Jerusalem. Artaxerxes issued a second decree to Nehemiah in the king's twentieth year (Nehemiah 2:1), which would make it 445 B.C. This letter, although not recorded in Nehemiah, supported the efforts to complete the wall of the city. The first decree to actually restore and rebuild the city of Jerusalem was the one issued in 458 B.C. This is most likely the one referred to in Daniel 9:25.

If the seventy "sevens" refer to years, then, adding four hundred and ninety years to 458 B.C. would give the year A.D. 32. Actually, that is wrong, as there was no year 0 B.C., so four hundred and ninety years after the decree to rebuild Jerusalem was A.D. 33. That is a very familiar year to anyone who knows the story of Jesus Christ. Actually, if one reads Daniel 9:25 more carefully, one will find the prediction that the Messiah will come to Jerusalem during the last week; *"there will be seven 'sevens' and sixty-two 'sevens.'"* To be honest with the text, it predicts that the Messiah will come to Jerusalem to atone for wickedness, to be anointed and to bring in everlasting righteousness somewhere between A.D. 26-33. The most likely date for the crucifixion is actually A.D. 29, rather than the traditional A.D. 33.[14]

To summarize, not only did Daniel predict that the Messiah would bring forgiveness of sins to Israel; he told us when to expect him to come! It is not as if the gospel writers could have faked Jesus' fulfillment of this prophecy! History tells us when Pontius Pilate ruled Judea and Tacitus reported that *"Chrestus"* was executed under Pontius Pilate. This is an amazing prophecy! Think, for a moment, about the implications. God told us the year Jesus would be crucified almost six hundred years before it happened. The death of Jesus was no afterthought.

The prophecy in Daniel chapter nine goes on to predict events in A.D. 70 when the Roman armies surrounded Jerusalem, broke through the walls, destroyed the city and burned the Temple to the ground, bringing a final *"end to sacrifice and offering"* (v. 27). Jesus Christ also prophesied concerning these events as recorded in Luke 21:20-24 and Matthew 24:15-25, but since this is not messianic prophecy, we will move on.

Micah 5:2

> *"But you, Bethlehem Ephrathah*
> *though you are small among the clans of Judah,*

> *Out of you will come for me*
> *one who will be ruler over Israel,*
> *whose origins are from of old,*
> *from ancient times."*

Micah prophesied to Israel in the eighth century B.C. He was a contemporary of Isaiah. That this is a prophecy of the Messiah is obvious from the text: *"one who will be ruler over Israel, whose origins are from old."* There is no doubt that the Jews in Jesus' time acknowledged that this was a messianic prediction, as they confronted Jesus with this very passage. *"How can the Christ come from Galilee? Does not the Scripture say that the Christ will come from David's family and from Bethlehem, the town where David lived?"* (John 7:41,42). Apparently the crowd was aware of Micah 5:2, and of the fact that Jesus was from Galilee (as required by Isaiah 9:1), but they were not informed about where Jesus was born. Here again we have a specific prophecy of the Messiah which was fulfilled by Jesus but which it was not in his (human) ability to control and which even historians will acknowledge is true of Jesus. How many people running around in Israel at the right time (A.D. 26-33) were born in Bethlehem but came from Galilee? Probably very few. Throw in the requirement to be a Nazarene (branch) and you are probably down to exactly one.

By the way, there were actually two small cities in Palestine named Bethlehem at the time Micah wrote. One was the now-famous Bethlehem which is a few miles south of Jerusalem. The other was in Northern Israel (Joshua 19:15). Jesus was born in the right one: Bethlehem Ephrathah.

Zechariah 6:9-15

> *The word of the Lord came to me: "Take silver and gold from the exiles Heldai, Tobijah and Jediah, who have arrived from Babylon. Go the same day to the house of Josiah son of Zephahiah. Take the silver and gold and make a crown, and set it on the head of the high priest, Joshua son of Jehozadak. Tell him this is what the LORD Almighty says: 'Here is the man whose name is the Branch, and he will branch out from his place and build the temple of the LORD and he will be clothed with majesty and will sit and rule on his throne. And he will*

> be a priest on his throne. And there will be harmony between the two.'"

This is one of the lesser-known Old Testament prophecies of the Messiah. We can be sure that it is a prophecy of the savior of Israel because of some familiar themes in the passage. Zechariah mentions that the name of the man to be crowned is *"the Branch."* He also says that the Branch will sit and rule on his throne. This passage, as well as Micah 5:2 (and Jeremiah 33:14-22) could be categorized as kingly, Davidic messianic passages—ones which the Jews were more likely to acknowledge as referring to the Messiah than servant passages such as Isaiah 53.

In this prophetic scripture, God tells Zechariah to place a crown on the head of the high priest Joshua, son of Jehozadek. This is a symbolic acting out of the crowning of the Messiah as king. Remember that the Hebrew word Joshua is Jeshua in Aramaic and Jesus in Greek. This is not the first time in Zechariah that God uses the high priest Joshua as a symbolic foreshadowing of the Messiah. Zechariah sees Joshua the high priest in messianic vision acting out the role of the Savior of Israel in Zechariah 3:1-4 as well.

We have some new details about the Messiah here. First, he will build the temple of the LORD. Jesus made a similar statement about himself. *"Destroy this temple, and I will raise it again in three days"* (John 2:19). In this statement, Jesus was referring to his own body, which was the Temple of God. We also know from our study of the Tabernacle and the Temple in chapter three that Jesus restored access to the true Temple/Tabernacle in heaven through his sacrifice on the cross.

Another important part of this prophecy is that, after describing the Messiah as a king, it also calls him a *"priest on his throne."* God tells Zechariah that *"there will be harmony between the two."* "The two" are the priesthood and the kingship. As has been said previously, the Jews had three offices: priest, prophet and king. This prophecy states that in the Messiah, priest and king will come together in one person. For the Jews, the idea of crowning the high priest Joshua as a king must have been shocking, but God is trying to tell us something about the Messiah. Never in the history of Israel did a priest occupy the throne. Jesus certainly fulfilled this prophecy as a priest "in the order of Melchizedek" (Psalms 110:4), and as king (John 18:37).

Zechariah 9:9-11

Rejoice greatly, O Daughter of Zion!
  Shout, daughter of Jerusalem!
See, your king comes to you,
  righteous and having salvation,
Gentle and riding on a donkey,
  on a colt, the foal of a donkey....
He will proclaim peace to the nations.
His rule will extend from sea to sea
  and from the River to the ends of the earth.
As for you, because of the blood of my covenant with you,
  I will free your prisoners from the waterless pit.

For us in the modern world, the donkey is not a symbol of anything great, but in the ancient Near East, riding into a city in procession on a donkey was a symbol of royalty.[15] Again we have a prophecy which is undoubtably messianic. *"He will proclaim peace to the nations: His rule will extend from sea to sea... to the ends of the earth."* According to Zechariah's oracle, the Messiah will ride into Jerusalem on a donkey. No, that is not right. He will ride into Jerusalem on a colt—a very young donkey. Which is it, a donkey or a colt? This is reminiscent of Psalms chapter twenty-two which had the Messiah's garments divided up and gambled. Which is it? Both!

As Jesus said, *"everything must be fulfilled that is written about me in the Law of Moses, the Prophets and the Psalms."* (Luke 24:44). Zechariah chapter 9 is no exception. Jesus had been to Jerusalem many times before. However, because he knew *"my time has not yet come"* (John 2:4), he entered and left very quietly. His last entry into Jerusalem was a dramatic exception to this rule. *"Go to the village ahead of you, and at once you will find a donkey tied there, with her colt by her. Untie them and bring them to me"* (Matthew 21:3). Which did Jesus ride on? *"They brought the donkey and the colt, placed their cloaks on them and Jesus sat on them"* (Matthew 21:7). During the journey, Jesus probably rode them both. Jesus entered Jerusalm as a king. The Messiah has come, bringing salvation.

Zechariah 11:10-14

> Then I took my staff called Favor and broke it, revoking the covenant I had made with all the nations. It was revoked on that day, and so the afflicted of the flock who were watching me knew it was the word of the LORD.
> I told them, "If you think it best, give me my pay; but if not, keep it." So they paid me thirty pieces of silver.
> And the LORD said to me, "Throw it to the potter"—the handsome price at which they priced me! So I took the thirty pieces of silver and threw them into the house of the LORD to the potter."

Someone is being paid thirty pieces of silver here. What is the money buying? *"And the LORD said to me, 'Throw it to the potter'—the price at which they priced me!"* Someone sold God for thirty pieces of silver. Most of us have heard stories of a painting by one of the masters, worth many millions of dollars, being sold for twenty bucks at a garage sale, but this has to be the most foolish sale since Esau sold his birthright to Jacob for a bowl of lentil stew (Genesis 25:29-34). When he looked at what he had put on papyrus, Zechariah must have really been baffled to imagine what he was writing about. With historical hindsight, we know exactly what this is about. Talk about a specific prophecy!

> Then one of the Twelve—the one called Judas Iscariot—went to the chief priests and asked, "What are you willing to give me if I hand him over to you?" So they counted out for him thirty silver coins. From then on Judas watched for an opportunity to hand him over (Matthew 26:14-16).

Zechariah hit the price on the nose, five hundred and fifty years before the event.[16] What are the chances of accurately predicting that God would be sold, never mind getting the exact price, hundreds of years before the event? And who would have the nerve to put his prediction down in writing as Zechariah did? Jesus could not have arranged for the price of his betrayal. Again, we see God using those who opposed Jesus to fulfill prophecies of the Messiah.

The skeptic might argue that Matthew made up this detail about the price to make it appear that Jesus fulfilled this prophecy. However that argument does not hold up to scrutiny. If Matthew were making up a story, why would he include a detail that hundreds of people still alive when he wrote the gospel could publicly refute? A liar generally is vague about the details.

In Zechariah 11, the one who sells God for thirty pieces of silver seems hesitant to take the money: *"If you think it best, give me my pay, but if not keep it."* Then Zechariah supplies a detail which must have been even more mystifying to him when he wrote it than the thirty pieces of silver. *"'Throw it to the potter'—the handsome price at which they priced me. So I took the thirty pieces of silver and threw them into the house of the LORD to the potter."* The mystery is removed when one looks at what happened to Judas after his betrayal of Jesus. Perhaps Judas had betrayed him in order to force his hand to bid for political power in Judea. It is hard to believe he did it simply for the money. When he saw his plan backfiring, and realized that Jesus would not defend himself, but would instead be condemned, Judas was seized with remorse. He had misunderstood Jesus all along. When Judas tried to return the money to the chief priests, they refused to accept it, so he threw the money into the temple—the house of the LORD—exactly as Zechariah had prophesied. This is not the first time we have seen characters acting out a play on a divine stage without even knowing that they are being fed the lines by God.

> *The chief priests picked up the coins and said, "It is against the law to put this into the treasury, since it is blood money." So they decided to use the money to buy the potter's field as a burial place for foreigners. That is why it has been called the Field of Blood to this day* (Matthew 27:6,7).

When Matthew threw in the little detail about the field being called The Field of Blood *"to this day,"* it is as if he was saying, "If you have any doubt about it, just go ask the chief priests in Jerusalem, they will tell you all about it."

Let us not forget the main point here. The death of Jesus on the cross was no accident. Prophecies such as Zechariah 11:10-14 provide great evidence for the inspiration of the Bible, which is a great faith-builder. Even more significantly, this passage shows that God planned all along to send his son to be betrayed, to suffer, and to die so that every person could have access to forgiveness of sins and eternal life.

Zechariah 12:10

> "And I will pour out on the house of David and the inhabitants of Jerusalem a spirit of grace and supplication. They will look on me, the one they have pierced, and mourn for him as one mourns for an only child, and grieve for him as one grieves for a firstborn son."

The phrases *"I will pour out,"* and *"They will look on me, the one they have pierced,"* indicate that this is a messianic prophecy, as the use of I and me show that the passage is about deity being pierced.

Zechariah prophesied that the Messiah would pour out grace on the inhabitants of Jerusalem. The apostle John described Jesus as *"the one and only Son, who came from the Father, full of grace and truth"* (John 1:14). Jesus certainly poured out grace on the inhabitants of spiritual Jerusalem: those saved under the New Covenant.

We have already seen from our study of Isaiah 53 that "the one they have pierced" is a prophecy of the spear being thrust into Jesus' side after he died on the cross. Zechariah adds one detail to Isaiah. Notice the words "they" in the phrases, *"They will look,"* and *"they have pierced."* "They" is a reference to anyone who recognizes that his sin is responsible for the death of Jesus. In the first recorded gospel sermon as the church began, Peter pointed out to the crowd that, *"God has made this Jesus, whom you crucified, both Lord and Christ"* (Acts 2:36). The prophecy of Zechariah that the people would mourn deeply for the one who was pierced was fulfilled, both in the intense mourning of the witnesses at the foot of the cross, and in the response of the people to Peter's announcement that they had killed the Messiah. *"When the people heard this, they were cut to the heart"* (Acts 2:37). Revelation 1:7 reminds us of Zechariah 12:10.

> Look, he is coming with the clouds,
>   and every eye will see him,
> even those who pierced him;
>   and all peoples of the earth will mourn because of him.

Zechariah 13:7

> *"Awake, O sword, against my shepherd,*
>   *against the man who is close to me!"*
>   *declares the LORD Almighty.*
> *Strike the shepherd,*
>   *and the sheep will be scattered,*
>   *and I will turn my hand against the little one."*

At the moment of his greatest personal need, Jesus was abandoned by his closest friends in the world. These were the same men for whom he had poured out his life. That very night he had humbly washed their feet. Yet, when he asked them to stay with him while he prayed in the garden on the night he was betrayed, they fell asleep. *"Awake, O sword against my shepherd."* This is a prophetic reference to the Jewish temple guard who came with swords drawn to arrest Jesus. What did the sheep (the apostles) do when their shepherd was struck? Despite their vehement declaration that same night that they would never abandon their leader, all of the disciples fled to avoid arrest. *"Then everyone deserted him and fled"* (Mark 14:50).

Jesus was obviously well aware of this passage in Zechariah. Just a few hours before he told them that they would abandon him that very night. Jesus knew his fate from the very beginning, but he never wavered. The suffering servant of Isaiah 53 was about to begin his hour of greatest trial alone.

CONCLUSION

When one considers the historical messianic prophecies in the Old Testament, one thing is made abundantly clear. The death of Jesus was no spur-of-the-moment decision. God had planned from the very beginning to allow his Son to suffer and be killed at the hands of those for whom he had come to die. God made this truth very clear in the Old Testament, so we shouldn't be surprised. Jesus' claim that the entire Old Testament was written about him has been proven by the evidence. Jesus Christ is the Messiah, sent by God into the world to save sinners. He is the man. How can we be sure? According to the Old Testament, the Messiah would:

- Be born in Bethlehem Ephethrah,
- Come from Galilee, in the region of Zebulun and Naphtali,
- Come to Jerusalem to bring salvation in about A.D. 33,
- Be despised and rejected by men,
- Remain silent when accused, even upon threat of death,
- Be pierced, and
- Be crucified,
- Have his clothes divided and gambled over,
- Be sold for 30 pieces of silver,
- Ride into Jerusalem on a donkey and its colt,
- Be abandoned by his followers,
- And most difficult of all: Be resurrected from the grave.

Has any man who ever lived experienced more than, say, three of these? Is there the slightest possibility that the Bible is not inspired by God? Do non-believers have an answer to this challenge? Clearly not.

This is faith-building, but let us not forget the main point. God sent his Son, Jesus Christ, to die for the sins of the whole world. The message of the Old Testament is that the Messiah is coming, bringing salvation. In the words of the Apostle Paul in 2 Corinthians 6:1, *"I tell you, now is the time of God's favor, now is the day of salvation."* Or as Peter put it in 2 Peter 1:19, *"And we have the word of the prophets made more certain, and you will do well to pay attention to it."*

Endnotes

1 This summary of the work of the Messiah is taken from Phillip Lester, *The Jewish Messiah: Jesus, Judaism and Messianic Prophecy* (unpublished, PPLester@aol.com).

2 John M. Oakes, *Reasons for Belief—A Handbook of Christian Evidences* (2001), chapter four.

3 See *Reasons for Belief—A Handbook of Christian Evidences* (2001), for specific references to Tacitus, Pliny, Josephus and the Talmud.

4 The Jewish historian Josephus described the martyrdom of the apostle James in *Antiquities, xx.9.1*. Fourth century church historian Eusebius claimed that all the apostles except for John were martyred, providing details of varying reliability to support the claim.

5 *Targum Neofiti, 3:14b-15*, which reads: 'But when they forsake the commandments of the Law you will aim and bite him on his heel and make him ill. For her sons, however, there will be a remedy, but for you, O Serpent, there will not be a remedy, since they are to make appeasement in the end, in the day of King Messiah.' (As translated by M. McNamara, Targum Neofiti 1: Genesis, The Aramaic Bible 1A [T. T. and Clark, Edinburgh, 1992] p. 61).

6 Antiochus Epiphanes was the Greek king who desecrated the temple in 167 B.C., sacrificing a pig in the Most Holy Place. For details on this, see John M. Oakes, *Daniel, Prophet to the Nations* (available from www.ipibooks.com), especially in its treatment of Daniel chapters seven and eleven.

7 Josephus, *Antiquities, xviii.3.3*, Babylonian Talmud, *Sanhedrin, 43a*.

8 Examples are found in Barry Rubin, *You Bring the Bagels, I'll Bring the Gospel* (Lederer, Baltimore, Maryland, 1997), pp. 73-79.

9 For many years, skeptics scoffed at the story in Matthew of Joseph and Mary having to travel to their ancestral home to register for a census. The skeptics said first of all that there was no evidence of Augustus calling a general census, and second that even if he had, the idea that people would travel great distances to be counted had no ancient precedent. That skepticism was shown for what it is when an inscription was found in Egypt which mentions a census called by Augustus in 8 B.C. which specifically stated that all peoples had to return to their native towns to register.

10 From the *Baraila Talmud*, Babylonia Sanhedrin 43a.

11 An example of a Jewish writing which identified this section of Isaiah as messianic is in the Talmud, Sotah 14a, which describes the suffering servant as a fulfillment of the second Moses prophecy in Deuteronomy 18:15-19.

12 Modern medical science would interpret the flow of both blood and "water" to indicate that Jesus had already died, as blood and serum separate soon after death.

13 John M. Oakes, *Daniel, Prophet to the Nations* (available from www.ipibooks.com) .

14 See *Daniel, Prophet to the Nations*, p 154,155.

15 See 1 Kings 1:33.

16 Zechariah 1:1 dates the visions he received from God to the second year of Darius, king of Persia, which would be 520 B.C.

Old Testament Prophecies Announce the Coming of the Kingdom of God

> *"In the time of those kings* (i.e. the time of Rome), *the God of heaven will set up a kingdom that will never be destroyed, nor will it be left to another people. It will crush all those kingdoms and bring them to an end, but it will itself endure forever."*
> — Daniel 2:44

We have already seen a number of prophecies which describe the Messiah as a king. Having the title of king isn't all that impressive unless one has a kingdom and subjects to rule over. When Jesus rode into Jerusalem on a donkey, he was announcing the coming of a king, and the birth of a kingdom. When asked by Pilate if he was a king, Jesus responded, *"My kingdom is not of this world."* So what is the kingdom ruled by the Messiah to be like? To answer this question, one need look no farther than the Old Testament. There one will find a number of prophecies concerning the messianic kingdom of God. The Old Testament has prophecies describing the "constitution" of this kingdom, as well as its growth and the extent of its dominion. There are also prophecies concerning the power of this kingdom and its "foreign relations," as well as the relationship between the king and his subjects.

In the previous chapter we saw messianic prophecies involving the general nature of the Messiah, but also ones providing specific details about his life such as where he would live, when he would come to Jerusalem; even the exact price for which he would be betrayed. Prophecies of the Kingdom of God in the Old

Testament are not as detailed or specific because the Kingdom of God is a broad concept, rather than an entity which is limited by time and space. Having said that, however, there is plenty of Old Testament source material about the coming kingdom of God. Jesus expounded on the subject when he appeared over a forty day period after his resurrection during which he *"spoke about the kingdom of God"* (Acts 1:3).

A BIBLICAL VIEW OF THE KINGDOM OF GOD

Before examining some of the prophetic descriptions of the Kingdom of God in the Old Testament, it will be helpful to establish a biblical definition of this kingdom. Some would say that the Kingdom of God is the church of Jesus Christ on the earth. Others would say that the kingdom of God is heaven. In truth, God's kingdom expresses itself in different ways at different times. In broadest terms, the Kingdom of God is anyone or anywhere over which God rules.

Certainly the Jews under the Mosaic covenant saw themselves as the Kingdom of God. One of the reasons God did not want Israel to have a human king is that He wanted to be king over his people—one without rival. When invited to be king over the tribes of Israel, Gideon replied: *"I will not rule over you, nor will my son rule over you. The LORD will rule over you"* (Judges 8:23). Samuel admonished Israel, *"But when you saw that Nahash king of the Ammonites was moving against you, you said to me, 'No, we want a king to rule over us'—even though the LORD your God was your king"* (1 Samuel 12:12). The greatest king of Israel, David, acknowledged that God was the real king of Israel. *"Yours, O LORD is the kingdom; you are exalted as head over all"* (1 Chronicles 29:11). Jesus acknowledged that his fellow Jews were part of the Kingdom of God in Matthew 8:12. So Israel, and later Judah, was a manifestation of the kingdom of God on earth at that time.

However God's people were not faithful, and God intended all along to set up a spiritual kingdom to include both Jew and Gentile. That is the point of this chapter. We will see many prophecies of this kingdom. The spiritual kingdom on earth which superseded the kingdom of Israel was the church. Indeed, the physical kingdom of Israel was a foreshadow of the spiritual Kingdom of God—the church of Jesus Christ. A number of New Testament passages seem to equate the Kingdom of God with the church—the body of Christ. One example is Matthew 16:18,19, where Jesus explicitly connects the two as he speaks to Peter. But we should be aware that while the church which Jesus died for may be the kingdom of God, the kingdom is something greater than that, for while Jesus reigns over his church, he also reigns in Heaven. To use a crude description, the church is "part" of the kingdom of God.

So the church is the Kingdom of God, but surely the greatest expression of the kingdom is heaven itself. In heaven, God reigns, with Jesus at his right hand. As Jesus said, *"Then the King will say to those on his right, 'Come, you who are blessed by my Father; take your inheritance, the kingdom prepared for you since the creation of the world"* (Matthew 25:34). The book of Revelation is replete with royal scenes in heaven, such as Revelation chapter four: *"At once I was in the spirit, and there before me was a throne in heaven with someone sitting on it...Surrounding the throne were twenty-four other thrones...In the center, around the throne were four living creatures...the twenty-four elders fall down before him who sits on the throne, and worship him who lives forever..."* (Revelation 4:2,4,6,10). To summarize, in ascending order, physical Israel as a kingdom is a foreshadow of spiritual Israel—the church, while the church as a kingdom is a foreshadow of the Kingdom of God in heaven.

More evidence of the parallel and complementary nature of the different aspects of the Kingdom of God is found in the use of the number twelve in the Bible. The physical kingdom of Israel was divided into twelve tribes. Jesus chose twelve apostles who had special spiritual authority in the spiritual Kingdom of God on the earth. The parallel is carried into the future Kingdom of God in Revelation 21:12,13:

> *It* (the New Jerusalem) *had a great, high wall with twelve gates and with twelve angels at the gates. On the gates were written the names of the twelve tribes of Israel. There were three gates on the east, three on the north, three on the south and three on the west. The wall of the city had twelve foundations, and on them were the names of the twelve apostles of the Lamb.*

Twelve is the number associated with God's kingdom in its three most obvious manifestations. The throne scene in heaven in Revelation chapter four has twenty-four elders laying down their crowns before the throne of God, declaring him to be worthy to receive glory and honor and power. The twenty-four elders in this scene may represent the twelve tribes and the twelve apostles. James was not making a mistake when he wrote his letter to the church as a whole, describing them as *"the twelve tribes scattered among the nations"* (James 1:1).

Much more could be said about the Kingdom of God.[1] The earth itself, with all its flora, and fauna, is part of God's kingdom. The kingdom is God's rule over anyone who takes him as King. With this broad understanding we will narrow our focus in this chapter to Old Testament prophecies which refer to the kingdom as it is manifested in the church. That the passages we examine refer to the church may not always be completely clear cut. Some prophecies of the kingdom may refer principally to the church, but also have some reference to physical Israel. Others will be predictions of the church, but have prophetic overtones referring to heaven.

We have already seen this phenomenon, where prophecy has a dual reference. One example we have seen is 2 Samuel 7:11,12, in which one finds a dual prophecy of the kingship of Solomon over physical Israel and of the kingship of the Messiah over spiritual Israel. An example of a prophetic passage which seems to slip back and forth between reference to the church as a kingdom and to heaven is the extensive prophecy given by Jesus in Matthew 24:1-25:13, in which Jesus moves from predicting the destruction of Jerusalem in A.D. 70 to describing his return at the trumpet call of God at the end of days without providing a clear transition. In Jesus' prophecy, it is sometimes hard to be sure if he is describing the destruction of Jerusalem or his second coming.

Now that we have a working definition of the Kingdom of God, we will look at a number of the Old Testament prophecies of the kingdom. Not all of these verses will actually include the word "kingdom," but all will refer to a new dispensation to be offered to humanity at some point in the future. In the study of messianic prophecies in the previous chapter, we worked from the front to the back of the Old Testament. In this treatment, the kingdom prophecies will be divided according to subject matter.

Prophecies of the Kingdom of God

Prophesied Quality of the Kingdom of God	Old Testament Prophecies (& New Testament Fulfillment)
Establishment of the Kingdom.	Jeremiah 31:31-34 (Hebrews 9:15) Ezekiel 36:24-27 (John 16:13-15, Acts 2:39)
Who will be the King?	Ezekiel 34:23,24 (John 10:14, Ephesians 1:22,23) Hoseal 3:5 Joel 2:28-32 (Acts 2:16-21) Zechariah 13:1,2
Extent of the Kingdom of God.	Isaiah 49:6, 42:6 Isaiah 2:2-4 Isaiah 54:1 (Galatians 4:26-28) Ezekiel 17:22-24 Zechariah 2:10,11
Relationship between King and subjects.	Exodus 19:5,6 (1 Peter 2:9, 1 Timothy 2:5) Exekiel 37:24-28 (2 Corinthians 6:6) Ezekiel 11:19,20 Hosea 1:10,11, 2:23 (Romans 9:25,26)
Relationships between subjects in the Kingdom of God.	Isaiah 11:6-10 (Galatians 3:26-28)
Persecution of the Kingdom of God.	Daniel 7:6-8 Daniel 7:19-25
Power and Endurance of the Kingdom of God.	Daniel 7:26,27 Amos 9:11 2 Samuel 7:12-14 Daniel 2:44

ESTABLISHMENT OF THE KINGDOM OF GOD

Let us begin by looking at passages that predict the establishment of a new covenant for the kingdom of God. The most well known of these is Jeremiah 31:31-34:

> "The time is coming," declares the LORD, "when I will make a new covenant with the house of Israel and with the house of Judah. It will not be like the covenant I made with their forefathers when I took them by the hand to lead them out of Egypt, because they

> broke my covenant, though I was a husband to them," declares the LORD.
>
> "This is the covenant I will make with the house of Israel after that time," declares the LORD. I will put my law in their minds and write it on their hearts. I will be their God and they will be my people. No longer will a man teach his neighbor or a man his brother, saying, 'Know the LORD,' because they will all know me, from the least of them to the greatest," declares the LORD. "For I will forgive their wickedness and will remember their sins no more."

This is a wonderful prophecy! It could serve as a summary statement of what this entire book is about. In this passage, God tells his people that he will establish a New Covenant some time in the future.[2] It will be very different from the one he gave to them at Mt. Sinai after they left Egypt. This New Covenant will be based on a personal relationship with God, rather than on obedience to a set of laws. People who were born into the first covenant had to be taught to know about God because they were born as infants into Israel, but the people in the New Covenant will all know him from the start. In the Old covenant, some, such as priests, knew God more intimately than others, but that will not be the case in the new covenant. All will know God and all will be forgiven of their sins.

The Jews who read Jeremiah must have found this description of a future covenant to be very different from their own experience. To the Jews, God loved them, but from a distance. The non-Levites had no access into the Most Holy place. God had taught them, through Moses (Deuteronomy 6:6-9), to teach their children carefully about God, but in this New covenant, all will be close to God, and all will be born (again) already knowing about him.

The church, the Kingdom of God, is the place where this New Covenant prophecy finds its fulfillment. *"For this reason Christ is the mediator of a new novenant, that those who are called may receive the promised eternal inheritance—now that he has died as a ransom to set them free from the sins committed under the first covenant"* (Hebrews 9:15). Galatians 4:9 describes those who are in Christ as those who know God—or rather are known by him.

Another passage that prophesies the coming of a new relationship with God is Ezekiel 36:24-27:

> *"For I will take you out of the nations; I will gather you from all the countries and bring you back into your own land. I will sprinkle clean water on you, and you will be clean; I will cleanse you from all your impurities and from all your idols. I will give you a new heart and put a new spirit in you; I will remove from you your heart of stone and give you a heart of flesh. And I will put my Spirit in you and move you to follow my decrees and be careful to keep my laws."*

Verse twenty-four is a reference to the return of the Jews to the Promised Land after their captivity in Babylon. But, as we will see, God also used the return of the diaspora Jews to Jerusalem as a prefigure of the bringing of Gentiles from every nation into the kingdom of God. When Ezekiel continues by describing being sprinkled with clean water and being given a new heart and new spirit, he is definitely not talking about anything which God promised under the covenant at Sinai. Jesus announced the imminent fulfillment of this prophecy (and of Jeremiah 31:31-34) in John 16:13-15:

> *"But when he, the Spirit of truth comes, he will guide you into all truth. He will not speak on his own; he will speak only what he hears, and he will tell you what is yet to come. He will bring glory to me by taking from what is mine and making it known to you. All that belongs to the Father is mine. That is why I said the Spirit will take from what is mine and make it known to you."*

The giving of the promised Holy Spirit to all who come to believe in Jesus was foretold by the Christ and was announced by Peter the following Pentecost in Acts 2:38: *"Peter replied, 'Repent and be baptized, every one of you, in the name of Jesus Christ for the forgiveness of your sins. And you will receive the gift of the Holy Spirit.'"* Notice that Peter's statement includes water (baptism), the forgiveness of sins, and the reception of the Holy Spirit, all of which are predicted by Ezekiel.

To summarize the teaching found in John 16:13-15 and Acts 2:38 (and Jeremiah 31 and Ezekiel 36), one enters into this new manifestation of the kingdom of God by repenting of sins and by being baptized. At that time, one is forgiven of sins and receives the gift of the Holy Spirit who helps the believer to know God, to have a heart for him and to overcome sin in his/her life.

WHO WILL BE KING?

There will be a new kingdom, but who will be the king? The Old Testament gives this answer in Ezekiel 34:23,24:

> *"I will place over them one shepherd, my servant David, and he will tend them; he will tend them and be their shepherd. I the LORD will be their God, and my servant David will be prince among them. I the LORD have spoken."*

"Them" in this passage is God's people. The Jews of Jesus' day would have no problem understanding this prophecy. The Messiah will be over God's kingdom at some time in the (for them) future. The Jewish Mishnah identifies this passage as a reference to the messianic kingdom.[3] Jesus, the "Son of David," who was also called the *"Good Shepherd"* (John 10:14) will rule as king (actually prince in this passage) over his people. This is the New Testament view of the relationship between the church and Jesus Christ. *"And God placed all things under his feet and appointed him to be head over everything for the church, which is his body, the fullness of him who fills everything in every way"* (Ephesians 1:22,23).

Another passage which prophetically identifies the one to be over the kingdom is Hosea 3:5:

> *Afterward, the Israelites will return and seek the LORD their God and David their king. They will come trembling to the LORD and to his blessings in the last days.*

Of course, David was dead long before Hosea wrote. His readers knew that he was talking about the Son of David—the Messiah. Jesus is the Son of David, both physically, being directly descended from the former king David, and as a spiritual antitype, as the king of the spiritual Kingdom of God.

THE COMING OF THE KINGDOM OF GOD

Most people become subjects of a physical kingdom either by being born to one of the subjects of the king or by living in territory which is conquered by another ruler. How will one become a subject of what was, for the Jews, the future kingdom of God? And how will this kingdom get its start? We have already seen that *Shavoat*, the Feast of Pentecost, is an Old Testament foreshadow of the coming of the kingdom of God. Let us look at two specific prophecies fulfilled on the first Pentecost after Jesus was crucified:

> *"And afterward, I will pour out my Spirit on all people. Your sons and daughters will prophesy, your old men will dream dreams, your young men will see visions. Even on my servants, both men and women, I will pour out my Spirit in those days. I will show wonders in the heavens and on the earth, blood and fire and billows of smoke. The sun will be turned to darkness and the moon to blood before the coming of the great and dreadful day of the LORD. And everyone who calls on the name of the LORD will be saved; for on Mount Zion and in Jerusalem there will be deliverance, as the LORD has said, among the survivors the LORD calls"* (Joel 2:28-32).

Peter quoted this passage as part of the first gospel sermon preached on the Day of Pentecost. Like Jesus had said (Acts 1:5,8), and as Joel prophesied, the coming of the new dispensation was to be accompanied by a pouring out of the Holy Spirit and by miraculous signs. The Joel passage uses apocalyptic language, including dramatic imagery which should not be taken literally (the moon turning to blood and so forth). This prophecy was fulfilled in a great way when the Spirit was poured out on the apostles that day, causing a great wind and producing tongues of fire. The apostles were also given the miraculous ability to speak in many languages. Referring to the miracles, Peter said, *"This is what was spoken by the prophet Joel"* (Acts 2:16).

Not only does this prophecy in Joel announce a great pouring out of the Holy Spirit, it also predicts the arrival of salvation which will be available to all people. *"Everyone who calls on the name of the LORD will be saved."* At the end of his great sermon, Peter announced publicly for the first time salvation in the name of Jesus Christ, *"for all who are far off—for all whom the Lord our God will call"* (Acts 2:39). Of course, as prophesied by Joel, this great pouring out of the Spirit came on Mount Zion, in Jerusalem.

A second prophecy of the coming of the new dispensation from God is found in Zechariah 13:1,2:

> "On that day a fountain will be opened to the house of David and the inhabitants of Jerusalem, to cleanse them from sin and impurity.
> "On that day, I will banish the names of the idols from the land, and they will be remembered no more," declares the LORD Almighty.

The time of the arrival of this new way of salvation is variously called *"the last days"* (Joel 2:28, Isaiah 2:2), and *"that day"* (Zechariah 13:1, Isaiah 22:20, Hosea 2:16,18, Amos 9:11, Micah 4:6, Zechariah 3:10) in the Hebrew Scripture. Again, we have here a prophecy of a day on which a new way to receive cleansing from sin will come. As in the Joel passage, this will begin with the inhabitants of Jerusalem. The fountain of Zechariah 13:1 is a continuous stream of cleansing water—a reference to the cleansing water of baptism, as announced by Peter on the day of Pentecost when he declared the availability of forgiveness of sins for those who repent and are baptized, for all whom the Lord our God will call (paraphrasing Acts 2:38,39).

EXTENT OF THE KINGDOM OF GOD

One aspect of the future kingdom of God which was prophesied to the Jews involved the extent of its "borders." The unanimous testimony of these many prophecies is that with the advent of the messianic kingdom of God on earth, all nations and peoples will be welcomed into this new dispensation of God's will. There are far more prophecies of this aspect of the kingdom of God than any other. The Jews were very well aware of being the chosen people of God and were generally jealous of maintaining God's blessings to themselves alone. Throughout their history, the Jews were reluctant to welcome outsiders, thinking of all other peoples as "not the people of God." A good example of this is found in Jonah. God commanded Jonah to go and preach repentance to Nineveh. From a human perspective one can understand why Jonah would be reluctant to preach to the Ninevites because this was the capital of Assyria, the power which was at that time threatening the independence of the Northern Kingdom. When, under duress, Jonah finally went and preached repentance to Nineveh, he seems to have forgotten to include in his preaching the possibility of being saved from God's wrath if they repented. When the king of Nineveh and his people repented, fasting and wearing sackcloth, God relented and did not destroy Nineveh. Rather than rejoicing in God's mercy, Jonah threw a temper tantrum, telling God that was why he did not want to go there in the first place. The last thing Jonah wanted was for God to offer repentance and forgiveness to the Gentiles.

The story of Jonah is an historical prefigure of the offer of repentance to the Gentiles under Jesus. Let's examine some of the prophecies announcing this amazing development.

> *"It is too small a thing for you to be my servant to restore the tribes of Jacob and bring back those of Israel I have kept. I will also make you a light for the Gentiles, that you may bring my salvation to the ends of the earth"* (Isaiah 49:6).
>
> *"I, the LORD, have called you* (the Messiah, in the context of the passage) *in righteousness; I will take hold of your hand. I will keep you and will make you to be a covenant for the people and a light for the Gentiles"* (Isaiah 42:6).

God tells his people in these passages that the Messiah will restore the (spiritual) fortunes of Israel, of the Jewish people, but that he would also be a light to the Gentiles: *"to the very ends of the earth."* This must have come as a surprise to those who heard the preaching of Isaiah.

This is not the first time Isaiah mentioned in his book the offer of salvation to the nations, nor the last.

> *In the last days the mountain of the Lord's temple will*
>   *be established as chief among the mountains;*
> *it will be raised above the hills,*
>   *and all nations will stream to it.*
> *Many peoples will come and say,*
>   *"Come let us go up to the mountain of the LORD,*
>   *to the house of the God of Jacob.*
> *He will teach us his ways,*
>   *so that we may walk in his paths."*
> *The law will go out from Zion,*
>   *The word of the Lord from Jerusalem.*

> He will judge between nations
>   and will settle disputes for many peoples.
> They will beat their swords into plowshares
>   and their spears into pruning hooks.
> Nation will not take up sword against nation,
>   nor will they train for war anymore (Isaiah 2:2-4).[4]

Here the prophet predicts that the mountain of the Lord's temple, symbolic of the spiritual power of the kingdom of God, will go out to all nations in the last days. He also specifies that the call to this new spiritual government will go out beginning at Mount Zion, in Jerusalem. It was on Mount Zion, in the temple precincts, that Peter gave that famous first public gospel sermon at Pentecost, as recorded in Acts chapter two. Little did Peter and the other apostles understand at that time the full implication of Isaiah chapter two. It required two visions and a second pouring out of the Holy Spirit a few years after the Pentecost event (see Acts chapter ten) to finally convince Peter that Jesus was serious about offering salvation to all nations. Only then did the exclusively Jewish church welcome Gentiles into the fold.

Isaiah further prophesies, using apocalyptic imagery, that in this new Mountain of the Lord, nations who would normally only think of fighting and destroying one another will come together in peace. *"They will beat their swords into plowshares and their spears into pruning hooks."* During Roman times, and even today, only in the church established by Jesus Christ can all nations and peoples, races and cultures come together in harmonious brotherhood. If only this prophecy would apply to the physical nations of the earth!

Isaiah is not yet done informing God's people that the future messianic kingdom will not be an exclusive club:

> "Sing, O barren woman,
>   you who never bore a child;
> burst into song, shout for joy,
>   you who were never in labor;
> because more are the children of the desolate woman
>   than of her who has a husband,"
>   says the LORD" (Isaiah 54:1).

Paul quotes this passage in the letter to the Galatians (4:26-28), identifying the children of the one who was never in labor—of the desolate woman—as those who are saved under the New Covenant. In this passage, Isaiah foresees that the spiritual children of Abraham through his barren wife Sarah—the Gentile Christians—will eventually outnumber the natural children of Abraham by Hagar. This is exactly what happened. At first, the church only offered salvation to the Jews—the natural born children of God under the old kingdom. Once God finally convinced Peter to offer salvation to the Gentiles, it was like a starting gun. Within one generation, especially through Paul's ministry, the Gentile followers of Jesus outnumbered the Jewish Christians: a pattern which has continued to this day.

Perhaps the Jews did not get the hint that new times were coming in God's kingdom from Isaiah's preaching. Perhaps they will listen to Ezekiel:

> "This is what the Sovereign LORD says: 'I myself will take a shoot from the very top of a cedar and plant it; I will break off a tender sprig from its topmost shoots and plant it on a high and lofty mountain. On the mountain heights of Israel I will plant it; it will produce branches and bear fruit and become a splendid cedar. Birds of every kind will nest in it; they will find shelter in the shade of its branches. All the trees of the field will know that I the LORD bring down the tall tree and make the low tree grow tall'" (Ezekiel 17:22-24).

This is beautiful imagery describing the tender sprig from the cedar tree. This tender sprig, of course, is the church; the Kingdom of God. The imagery was probably not so beautiful to those Jews who did not accept Jesus Christ—who saw the new cedar outgrow the original. In A.D. 70 they saw the cedar wood in the temple literally burned to the ground. As Ezekiel prophesied, the little, fresh sprig will grow into a great tree and birds of every kind will nest in it. Again in this scripture, we have a relationship with God being offered to all nations.[5]

To bring home his point, God also spoke to his people concerning a future bringing in of the nations in the "minor" prophets. For example, consider Zechariah 2:10,11:[6]

> "Shout and be glad, O Daughter of Zion. For I am coming, and

I will live among you," declares the LORD. "Many nations will be joined with the LORD in that day and will become my people. I will live among you and you will know that the LORD Almighty has sent me to you."

This passage summarizes the others. In *"that day,"* i.e. beginning at the Pentecost event, God will establish a kingdom. The subjects of this kingdom will be joined to (reconciled with) God through Jesus Christ. God, the Holy Spirit, will live in all those who are in Christ. The amazing thing, at least to the Jews, is that this offer will go out to many nations. May this vision be brought to its final fulfillment!

RELATIONS BETWEEN KING AND SUBJECTS

We already have some hints, but what will the nature of the relationship between the king and his subjects in the spiritual Kingdom of God? The Old Testament gives us insights.

The first prophetic hint of a new kind of relationship between king and subject is found in the book of Exodus:

"Now, if you obey me fully and keep my covenant, then out of all the nations you will be my treasured possession. Although the whole earth is mine, you will be for me a kingdom of priests and a holy nation" (Exodus 19:5,6).

When he gave the Law of Moses to physical Israel, God had in mind a special relationship. However, did they ever fully obey the laws and keep the covenant? Were they truly a nation of priests—a holy nation? The answer, unfortunately, is no. However, this passage is a veiled reference to what God would do for his people in the spiritual Kingdom of God. Peter reminded followers of Jesus that this prophecy applies to them: *"But you are a chosen people, a royal priesthood, a holy nation, a people belonging to God"* (1 Peter 2:9). Only under the New Covenant did all the people of God become priests. That is the focus of chapter four of this book. As Paul put it in 1 Timothy 2:5, *"For there is one God and one mediator between God and men, the man Christ Jesus, who gave himself as a ransom for all men."* Only in Christ do the words in Exodus 19 find their fulfillment. Those who are in Christ do not need a human to intercede between them and God. We do have a high priest, Jesus Christ (Hebrews 8:1,2), through whom we can enter boldly as priests of God into the presence of the Almighty in the heavenly tabernacle (Hebrews 10:19,20). The Jews could only dream of such a relationship.

A related passage—one which provides even more information about the relation between Lord and liege in the Kingdom of God—is found in Ezekiel 37:24-28:

> "My servant David will be king over them, and they will all have one shepherd. They will follow my laws and be careful to keep my decrees. They...will live there forever and David my servant will be their prince forever. I will make a covenant of peace with them; it will be an everlasting covenant. I will establish them and increase their numbers and I will put my sanctuary among them forever. My dwelling place will be with them; I will be their God and they will be my people. Then the nations will know that I the LORD make Israel holy, when my sanctuary is among them forever."

We have already seen that David, i.e. Jesus, the son of David, will be king over this kingdom. Here we also see that his sanctuary will be among his people. Putting their confidence in the flesh, the Jews declared, *"This is the temple of the LORD, the temple of the LORD, the temple of the LORD"* (Jeremiah 7:4). From the time of Moses, God lived near his people. Here we see something far greater. As Paul put it, in Christ, *"we are the temple of the living God"* (2 Corinthians 6:6). In a fantastic way, God's sanctuary is truly with his people forever. The prophecy will find its ultimate fulfillment in the heavenly kingdom.

Another very encouraging prophecy of the relationship between king and subject is found in Ezekiel 11:19,20:

> "I will give them an undivided heart and put a new spirit in them; I will remove from them their heart of stone and give them a heart of flesh. Then they will follow my decrees and be careful to keep my laws. They will be my people and I will be their God."

This prophecy speaks of a people with a new heart, and a new spirit—people who will follow God with a sincere desire rather than from obligation. These are a people who, as Jesus put it, have been born again. Despite the fact that these people were not born into the physical kingdom of God, they will be called God's people.

This concept is developed more fully by the Old Testament prophet, Hosea:

"'Yet the Israelites will be like the sand on the seashore, which cannot be measured or counted. In the place where it was said to them, 'You are not my people,' they will be called 'sons of the living God.' The people of Judah and the people of Israel will be reunited, and they will appoint one leader and will come up out of the land, for great will be the day of Jezreel...' 'I will plant her for myself in the land; I will show my love to the one I called 'Not my loved One.' I will say to those called 'Not my people,' 'You are my people'; and they will say, 'You are my God'" (Hosea 1:10,11, 2:23).

In order to create this prophecy, God had Hosea name his two daughters, Lo-Ruhamah and Lo-Ammi, which meant "not loved" and "not my people." Imagine being one of these girls! The point of this prophecy, as Paul points out in Romans 9:25,26 and Peter reinforces in 1 Peter 2:10, is that, though the Gentiles were not God's people, a future time and kingdom would come in which the Gentiles would be called God's people. As Peter put it, *"Once you were not a people, but now you are the people of God."* This is great news!

RELATIONSHIPS IN THE KINGDOM OF GOD

The subject has been covered to some extent already, but it is hard to resist bringing up Isaiah 11:6-10 as a prophecy of the relationships between people found in the messianic kingdom:

The wolf will live with the lamb,
  the leopard will lie down with the goat,
the calf and the lion and the yearling together;
  and a little child will lead them.
The cow will feed with the bear,
  their young will lie down together,
  and the lion will eat straw like the ox.
The infant will play near the hole of the cobra,
  and the young child will put his hand into the viper's nest.
They will neither harm nor destroy
  on all my holy mountain,
for the earth will be full of the knowledge of the LORD
  as the waters cover the sea.

This is not a prophecy about tame animals. It is about the relationships between people. In the messianic kingdom, there will be a new kind of relationship. No longer will such distinctions as rich or poor, slave or free, male or female matter (Galatians 3:26-28). Nation will not matter, and neither will race or ethnicity. Natural enemies will be the best of friends. Huttu will hug Tutsi. All will be one because they have one king who joins them together. The way Jesus put it, *"Therefore, whoever humbles himself like this child is the greatest in the kingdom of heaven"* (Matthew 18:4). This is an ideal which, unfortunately, no group inhabited by human beings will ever fully achieve. However, from the author's own experience this kind of relationship finds its greatest fulfillment in a New Testament church devoted to establishing Galatians 3:26-28 relationships.

PERSECUTION OF THE KINGDOM OF GOD

So far, the spiritual Kingdom of God seems like a really great place, and so it is, but the Old Testament warns prophetically that the world will not always see the church as a great thing. Kings are not generally willing to share power with other kings, even if their territory is spiritual. The Old Testament warns of great persecutions that the saints will endure.

The most direct prophecy of persecution against the citizens of the Kingdom of God is found in Daniel chapter seven. *"In the first year of Belshazzar, king of Babylon* (553 B.C.), *Daniel had a dream"* (Daniel 7:1). In the dream, Daniel saw four beasts. As the angel told him (v. 17), the four beasts were four kingdoms. The four kingdoms: the lion, the bear the leopard and the terrible, indescribable beast were Babylon, Persia/Media, Greece and Rome.[6]

The dream provides specific prophetic detail about the Medo-Persian empire and the Greek empires, but it focuses principally on the fourth beast.

> *"After that, in my vision at night I looked, and there before me was a fourth beast—terrifying and frightening and very powerful,...and it had ten horns.*
>
> *While I was thinking about the horns, there before me was another horn, a little one, which came up among them; and three of the first horns were uprooted before it. This horn had eyes like*

the eyes of a man and a mouth that spoke boastfully" (Daniel 7:6-8).

Daniel must have wondered what the meaning of this strange vision could be. He asked one of the angels who stood nearby during his vision and the angel told him the meaning of this very strange vision:

> *"Then I wanted to know the true meaning of the fourth beast...I also wanted to know about the ten horns on its head and about the other horn that came up, before which three of them fell...As I watched, this horn was waging war against the saints and defeating them, until the Ancient of Days came and pronounced judgment in favor of the saints of the Most High, and the time came when they possessed the kingdom.*
>
> *He gave me this explanation: 'The fourth beast is a fourth kingdom that will appear on earth....The ten horns are ten kings who will come from this kingdom. After them another king will arise, different from the earlier ones; he will subdue three kings. He will speak against the Most High and oppress his saints and try to change the set times and the laws. The saints will be handed over to him for a time, times and half a time'"* (Daniel 7:19-25, excerpts).

The vision of the fourth beast is includes a king who will attack and oppress the saints who possess the Kingdom of God. This king is the eleventh king of the fourth kingdom: one who will remove three former kings.

The vision and its interpretation may seem mysterious at first glance, but a second glance at the history of ancient Rome will clear up the vision readily. The little horn was the eleventh emperor of Rome—Domitian. Domitian was the first Roman emperor to systematically attack the Christian church throughout most of his empire. Domitian was the son of Vespasian, the ninth emperor of Rome. While his father was off fighting the rebels in Jerusalem in A.D. 68, Domitian was the dominant force in removing Galba, Otho and Vitellius, the sixth, seventh and eighth emperors of Rome, each of whom had led military coups, but only ruled for a few months. These are the three horns removed by the eleventh horn in the vision. Amazing accuracy for a prophet who wrote over six hundred years before the events. But God's plan is not

DOMITIAN, EMPEROR OF ROME AD 81-96

simply to impress the readers with how good a prophet Daniel is. God's plan is to prepare the saints of his kingdom for a great persecution which is to come.

By coincidence, as I am writing this chapter, I am in Rome. Just yesterday, my wife and I visited the Palatine Hill where the ruins of Domitian's massive ampitheatre and personal residence are still easily seen. Domitian built a huge complex for his personal pleasure: a place to view the spectacle as many followers of Jesus were thrown to the hungry beasts. Domitian's personal arrogance became proverbial for the Romans. As Daniel put it, he had *"a mouth that spoke boastfully."* As the vision states, Domitian spoke boastfully against the Most High God. In fact he forced his subjects to worship him as a god. Roman historians report that Domitian insisted on being addressed as *dominus et deus* (lord and god). Believers in the one true God were executed by Domitian for "atheism."

The angel said that this eleventh horn would change the set times and the laws. That is exactly what Domitian did. In his arrogance, he added a month to the Roman calendar, naming it Domitiainus! He also cancelled the entire Roman legal code—the most respected code of law in the ancient world—and established his own code of laws, which gave him a greatly expanded power. The day after Domitian died, the Roman senate removed the month Domitiainus from the calendar, and repealed all the laws he had established.

The First Eleven Emperors of Rome

Emperor	Dates of Rule	Significance to Biblical Events
Augustus	27 B.C.-A.D. 14	Birth of Christ
Tiberius	A.D. 14-37	Crucifixion of Christ
Gaius (Caligula)	A.D. 41-54	Attempted to put a statue of himself in the temple
Claudius	A.D. 54-68	Jews Exiled from Rome
Nero	A.D. 68-69	First serious persecutions, Execution of Paul & Peter
Galba	A.D. 69-70	One of the three overcome by Vespaisan/Domitian
Otho	A.D. 69-70	One of the three...
Vitellius	A.D. 69-70	One of the three...
Vespasian	A.D. 70-79	Attack on Jerusalem
Titus	A.D. 79-81	The general who destroyed Jerusalem
Domitian	A.D. 81-96	First Systematic Persecutor of the Church

By precise and detailed fulfillment of Daniel's prophecy, the Old Testament warns in a striking way that it will not be all sweetness and light for the saints in the Kingdom of God. There will be times when the citizens of the heavenly kingdom will be attacked by the earthly kingdoms. At times, the worldly king will even appear to be defeating the saints (v. 21). However, the great persecution will not continue indefinitely; it will last for, *"a time, times and half a time."* The number three and one-half in Jewish apocalyptic symbology represents a limited amount of time. After that time, God will judge the persecutor and the saints will ultimately be victorious.

THE POWER AND ENDURANCE OF THE KINGDOM OF GOD

Although Daniel seven presents what could be a discouraging picture of persecution and oppression of the saints, it also presents a picture of ultimate eternal victory for the saints in the Kingdom of God.

> "*But the court will sit, and his power will be taken away and completely destroyed forever. Then the sovereignty, power and greatness of the kingdoms under the whole heaven will be handed over to the saints, the people of the Most High. His kingdom will be an everlasting kingdom and all rulers will worship and obey him*" (Daniel 7:26,27).

With these words the angel assured Daniel that the Kingdom of God will have ultimate victory over its persecutors and against the forces of darkness in this world. Given the fact that Daniel described, in spectacular detail, the reign and the persecutions of Domitian hundreds of years before they happened, the saints in the kingdom can be assured that even in the hardest times, God is in control. Also, given that Daniel accurately predicted such details as the three kings who would be removed by Domitian and even the fact that he would change the times and laws of his kingdom, the saints can be assured that *"the court will sit and his power will be taken away and completely destroyed forever."* It will happen just as God told Daniel in the vision.

Historically, the persecutions of the Roman Empire against the saints of the Most High did not end with Domitian. In fact, although there were periods of relative peace, the persecutions actually got even worse at certain times, culminating with the last great persecutor of the Christian church, Diocletian. Diocletian ruled Rome in the years A.D. 284-305. He forced all his subjects to offer a sacrifice to the Roman god. Many at that time were defeated (v. 21), but God sat in judgment, and removed the pagan rulers of Rome. From the time of Constantine (A.D. 312-337), the pagan religions in Rome were oppressed and eventually eliminated, but the saints experienced a time of unprecedented peace.

The message of this prophecy is that either way, whether experiencing a time of peace and relative prosperity, or a time of great attacks and even apparent defeat, the Kingdom of God and the saints who remain faithful will endure with God forever. His will be an everlasting kingdom.

The endurance, the power and the ultimate victory of the saints and the Kingdom of God is prophesied in a number of other passages in the Old Testament.

> *"In that day I will restore David's fallen tent. I will repair its broken places, restore its ruins"* (Amos 9:11).

> *"I will raise up your* (David's) *offspring to succeed you, who will come from your own body, and I will establish his kingdom. He is the one who will build a house for my Name, and I will establish the throne of his kingdom forever. I will be his father, and he will be my son"* (2 Samuel 7:12-14).

> *"In the time of those kings* (the kings of Rome), *the God of heaven will set up a kingdom that will never be destroyed, nor will it be left to another people. It will crush all those kingdoms and bring them to an end, but it will itself endure forever"* (Daniel 2:44).

These prophecies find their fulfillment even now. From the time the messianic Kingdom of God dramatically began at Pentecost, many have attempted to defeat the church of the living Christ. Those who would obey Jesus and his Word have experienced persecutions and ridicule from political authorities and even from pseudo-Christians who have rejected the basic teachings of the Bible to follow human tradition. But David's fallen tent will rise. God will establish the throne of his kingdom forever. The church—the Kingdom of God on the earth—will crush those kingdoms and bring their power to an end. Victory belongs to the kingdom of God.

CONCLUSION

The Kingdom of God finds its fulfillment in physical Israel, in spiritual Israel and in the future eternal kingdom in heaven. God made it clear through the prophets that after the time of the physical kingdom, a spiritual kingdom would arise, beginning in Jerusalem, spreading to cover the entire earth. This kingdom would include both Jew and Gentile. The saints in the kingdom were to be persecuted, but in the end, let us be assured that every power and authority which sets itself against God's eternal kingdom will come into judgment. And let us not forget the wonderful prophecy in Daniel:

> *"Multitudes who sleep in the dust of the earth will awake: some to everlasting life, others to shame and everlasting contempt. Those who are wise will shine like the brightness of the heavens, and those who lead many to righteousness, like the stars for ever and ever"* (Daniel 12:2,3).

The prophecies of the Kingdom of God will find their ultimate fulfillment in the still-future kingdom, where the saints will reign with God in heaven forever. And to God be the glory.

Endnotes

1 Reference Jim McGuiggan's *The Kingdom of God and the Planet Earth* (International Bible Resources, 1978), and *The Reign of God: A Study of the Kingdom of God* (Star Bible Publications, 1992).

2 Actually, just over six hundred years in the future, as Jeremiah wrote during the generation before and after 600 B.C.

3 *Bereshith Rabbah*, 97.

4 Also see the parallel passage in Micah 4:1-8.

5 See also Ezekiel 34:10-14.

6 See also Zechariah 10:4-12.

7 See my book on Daniel for details. John M. Oakes, *Daniel, Prophet to the Nations* (available from www.ipibooks.com), especially chapter nine.

Appendix One: The Limits of Biblical Interpretation

This section which follows is included as an appendix because some readers may not find it necessary to the topic at hand. For some who are not inclined to spend a lot of energy worrying about technical details, it could even distract from the main message of the book. However, a number of questions will naturally arise for many readers which deserve to be addressed. How can one know for sure that God intended that the Feast of Trumpets be a foreshadow of Judgment Day? Is it possible we are only imagining that the lampstand in the tabernacle is a purposeful type of the Holy Spirit—that we are putting words in God's "mouth?" Based on examples which will be given below, it definitely is possible to over-interpret the Bible. It is a too-common occurrence for preachers and teachers to pull messages from particular passages of scripture which are not justified by their local or global context in the Bible. Given that some prophetic interpretation is clearly justifiable, and that some is debatable, where does one begin to admit that a particular application is of only borderline certainty, and therefore better left out of a sermon or a book like this one?

The purpose of this appendix is to attempt to at least provide a preliminary answer to these questions. The approach taken will be to list examples, both good and bad, to provide

provide a bit of history of Bible interpretation, especially as it relates to symbols, foreshadows and prophecy, and to give a fairly simple set of rules to guide the reader into deciding for themselves what are the limits of Bible interpretation.

Having taught parts of the material in this book to various groups, I have had the experience of an enthusiastic hearer attempting to dig into the Bible on their own and share their own discoveries of types and antitypes in the Old and New Testament. Some of these discussions have been very helpful and encouraging. Others have caused an uncomfortable moment. I have had to cringe at some interpretations which are, in my opinion, definitely not justified by the context of the scripture, no matter how enthusiastic or sincere the attempt. When such a person asks, "do you agree that this is a good example of Old Testament foreshadow?" it can be time to work hard on one's diplomacy.

It is clear that the New Testament writers used the method of finding types and antitypes in the Old Testament and in the gospel message as one of their chief means of exegesis of the Old Testament. Many examples of this have been given in this book. Jesus saw the miracle of Jonah being inside the big fish as a prefigure of his own death and resurrection (Matthew 12:39-42). Paul saw Ishmael and Isaac as foreshadows of physical Israel (the Jews) and spiritual Israel (the church) (Galatians 4:21-31). The Hebrew writer saw the Jewish Tabernacle as a foreshadow of the kind of relationship followers of Jesus have with God through Jesus Christ (Hebrews 9:23-28). Many examples could be added to this list.

Early Christian writers continued this trend of finding types and antitypes on the Old and New Testaments. (Ignatius, *Letter to the Magnesians,* 7:2, 10:2, *Letter to the Philadelphians,* 9:1, *The Epistle of Barnabas,* 7:10ff, Justin Martyr, *Dialogues,* 3). However, even quite early, the church fathers began to move beyond clear historical type/antitype interpretation. They began to make what appear to be rather speculative application of superficial details in the Old Testament to New Testament teachings which do not seem justified by the text. For example, in *The Epistle of Barnabas,* when Moses prayed before the people with outstretched hands (Exodus 17:8-13), it is interpreted as a foreshadow of Jesus hanging on the cross (The Epistle of Barnabas, 12:2ff). Clement of Rome (Clement, 1 Clement 12:7) interpreted the scarlet cord which Rahab tied to her window (Joshua 2:17-20) as a foreshadow of the blood of Jesus. Origen interpreted the story of the witch of Endor calling up Samuel from the dead (1 Samuel 28) as a foreshadow of the resurrection of Jesus.

Present-day Bible interpreters are not immune to the tendency to over-interpret passages of scripture. An example of biblical over-interpretation today is found in the way some interpret the parables of Jesus. In the parable of the lost son, clearly the father is God and the lost son is a person who has wandered off. However, when one tries to find specific significance in the fact that the son was eating pods or in the ring the father gave the son, one is quickly moving towards speculative interpretation.

Another trend among both Jewish Rabbis and early Christian teachers was to interpret the Old Testament as an allegory. The word allegory deserves a careful definition. In classical literature, an allegory was a writing in which the actions or persons in a story are intended to be interpreted symbolically. Allegory was one of the chief forms of expression of medieval writers. I can distinctly remember in my twelth grade English class studying the story Everyman. In this story, the characters have names such as Everyman, Death, Fellowship, Good Deeds and so forth. The characters and the actions in this story are clearly to be taken by the reader as symbols. All that is fine, but what about interpreting the Old Testament allegorically? Interpreting the text of the Bible allegorically is justified as an exegetical technique only if it can be established that the original writer intended the material to be taken principally as symbolic. Perhaps this is justifiable in interpreting some of Jesus' parables, but outside these examples, allegorical interpretation of the Bible is rarely justified.

A useful definition of allegorical exegesis is given by Leonhard Goppelt.[1] "By allegory is meant a kind of exegesis, which, in addition to the literal sense of the text, and, at times, even to the exclusion it (i.e., of the literal sense), finds another different and supposedly deeper meaning, although the context does not indicate the presence of any figurative language." Allegorical interpretation is rarely justified, but type/antitype interpretation of the Old Testament is justified under conditions which are described below. Type/antitype exegesis begins by accepting the physical reality of the Old Testament event and then looking for parallels in the Gospel. Israel passed through the Red Sea under the leadership of Moses. The question is to what, if any, New Testament reality does this actual event in the Old Testament prophetically correspond? On the contrary, allegorical exegesis begins by looking for a symbolic meaning behind a physical reality without justification in the text. As Goppelt put it,[2] "Allegory goes its own way regardless of the literal interpretation, while the typological use of Scripture begins with the literal interpretation." and "Allegorical interpretation, therefore, is not concerned with the truthfulness or factuality of the things described. For typological interpretation, however, the reality of the things described is indispensable. The typical meaning is not really a different or higher meaning, but a different or higher use of the same meaning that is comprehended in type and antitype."[3]

Examples of allegorical interpretation are found in the Jewish writer/theologian/philosopher Philo of Alexandria. Philo lived in Alexandria in Egypt from about 20 B.C. to A.D. 50. His method was to detect underlying spiritual symbolism in the literal descriptions in the Old Testament, especially in the Pentateuch. To quote Philo, "we must now speak of that which may be given if the story be looked at as figurative and symbolical."[4] As a specific example, consider Philo's interpretation of the rib being taken from Adam in order to form Eve; "'He took one of his ribs.' He took one of the many powers of the mind, namely, that power which dwells in the outward senses. And when he uses the expression, 'He took,' we are not to understand it as if he had said 'He took away,' but rather as equivalent to 'He counted, He examined.'"[5] Philo continues by interpreting the taking of the rib to be symbolic of God examining our conscious thoughts.

Philo, in his book *De Abrahamo* interpreted the four kings of Genesis 14 to signify the four passions—pleasure, desire, fear and grief. The other five kings in this passage represent the five senses, because they rule over us. In Genesis 14, the five are subject to the four and pay them tribute; so from our senses arise the passions of pleasure, fear, etc which dominate our senses. In Genesis 14, two kings fell into the well. Philo interprets this to mean, that touch and taste penetrate to the interior of the body. The other three who "took to flight" are the other three senses which are directed outside the body. "The wise man attacked them all" means that reason rushed upon them and conquered them. Using this form of interpretation, it becomes easy to read any philosophy one likes into the biblical text. That is exactly what Philo did—finding the teachings of the Stoics and the disciples of Plato in the Hebrew Scripture.

Such methodology of interpretation has not been limited to Jewish interpreters. By the early third century A.D., many early Christian writers began to use allegorical interpretation of both the Old and the New Testament, with dubious result. Origen of Alexandria (A.D. 185-254) is best known for his allegorical interpretation of the Old Testament. It is probably not a coincidence that Origen was from Alexandria, the home of Philo. A whole school of Bible interpreters rose up at that time (including Lucian and Eustathius of Antioch) to defend historical interpretation as opposed to Origen's allegorical exegesis of the Bible.

This brings us to the bottom line. Why is the writer of *The Epistle of Barnabas* not justified in interpreting Moses holding out his arms as a prefigure of the crucifixion of Jesus, yet in this book I claim that the blood spread on the cross-beam above the doors on the Passover eve is a foreshadow of Jesus' blood on the cross? What is the essential difference?

In order to determine how one can be confident in finding a foreshadow, a type/antitype relationship a prefigure or a legitimate historical prophecy in the Old Testament, I would propose the following fairly simple rules:

1. If a New Testament writer says a particular passage in the Old Testament is a foreshadow/prophecy/prefigure/type, then it is.

2. If an Old Testament passage works as a foreshadow/prophecy/prefigure/type both in the general sense and in the specifics, then it is probably legitimate.

3. If one already knows that a general event in the Old Testament is a foreshadow/prophecy/prefigure/type, then it is safer to assume that the details are foreshadows as well.

Let us consider specific applications of these rules to the interpretation of types, foreshadows and prophecies in the Old Testament. Perhaps one could question whether it is mere coincidence or a historical foreshadow that Jonah was in the belly of the fish for three days, which happens to be the amount of time that Jesus was in the tomb. When Jesus said in Matthew 12:39-42, *"For as Jonah was three days and three nights in the belly of a huge fish, so the Son of Man will be three days and three nights in the heart of the earth"* it settles the issue. Similarly, consider the parallel between Moses holding up the snake in the desert to save people from physical death and Jesus being lifted up on the Cross to save people from spiritual death. One could debate whether the parallel between the events is coincidence or a sign of an inspired foreshadow. The question seems to be settled by Jesus' statement in John 3:14,15: *"Just as Moses lifted up the snake in the desert, so the Son of Man must be lifted up, that everyone who believes in him may have eternal life."* As a third example, we can be sure that the thrusting of the spear into Jesus' side is a fulfillment of Zechariah 12:10, because John said that it is (John 19:37). Many other examples of this principle could be given. It is a chief criterion used in choosing material to be presented in researching this book.

The explanation of rule number two requires a bit more careful thought. It is best explained by use of an example. When the snake was lifted up in the desert by Moses, it was a foreshadow of the saving effect of the crucifixion of Jesus. We already know this to be true because of application of rule number one. Nevertheless, let us apply rule number two to this passage. The two (lifting up of the snake on the pole and of Jesus on the cross) agree in the specifics, in that both involve someone or something being lifted up. They also agree in the general sense, because both involve a person being saved from death by looking at the object. Both are about salvation.

As a counter example, consider the (questionable) application in *1 Clement* 12:7. Here Clement attempts to draw a prefigure from the red rope Rahab tied to her window to the blood of Jesus. Both the blood of Jesus and the scarlet rope saved someone from death, so the general sense of the two agree, but the parallel between the specifics is specious. It is true that the rope was red, and that Jesus' blood was red, but the parallel between the specifics of blood flowing out and a rope being tied to a window is questionable. One could argue that Joshua 2:17-20 is a foreshadow of the blood of Jesus, but it is debatable at best. The same could be said for Origen's application of the calling of Samuel by the witch of Endor as a foreshadow of the resurrection of Jesus. In the general sense, both involve someone appearing on the earth after death, but in the specifics, the parallel does not work at all. A careful student of the Bible will avoid such over-interpretation.

Returning to some positive examples, one could mention such prophecies as Psalms 22 or Isaiah 9. In Psalms 22, the details (piercing of hands and feet, gambling and dividing) match with the death of Jesus, but also the general context does as well. Both involve suffering and being forsaken by God. In Isaiah 9:1-7, both the historical details (a child being born, the land of Zebulun and Naphtali) and the general idea (prince of peace, being over the kingdom) agree.

Another example is found in seeing the Tabernacle as a foreshadow of the ministry of Jesus. The details agree (altar of sacrifice = sacrifice of Jesus, water in the laver = baptism, bread on the right = Jesus, the Bread of Life, lampstand on the left = The Holy Spirit, etc.), but the general idea is parallel also. Both the Tabernacle and the work of Jesus and of the Holy Spirit are about how to have a relationship with God.

Let us consider the third rule. We know that the life of Jonah can serve as a prefigure of Jesus because of rule number one. We are therefore safer in looking at other details in the life of Jonah for parallels in the life of Christ, even if they are not specifically mentioned by Jesus (gambling, announcing repentance to the Gentiles, being from Galilee, etc.) We know for sure that Passover is a foreshadow of the death of Jesus by Rule # one. In 1 Corinthians 5:7, Paul says,

"For Christ, our Passover Lamb, has been sacrificed." This being true, one is safer in looking for other parallels between the Passover and the work of Jesus. If one can establish that not only the festival of Passover, but also the festival *Yom Kippur* is a foreshadow of salvation in the New Testament, then one is fairly safe in looking for type/antitype relationships between all seven Mosaic festivals and their New Testament counterparts. As a third example of rule number three, we know from Hebrews 3:16-4:2 that entering the Promised Land is a foreshadow of entering the eternal rest of heaven with God. We are therefore more likely justified in looking for other foreshadows in the events of the Exodus, the wandering in the wilderness and the entrance of Israel into Canaan.

In summary, as Paul admonished Timothy, anyone who studies the Bible, and especially one who would teach others should learn to *"correctly handle the word of truth"* (2 Timothy 2:15). We can see from history, that many have done a poor job of this, including those who have tried to extract prophetic details from Old Testament events. We have seen that allegorizing and over-interpreting can lead to dubious use of scripture. Having said that, let us not be discouraged. We have seen that there is a great deal of evidence for the inspiration of the Bible in Old Testament/New Testament prophecies and foreshadows. It is truly inspiring to consider how God revealed so much of the gospel truth in the Old Testament. However, one is well advised to exercise caution against over-interpreting and fiding parallels that God never intended. If the student of the Bible will apply a few simple rules, most of the mistakes will be easily avoided and the inspiring aspects of this subject can come out. In the writing of this book, I have attempted to faithfully apply the principles listed above. I will leave it to the reader to decide how well this goal has been realized.

Endnotes

1 Leonhard Goppelt, *Typos* (Eerdmans, Grand Rapids, Michigan, 1982), p. 16.

2 Ibid, p. 16.

3 Ibid, p. 13.

4 Philo, *De Abrahamo*, 119.

5 Philo, *Allegorical Intepretation, II. X* (From the translation of C.D. Yonge, Hendrickson Publishers, 1993).

Appendix Two: References

Phillip E. Satterthwaite, Richare S. Hess and Gordon J. Wenham, *The Lord's Anointed* (Baker Books, Grand Rapids, Michigan, 1995).

Leonhard Goppelt, *Typos: The Typological Interpretation of the Old Testament in the New* (Eerdmans, Grand Rapids, Michigan, 1982).

Sir Robert Anderson, *Types in Hebrews* (Kregel, Grand Rapids, Michigan, 1978).

P. Fairbairn, "The Old Testament in the New," *The Typology of Scripture* (New York, 1900) p. 363-95.

D. L. Baker *Two Testaments, One Bible: A Study of the Theological Relationship Between the Old and New Testaments* (Apollos, Leicester, 1991) pp. 179-299.

Lessons from Daniel: Prophet to the Nations

Illumination Publishers Intl.
ISBN: 978-0-978803906
Author: Dr. John M. Oakes
Price: 2-CDs in hard case
$10.00

Available at: www.ipibooks.com

This audio series by Dr. John Oakes will make the book of Daniel come alive for you. The series is divided into two parts. In Part 1, John relates the practical lessons of staying pure in a corrupt world. He looks at the examples of Daniel, Shadrach, Meshach and Abednego and makes application to our Christian walk.

In Part II, John examines the prophecies of Daniel and how they were fulfilled. Your faith will increase as you see vision after vision fulfilled and learn that God controls the nations and can control the circumstances of our lives.

Also included on CD 1 are classroom notes on Daniel, Prophecies in Daniel (word documents and pdfs) and also a Powerpoint presentation on the book of Daniel.

CD 1: Staying Pure in a Corrupt World

CD 2: God Rules the Nations: Do Not Fear

Illumination Publishers Intl.
Author: Dr. John M. Oakes
Price: 1-CDs (w/downloads) $5.00

Available at: www.ipibooks.com

Illumination Publishers Intl.
Author: Dr. John M. Oakes
Price: 1-CD (w/downloads) $5.00

Available at: www.ipibooks.com

Without a doubt, faith is at the heart of Christianity. *"Without faith it is impossible to please God"* (Hebrews 11:6). This book is intended to provide a basis in fact for belief in the Bible as the inspired word of God. It will be helpful, both to deepen the faith of those who already believe and to establish a factual basis for belief to those who do not yet accept that the Bible is the inspired word of God.

Illumination Publishers Intl.
ISBN: 0-9767583-3-4
Author: Dr. John M. Oakes
Price: 256 pages, $15.00
Available at: www.ipibooks.com

About the Publisher

Toney Mulhollan has been in Christian publishing for over 30 years. He has served as the Production Manager for Crossroads Publications, Discipleship Magazine/UpsideDown Magazine, Discipleship Publications International (DPI) and on the production teams of Campus Journal, Biblical Discipleship Quarterly, Bible Illustrator and others.  He has served as production manager for several printing companies. Toney serves as the Managing Editor of Illumination Publishers International, and is the writer and publisher of the weekly "Behind the Music" stories and edits other weekly newsletters. Toney is happily married to the love of his life, Denise Leonard Mulhollan, M.D.

For the best in Christian writing and audio instruction, go to the Illumination Publishers website. Shipping is always free in the United States. We're commited to producing in-depth teaching that will inform, inspire and encourage Christians to a deeper and more committed walk with God.

www.ipibooks.com

Illuminations Publishers International

www.ipibooks.com

ipi

For the latest news and teaching from Dr. John M. Oakes, visit his website at:

http://www.EvidenceForChristianity.org

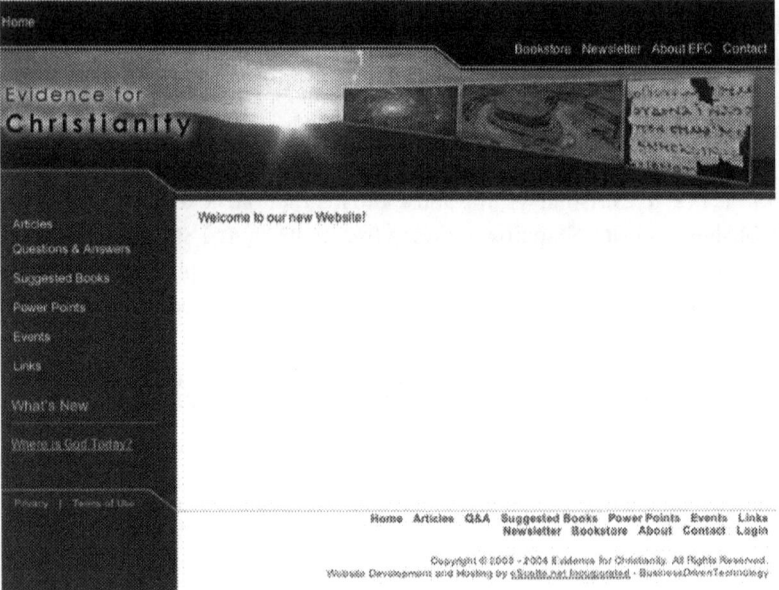

www.ingramcontent.com/pod-product-compliance
Lightning Source LLC
Chambersburg PA
CBHW031411290426
44110CB00011B/334